A great read for anyone trying to make sense of cultural whiplash over the last few years, Nancy French's journey from poverty-stricken mountains to a presidential-campaign plane is a joy. *Ghosted* tries to understand this tumultuous, strange world and finds a beautiful peace amid the chaos.

—JAKE TAPPER, CNN anchor and chief Washington correspondent

I didn't know writing could be this haunting and hilarious, heartbreaking and exhilarating all at the same time. I did not want it to end. This tour de force of storytelling and sense-making is one of the most gripping and beautiful memoirs in a generation. In these pages, Nancy French takes us beyond this confusing American moment right into the soul of our shared human condition, full as it is of gore and glory. You will not close this book the same as you were when you opened it.

—RUSSELL MOORE, *Christianity Today*

I picked up *Ghosted* only once, not putting it down until I had read every page. This is a captivating account of a child, a girl, and then a woman buffeted by unthinkable betrayals who withstood despair and surrender and remained true to her values. Her uncommon character and integrity educate and inspire.

—MITT ROMNEY

Ghosted is an incredible story of a woman facing abuse and betrayal with courage throughout isolation who comes out strong as steel on the other side. Nancy French is a role model for every woman who strives to stand by her convictions even when times get tough. This book is for anyone who has ever felt like an outsider yearning for the truth and what's right.

—GRETCHEN CARLSON, acclaimed journalist; bestselling author; female empowerment advocate; cofounder, Lift Our Voices

The world Nancy French introduces us to is so unfamiliar that it reminds me of my collegiate study-abroad experience in Japan. The young girl we meet at the beginning of the book's journey and follow over the years captured my heart and imagination. Through tears, sighs, prayers, laughter, fears, and cheers, I eagerly devoured every page of *Ghosted* until there were no more.

—SYBIL JORDAN HAMPTON, EdD, president emeritus, The Winthrop Rockefeller Foundation

GHOSTED

GHOSTED

An American Story

NANCY FRENCH

ZONDERVAN
BOOKS

ZONDERVAN BOOKS

Ghosted
Copyright © 2024 by Nancy French

Published in Grand Rapids, Michigan, by Zondervan. Zondervan is a registered trademark of The Zondervan Corporation, L.L.C., a wholly owned subsidiary of HarperCollins Christian Publishing, Inc.

Requests for information should be addressed to customercare@harpercollins.com.

Zondervan titles may be purchased in bulk for educational, business, fundraising, or sales promotional use. For information, please email SpecialMarkets@Zondervan.com.

ISBN 978-0-310-36746-8 (audio)

Library of Congress Cataloging-in-Publication Data

Names: French, Nancy, 1974- author.
Title: Ghosted : an American story / Nancy French.
Description: Grand Rapids : Zondervan Books, 2024.
Identifiers: LCCN 2023047026 (print) | LCCN 2023047027 (ebook) | ISBN 9780310367444 (hardcover) | ISBN 9780310367451 (ebook)
Subjects: LCSH: French, Nancy, 1974- | Ghostwriters—United States—Biography. | Women ghostwriters—United States—Biography. | BISAC: BIOGRAPHY & AUTOBIOGRAPHY / Personal Memoirs | POLITICAL SCIENCE / Political Process / Political Parties
Classification: LCC PN149.9.F74 A3 2024 (print) | LCC PN149.9.F74 (ebook) | DDC 070.92 [B]—dc23/eng/20240108
LC record available at https://lccn.loc.gov/2023047026
LC ebook record available at https://lccn.loc.gov/2023047027

Any internet addresses (websites, blogs, etc.) and telephone numbers in this book are offered as a resource. They are not intended in any way to be or imply an endorsement by Zondervan, nor does Zondervan vouch for the content of these sites and numbers for the life of this book.

Published in association with Stéphanie Abou of Massie & McQuilkin Literary Agents.

Cover design: Faceout Studio, Jeff Miller
Cover photos: Stocksy and Shutterstock
Interior design: Sara Colley

Printed in the United States of America

24 25 26 27 28 LBC 5 4 3 2 1

To David

I was lonely. Yeah, that's the word. But the unassuming sidewalk where we met turned out to be the road less traveled. In spite of protests, we took it.

Life propelled us, hand in hand, toward destinations I never imagined—surprised at every turn, delighted by your jokes, bored by your movie choices, comforted by your presence.

Then, life—war—pushed us apart. But that didn't matter because—by then—home was no longer a destination, it was a person.

I just love you.

CONTENTS

ACKNOWLEDGMENTS

To my wonderful, glamorous French agent, **Stéphanie Abou**, who took this meeting with this publisher after wearing gigantic sunglasses, sporting windblown hair, fresh off a beach in France. For years, you believed, listened, comforted, challenged, and persevered. Thank you for being so smart, clever, and fun.

Thank you, thank you, **Webb Younce**, for partnering with me on this book. I've appreciated your wisdom, faith, and openheartedness throughout this process and could not imagine entrusting this story to anyone else.

To my amazing editor, **Carolyn McCready**: you know exactly how to gently point out that something needs to go—and fast. ("This part is confusing," I determined, means, "Um, nope.") You're great at spotting extraneous, distracting, and boring aspects of stories, but on top of all that, your moral clarity and kindness are wonderful balms to the soul.

Paul Fisher, thank you for helping me figure out how best to place this book into the world. Your expertise and kindness are so invaluable.

Katie Painter, it makes sense—with your magnetic personality—that you have a job getting attention for books, because you are the life of all parties. I've enjoyed getting to know you and expect many more coffee dates to come.

Brian Phipps and Phil Newman, I appreciate your catching all of my mistakes. You make me look better than I am.

Curt Diepenhorst, I love the moody cover. Thank you for using your creativity to make this appealing!

INTRODUCTION

When I arrived home, I noticed a business card taped to my mailbox fluttering in the wind like a butterfly's wing.

I took it off, annoyed at whatever roofing company was trying to drum up business, and thumbed through my mail. But the card had a raised golden seal with five words printed beneath it: the Federal Bureau of Investigation.

"Contact me at your earliest convenience." The note on the back was written in slanted printed letters. "Urgent."

My chest tightened as I dialed my husband.

"The FBI?" David was on a business trip, and his voice sounded distant now. "What did the agent say when you called him?"

"You think I called him back?" I'd never been contacted by the FBI, but it seemed like an opening to a movie, the kind in which the unsuspecting woman ends up in a gas station bathroom cutting her hair with a knife and dyeing it with shoe polish hoping for a clean slate in Topeka.

"Did you rob a bank?" His voice was teasing, laced with impatient incredulity. "If not, call them."

"Does the FBI typically come to a person's house?" I asked.

"I don't know. Call him back, before it gets too late." It was already dark. "Whatever this is, it's not good."

I dialed the number.

"Thank you for calling, Mrs. French." The agent's formality caused my throat to thicken. "Are you familiar with the Cesar Sayoc case?"

Of course. Every news channel had been covering it around the clock for the past few weeks. In the days leading up to 2018's midterm elections, Sayoc sent prominent Democrats pipe bombs in a wave of attacks. Fear of political violence spread across the nation.

When the news first broke, I'd been on a job. I'm a ghost, but not the scary kind. The writer kind. Almost all celebrity books are written by ghostwriters like me, unknown writers who learn the minutiae of their celebrity clients' lives and toil in obscurity to meet tight deadlines. But it's true. Most famous people don't have the time, skill, or inclination to write a book while starring in a television show, running for office, or training for the Olympics. That's where I come in. I sit down, hear their stories, and go to their homes, studios, movie sets, weddings, or Olympic training centers and create books that will be in stores in twelve to eighteen months.

When Sayoc mailed his first pipe bombs, I was with a client in a hotel lobby. The television news anchor on a nearby TV described how the bomber had targeted Bill and Hillary Clinton, Joe Biden, several members of Congress, Barack Obama, George Soros, and Robert De Niro.

The other hotel guests and I got closer to the screen, which showed images of a cylindrical object wrapped in electrical tape, wires emerging from both ends. Black ISIS-like flags were taped to them, as well as photos of the recipients with a red X marked across their faces.

Someone was terrifying the nation right before the midterms. Bad news for democracy. My client shrugged and continued the interview. "Anyway, so let me tell you about why I support the president, even if people say he's divisive. He's a unifier, if anything."

Days after the first attack, the FBI identified this domestic terrorist as a stockily built Florida man who lived in a van covered with pro-Trump posters. The feds found binders full of media clippings, photo collages of people's faces, and writings that said, in a 180-degree twist on the words of Christ, "Kill your enemy."

He'd taken his cues from every serial-killer documentary ever made.

"I saw it on the news," I said to the FBI agent. "But what does any of this have to do with me?"

"We found your address on Sayoc's computer." He paused. "Your husband was on his list."

I sat down at the kitchen table. I'd never thought David, a conservative Iraq-war veteran, would ever be listed with Bill Clinton, Joe Biden, and Robert De Niro. We'd been Republicans our whole lives, and I'd helped many conservative leaders on book projects.

"He targets prominent critics of the president," he said. "Would that include your husband?"

It would. David, who wrote for the conservative magazine *National Review*, had been one of the only Republican thought leaders to oppose Trump. His name had even been briefly floated for a quixotic, third-party run for president of the United States. He declined, but not before his reputation among Republicans was sealed: traitor.

"What do we do?"

"He may have sent you a package we haven't intercepted yet," he explained. "We're working with the US Postal Service, but one could slip through."

I put my forehead in my hand, and my teenage son—who'd been hovering nearby—walked over, eyes wide with concern.

"Look out for nondescript manila envelopes you aren't expecting," the agent said. "And alert your neighbors. None of the packages have detonated, but they could."

I couldn't breathe. I've always prided myself on having a certain amount of emotional awareness and flexibility. Being a ghostwriter requires it. I'd worked with celebrities like Kim Kardashian, *The Bachelor*'s Sean Lowe, a Chinese political dissident, and prominent Republicans who had inhabited the nation's top political positions. As a ghost, I don't write "he hit Clara's daughter" but "he hit my daughter." I don't write "the car crash killed the passengers" but "the car crash killed my friends." I describe scenes in such detail that I sometimes experience secondary trauma vicariously living through the moment to capture it in the first-person written word.

But in 2016, I felt a different, more personal type of trauma. That's when things started to change in the GOP. Within a party proclaiming faith and freedom, an unsavory element bubbled to the surface.

David and I were doing what we'd always done: speaking out about our values, values which had not changed. But as the political climate shifted, we suddenly were at odds with our own community. Either you were with the GOP, or you weren't.

We'd been ostracized because we refused to support a president who made a cameo in the Playboy film *Playmate 2000 Bernaola Twins*. We'd been confronted at church because we didn't support a man who'd admitted to groping women. And now we'd been targeted by a domestic terrorist.

I sat at my kitchen table, my hands shaking. Someone had to point out that the emperor—not just the Bernaola Twins—had no clothes. But at what cost? Not only was I forced out of my tribe, I'd lost my main source of income. My political clients wanted a ghostwriter to write what they told them to write. That's the job. I was supposed to reflect their views for their books, not write my own.

Not only did I write their books, I traveled with them, wrote speeches, and even sat at Fox News headquarters to sharpen their talking points. I specialized in witty insults, clever turns of phrase, and political statements aimed to provoke liberals. Combativeness was part of the fun, delivered with a wink. People would argue during the day and have a drink together in the evening. But the wink was gone, replaced by mean tweets. Acrimony had settled into our brows, and people from different political parties actually loathed each other.

I tried to continue my political work but vowed not to twist the truth or bear false witness against my liberal neighbors. Because I lived in Franklin, Tennessee, I didn't have many actual liberal neighbors, but you get the idea. I wouldn't mischaracterize liberal positions, I wouldn't make generalizations about an entire group based on the craziest outliers, and I wouldn't assume the worst of every Democrat. Hadn't my own approach to politics contributed to the problem? Couldn't we all agree things had gone too far?

Though my political clients had previously respected my opinion and enjoyed our back-and-forth dialogue, they now resented my questioning their talking points and softening their forceful rhetoric. I soon quit, or was fired by, all of them.

That put me in a financially precarious situation. Now I was in a physically precarious one. I clutched the FBI agent's business card. Since my multiracial family had taken a stance against Trump, we'd been mocked by

Republicans, targeted by White nationalists, threatened with death, and alienated from our church community.

But the American story is one of defiance, especially of the political kind. My unwillingness to bow the knee to an unsuitable president was the most American thing I'd ever done. And the ensuing rupture allowed me to see my nation and fellow Americans in new, more accurate, and ultimately more meaningful ways.

I quit the GOP, which means I am no longer bound to toe the party line. Now I'm liberated from all expectations and can reveal what really happened.

That's what I'm doing now. Instead of writing for others, I'm telling my own story. As a ghost, invisible to the people around me, I'm coming out and making myself known. After floating along the outskirts of the powerful while our nation has digressed into unbelievable hatred, I've got a story to tell. It's not tidy, nor is it easy, and it's more than a little frightening.

All good ghost stories are.

1

ROUGH
AND READY

My grandmother took a knife to an apple, the snake of a peel curling until it fell in one piece on the linoleum floor. Half Cherokee, she had a long face, high cheekbones, and wrinkles like geological formations—deep and profound.

I stooped to get the peel.

"Not yet." She looked intently at it. My grandmother and aunts weaned babies, took jobs, and planned calendars according to the stages of the moon, the position of the stars, and the arbitrary alignments of common objects. The space between the physical and spiritual was thin on Monteagle Mountain, but the women in my family danced within it.

"Look for a letter," she said. "It'll be the first letter of the last name of the man you're going to marry."

At eleven years old, I didn't want this information. Surely when I married, it would be the result of a spark of romance, a well-considered life plan, love, not the remnants of a worm-eaten apple. But with trepidation, I tried to see a letter. C? Q? S? I was in love with Hank Higdon in my fifth-grade class, so I looked for ninety-degree angles, but my grandmother's knife had curled my destiny into a narrow path. Meanwhile, gravy bubbled in a skillet, and the chicken was frying.

I was glad I hadn't arrived earlier when she'd lulled the chicken from the run into her arms. I didn't want to witness her grabbing its feet, its wings flapping futilely to gain some space between the mountain and the sky before winding up on our plates.

"The peels ain't never wrong." Grandmother touched my crestfallen face. "But watch those men. They're like loaded guns . . . you never know when they'll go off."

The message, delivered in a melodic, southern tone, struck me: men were volatile, women were vulnerable. But my aunts were beautiful creatures with painted eyebrows who carried cigarettes in long skinny purses, more apt to deliver a beating than to receive one. The men were Paul Bunyan types, similar to lumberjacks in paper towel ads with towering pines in the background. Broad-shouldered men who wore red suspenders with calm manners belying their volcanic, chaotic impulses. My dad joked our family was famous, because gas stations hung "portraits" of them around the county. He meant wanted posters.

The mountain was a playground for mischief, with its coal mines, ubiquitous guns, and plentiful dynamite. My dad described his twenty-five cousins as "rednecks, rough and ready," and they drank, fought, and stole their way honestly onto those wanted posters.

My uncles were always kind to me, especially Uncle Jasper, who gave us nicknames and mussed our hair. He was a bigger version of my dad, wore overalls, and spoke with an almost indecipherable accent. He also was the most troubled.

I heard some variation of the same story several times. When Uncle Jasper was younger, he went to California and got in a fight. My dad and his siblings had to drive all the way across the country to plead his case with the judge. He'd been hit in the head with a baseball bat and was never the same. The bat was always a part of the story, though some claimed the fight happened on the mountain. Regardless, that bat changed Uncle Jasper. And he frequently called us when he was drunk. He stole vehicles. He drove a Jeep through a neighbor's fence.

My parents told these stories in whispered tones at church potlucks and late-night game nights with their friends. I lingered to hear the details and piece the stories together but got only the broad brushstrokes. On television, hillbillies were ignorant Jed Clampett types who managed to come out ahead. Our stories had to be whispered, but I overheard enough.

When my dad walked home from school, he'd sometimes find his drunk mom and dad shooting at each other, the gunshots puncturing the ceiling. While Grandmother was half Cherokee, with a little Creek thrown in, Grandfather had blood from the Blackfoot tribe, which he described as violent. I believed him. He broke my grandmother's leg at least once. Dad's cousin Fox once shot his brother Zeb's arm off.

My grandparents were almost entirely self-sufficient. They had to purchase coffee, tobacco, and sugar, three items they could not grow or manufacture themselves. Grandfather owned some land where he grew corn, which he made into moonshine. He was a coal miner and a logger but also ran a joint that sold bootlegged liquor. It had a slot machine in the back, illegal activity tucked out of sight of the police officers who stopped by and beat him with their batons.

Dad's job was to keep the peace during operational hours, and he slept in the car while the older boys of the family closed late at night. One night, Grandfather's cousins shot the windows out of the packed bar when he'd finally got tired of giving them his stash. People hit the decks, and everyone lived. Another time, a bar fight moved onto a neighbor's property, and one of the fighters died when he was nearly decapitated.

Ironically, these rowdy cousins were in charge of keeping the peace when customers got violent. But they figured out an ingenious strategy: They pulled out a rattlesnake's fangs with pliers and threw the snake on the floor when a fight erupted. As it slithered, customers stopped fighting and toppled chairs on their way out the door. Even drunk hillbillies know not to mess with a rattler.

I loved my family and never feared them, though my uncle Jasper pulled me aside and threatened to kill anyone who harmed me—or even dated me. I thought this was normal, but what is normal? Normal's what you know. And that's what I knew.

My parents were hillbillies, but my sisters and I were three-times-a-week, pantyhose-wearing churchgoers growing up in rural Kentucky. Still, I was drawn to the mountain. Chaos seemed to emanate from the iron furnace along with the heat. It was in the air, and I breathed it in.

"Now watch, hear?" Grandmother scooped up the peels. "I'm gonna drop this rag on the floor. If it falls flat, a woman will come to the house. If it wrinkles, a man."

She dropped the rag. Flat.

I sat at the table with my book, which I'd brought to pass the time. On the mountain, my grandfather didn't chat, but my aunts' conversation flowed like the waterfall into the Fiery Gizzard swimming hole. Jokes, laughter, compliments came freely, in singsong mountain accents. I read my book, about twins living in their fictional suburb of Los Angeles. As far as I knew, LA was fictional too as I stood in the kitchen with cast iron on the stove and loaded guns on the wall.

Aunt Zinnia stormed into the room holding a cardboard box.

"Reckon can I use your kitchen for my next client, Momma? My place is frozen solid." She took off her coat and slung it on the chair. "He's coming in ten minutes."

If the rag was truly prescient, no man was coming to the house today, but my aunt unpacked the box and placed a crystal ball and tarot cards in the middle of the table. Her dark hair framed her eyes, which were decorated with makeup the color of the sky.

I crept closer to the ball. This was the stuff of cartoon witches and cauldrons, and I wanted to peek into its swirling clouds of destiny.

"What do you see?" she asked.

Soft, prisms bounced around as I moved my head. Magical and mesmerizing.

"Rainbows." I twirled a tress of my dark hair. "What do you see?"

My aunt took a drag from her cigarette and peered into the ball with me. "I'm a seer, so I see a lot," she said. "But mostly, I see . . ."

I straightened and prepared to discover the secrets of the universe.

"Dollar signs."

I breathed out my disappointment but continued to look into the ball as the clock ticked. While we waited, my aunt told me about belonging to an Indian tribe and invited me and Grandmother to their next meeting.

"We wear Indian headdresses, do dances, and even have our own Indian names," she said, but Grandmother waved her off. She was the daughter of a Cherokee princess—one of our ancestors had been named Shield

Eater—but her generation didn't broadcast their identity on the mountain. When my dad left the mountain, we left behind all the Cherokee lore, the black magic, and the astrology. Still, I leaned in closer.

"You need an Indian name to go with your blood," Aunt Zinnia said. "Momma's one half, and you're one eighth, but I see it in you. Clear as day."

I shook my head. My dad would never let me attend any sort of Cherokee dancing rituals. We weren't allowed to do any kind of dancing, but I felt the pull. My aunt packed up her crystal ball. "Guess he stood me up."

"Didn't we know he wouldn't come?" I asked, hesitantly. Because of Grandmother's rag? Because my aunt was a seer? She tossed back her head and laughed.

"I like you." She flicked her ashes into a tray without looking. "Momma, she looks and talks like us, don't she?"

I shared their coloring, facial construction, and conversation style. I loved watching these women, whom I so resembled, move and talk. Fierce and beautiful.

"Your eyes will melt many a man's heart." Aunt Zinnia pulled out a cigarette from her case. "The color of those old blue bottles your daddy finds in the woods. Cobalt." Their own eyes were dark like coal, but my heart swelled at their sugarcoated insistence that I belonged in this stone house with magical apple peels and dishrags. I was one of them.

My aunt blew the smoke from her cigarette away from my face and leaned in closer. "And you have the gift, don't you?"

"What gift?"

"You can see."

I thought about it. My eyes worked. I clearly saw that the small home had provided shelter to two parents and seven tightly packed children. I saw the middle room, which had two beds—one for my grandparents and one for the two girls. I saw the room with dueling pianos where all five of the brothers had slept on one feather bed in a room with ice on the inside of the window in the morning. I saw what they still called the "new addition," a closet-sized space with a toilet which replaced the outhouse my dad dug.

When they got electricity and plumbing—reluctantly—they built a tiny addition with a single commode. My cousins stood over the toilet and watched the water flush away to parts unknown. Still, my grandfather didn't trust it and never used an indoor toilet even once in his life. "It's not my way," he said.

Aunt Zinnia always breezed in and out of our lives, and I felt honored to be in her presence, and I hung on her every word.

"You have the gift. To see things that are far off, have passed, or will come." As she took a drag from her cigarette, her eyes never left mine. "Reckon?"

I hesitated. At church we were warned against soothsayers and psychics, but deep down I wanted to be like these women, to be special. She put her hand on my knee. "You have it. Don't fight it."

For the second time in an hour, my destiny shifted. I had some sort of mystical power, and I only hoped my future husband—apparently a Mr. Quinn? Mr. Copeland? Mr. Shelby?—would appreciate that part of me.

Grandmother put the chicken into the oven to stay warm, and the gravy needed to cook a bit longer. We walked through the middle room, which had a two-handed saw painted with vibrant deer-filled vistas hanging on the wall, into the far room. It had a couch, two upright pianos, and a chair in the corner.

Grandfather had black lung disease from the deep-hole coal mines, but he smoked a pipe. The aroma—a blend of woods, vanilla, and tobacco—mixed with the smell of the stove. Slumped in his chair in his worn-out overalls, he bore an eerie resemblance to my father and uncles. While we waited on dinner, I tried to make conversation.

"I'm reading a good book." I held out my novel to my grandfather, who took in the pink cover without saying a word. Outside, the snow pelted in a horizontal pattern. Ice tapped the windows.

He beheld the book for a long time, and no one moved. I didn't know he couldn't read and could write only his first and last names, a skill Grandmother had taught him so he could sign his Tennessee Coal Company checks. Not for a second did I consider anything to be beyond their capabilities. They had that lived-through-the-Depression resourcefulness, which meant they never threw anything away and stared problems in the face until the sun came up the next morning. Their spines were as strong as steel, their hair as black as coal, and their bodies as unshakable as the mountain.

My dad broke the silence and addressed his mother. "Why don't ya play us a tune?" My grandmother shook her head. Before she'd gotten married, she played piano on gambling boats, but marriage and seven kids put a damper on all that. Uncle Jasper stood up.

"Come on now," he said, patting the bench beside him indicating a seat for me. Jasper wore a red and black flannel shirt under his overalls; his glasses were tinted so he looked like a hillbilly celebrity. "Let's play some music for these nice folks. They drove all this way."

They drove all this way. My sisters and I were on the mountain, but not of the mountain. He sat at one of the pianos and played the opening chords to "Your Cheatin' Heart."

My grandmother, unable to resist the pull of the notes, sat at the adjacent "dueling piano." Uncle Jasper could play the banjo, guitar, and piano. But Grandmother was a savant. Her hands pounded the keys, yellowed and some worn all the way to the wood. She played all eighty-eight keys, no matter the song.

"Your cheatin' heart," Uncle Jasper bellowed.

I took lessons from a Baptist lady. One finger played one note. A mistake would stand out during recitals. But there was no such thing as a wrong note here. Grandmother played from the heart, several keys at once, sweeping her hand over the piano with confidence and ease. The music was syncopated, the beat was loose. I never knew where the notes would take me.

My parents didn't normally allow us to sing about cheating hearts, but there I was—in a smoke-filled room—attempting the unfamiliar lyrics. Other family members joined in, taking the banjo and guitar from the corner.

For a moment, I imagined I was in a brothel or a Wild West saloon selling nickel beers at the bar, gunslingers temporarily lulled by the music. But Grandmother remembered the gravy, and everything stopped.

"Who has time for this foolishness?" she asked. "Supper's ready."

"Get it while the getting's good," Uncle Jasper said.

Grandfather rose from his chair and shuffled to the kitchen with his cane. He seemed like a gentle old soul whose main concern was packing his pipe with the right amount of tobacco. But as a coal miner, he'd packed dynamite. He'd lit a fuse long enough for my dad and his brothers to find shelter before the explosion, and hoped the miner on the surface turned the fan on fast enough to save him from the fumes. Jarred by the explosions, he sometimes didn't even know where he was. My dad and his brothers, though they were kids, were right there with him, hauling coal out of the hole in a mule-pulled cart.

Grandmother put a skillet down. I felt odd about eating their food, always in such short supply. After every scrap was eaten, my cousin Buck and I cleaned up. He filled his side of the sink with steaming water and soap smelling of freshly zested lemons.

"Uncle Bob was a boxer, but you're a knockout." He smiled as he brought the dishes over.

I rolled my eyes and filled my side with clean hot water. "We're first cousins."

"Don't mean nothing."

"Yes, it does," I said, but I wasn't sure of the rules.

He scraped the skillet. "You and your preacher daddy too good for your own family?" Because my dad no longer drank and we went to church, they viewed him as a puritan. But the mountain energy was wild and untamed by such things as laws, the government, or cultural norms. This place, forgotten, operated by its own rules. Buck tried to impress me, as his hands sank into the soapy water.

"This family," he said, "folks around here grow up tough, buddy." He was pointing out that I was growing up off the mountain and therefore had a toughness deficit.

"You're not even grown," I said.

"And I mean tough." He ignored me. "You do realize Uncle Jasper killed his wife, right?"

I let that be for a few moments. He was trying to shock me, and he did. I didn't let him know it. My family had been involved in illegal activities—bootlegging, fighting, and gambling—but murder?

I wiped a smudge off a knife and added it to the dry pile. "You're telling a story." I said it to the sink, without turning to him.

"I swear on the Bible." He took his right hand out of the water, soap suds running down his arm.

"You got a Bible in that water?" His water was the color of mud. The bubbles had mostly popped and food fragments floated on the surface.

The people in my orbit didn't drink alcohol, gaze into crystal balls, or shoot at each other. But Monteagle Mountain, even at two thousand feet, was big enough to cast a long shadow over us, no matter where we lived.

We tried to stuff that shadow in a mothball-filled closet back in Kentucky in a box labeled "Grandfather's KKK Robe." I'd heard stories about the "old" Ku Klux Klan, which—I'd always been told—kept law and order after the Civil War. My mother's grandfather had been a member. Back then, the KKK wore hoods and gowns so no one could identify them. However, there was a telltale way of knowing who was who: their pets. "You could tell it was Jim," my mother's mom explained, "because his ole dog would be curled at his feet."

We never were allowed to see the robe, but I would sneak peeks. It did not have a hood. The robes used on the mountain weren't to disguise members but to indicate who belonged. The klan was not presented to me as evil or a hate group but as a way to preserve the peace among lazy White people. There were few Black people on the mountain. Though my dad had seen one cross-burning, he said it was at the home of a White man who refused to support his wife and children.

But you can't really escape your shadow or stuff it in a box. It sticks to you.

The water in the sink cooled, and a chill ran through me. "Are there still klansmen today?"

"Standing right before your very eyes." Buck shrugged. "I'm a card-carrying member."

"The klan has business cards?"

"Membership cards." He laughed. "Only rich people like you have business cards." He washed a mug, pulled it out of the soapy water, and extended his pinky finger to imitate his imagined version of a rich person—though neither of us knew rich people in real life. My sisters and I didn't have air conditioning and lived well below the poverty line, but he made us seem like we flew in on a private jet.

All day, I thought about Uncle Jasper's dead wife and how Buck was in the KKK. And then, the sun dipped below the mountain and it was time to go. That's what made us different. We could leave. My mother sometimes used the word *escape* when she was talking to her friends.

I hugged Buck, aunts, and grandmother, but not Uncle Jasper. I waved at him awkwardly as I put on my jacket and climbed into our Marquis with velour seats and a ceiling that swooped to the top of my head. He'd been my favorite uncle, the one who'd put me on his broad shoulders, my legs dangling over his chest. He was a giant, but his size, his sturdiness, now didn't seem as fun. The knowledge that he'd killed his wife created a space between us I was afraid to cross.

I looked out the window to the runaway-truck ramps, which were used by eighteen-wheelers if their brakes went out. Monteagle Mountain is the top of one of the most hazardous stretches of interstate highway in America. The dangers of this stretch of I-24, between Nashville and Chattanooga, were so well known that Johnny Cash sang about the truckers who've died on its steep incline.

Our ride home was quiet. Our car didn't play cassettes, it played old eight-track cartridges. We had only one, which came with the car and played "Tennessee Waltz." But on this night, we sang "A Hundred Bottles of Beer on the Wall," edited to be Coke to avoid the appearance of evil. An hour or so into the trip, our car sputtered.

Dad gripped the steering wheel and listened for sounds from the engine. Our car had covers for the headlights, which were supposed to open. One had broken long ago. With the lights turned on, the car winked at oncoming vehicles, one headlight illuminating the falling snow. Suddenly, we heard a *thwap, thwap, thwap* from under the hood.

Dad white-knuckled it all the way down the mountain, but the car gave out when we got to Hurricane Mills. I don't remember what was wrong with it this time. In the summers, we couldn't even buy ice cream at the grocery store, we so frequently had to walk our purchases home.

Dad got off the interstate and slowly pulled into the parking lot of a dude ranch owned by country singer Loretta Lynn. There was an events center, cabins, and a coal mining museum. Dad got out and disappeared under the hood. I watched the snow fall in the beam of the one operational headlight. After about ten minutes, he sighed. "We're not going to make it home. Not tonight."

I had a momentary fantasy of walking into one of those cabins, sleeping on an actual bed, and using the towels from the clean bathroom. I'd never stayed at a hotel, but I imagined a dude ranch would be unimaginably fancy. Dad checked on the cost of a room but walked across the parking lot a few minutes later with his head down. But when he climbed into the front seat, he smiled.

"Who's ready for a campout?" He rubbed his hands together, like we were about to have an adventure.

My mother sighed.

"We can't pay full price for eight hours," Dad said, all fake enthusiasm gone from his voice.

Mom, accustomed to the car breaking down, got blankets from the trunk. My two sisters and I pulled the covers to our chins, closed our eyes, and tried to get comfortable without touching each other, a breach which could end in a fistfight during the best of times. I wasn't distressed by sleeping sitting up. The seats were deep and comfortable. But I was embarrassed at the thought of people walking by in the morning's light and seeing all five of us conked out in our junky land barge.

"Don't worry, your majesty," my mom said. "The windows will fog and no one will be able to tell who's in here. Shut your mouth and eyes."

I didn't want to be rich. I wanted to be able to sleep in a bed. I wanted a house with air conditioning. I wanted a car that drove, a foreign compact with a cassette player. The temperature dropped, and the blankets weren't heavy enough to take the edge off.

I wedged a quilt between my head and the frosted window. "With five people in the car," Dad said, "it'll warm up. I'll fix the car first thing."

I looked at the dude ranch, which probably had log cabins commemorating mountain life filled with stone fireplaces, fluffy quilts, iron kettles, and oversized coffee cups. But manufactured warmth was inaccessible to me. Lynn's famous song—"I'm proud to be a coal miner's daughter"—ran through my head. My dad now worked for a lumber company, but I guess I was technically a coal miner's daughter too. I wasn't proud. I was sad—about Uncle Jasper and his dead wife and the KKK and the ineffective crystal ball and my cousin's crush. All of that was my blood and in my blood. No matter how hard my parents had tried, we'd failed in our efforts to gain some space between us and the mountain.

In our car, the windows fogged over, I worried that we'd never find our way back home. Or away from it, either.

2

LOADED

The ranch house located at 602 Weda Avenue was the first home I remember.

"Memorize it in case you get kidnapped or something," Mom said. "Six-Oh-Two [clap] Weda Avenue. Six-Oh-Two [clap] Weda Avenue."

The singsongy address rang in my ears, but there was no chance I'd ever forget our fourteen-hundred-square-foot house, located in a three-block radius in Mayfield, Kentucky, which made up my entire world. Our living room had shiny black Naugahyde furniture, floral wallpaper, and macrame wall art. Without air conditioning, the breeze, mosquitos, and flies wafted in through the open windows and caressed our sticky skin. In the front, a towering tree held a tire swing dangling over a bald patch where our tiny feet had rubbed away the grass in a perfect dusty circle. We made dolls out of corn husks, toys out of locust hulls we plucked off tree bark, and jump ropes out of anything we could tie to a doorknob and twirl.

Cinderella, dressed in yella, went upstairs to kiss her fella. Made a mistake and kissed a snake. How many doctors will it take? On my best jumping day, it took eighty-three.

When my dad found a discarded washing-machine barrel in the woods, my sisters and I took turns wedging ourselves into it, rolling down the hill, puking, and running back for more. We made castles out of trees, whistles out of fescue, and crowns out of clover. We lured rabbits into boxes with carrots, pulled legs off daddy longlegs, and looked for ginseng like pirates

19

searching for treasure. My dad sold it because hippies and the Chinese believed it had healing qualities, so we didn't want to disabuse anyone of that notion.

We also found treasures in a fly-infested dump filled with discarded furniture and valuables. I baked mudpies in the sun, which I ate and eventually gave me pinworms. When I got an egregious case of lice, my mother cut my hair off and I resembled Dwight Eisenhower for the next few weeks. I was feral as an alley cat, "the stinky kid" at school.

Longfellow Elementary was a short walk from our house. There, I learned our home sat on the New Madrid geological fault, the most active fault in the central and eastern United States. Wasn't much we could do about that. But we did occasionally crouch under our desks, covering our heads, in case the Russians ever attacked western Kentucky.

But "show and tell" was scarier than a possible communist invasion. My friends brought plastic souvenirs from experiences known as "vacations"— palm tree magnets and coconut cups with straws. Some people, it turns out, stayed in hotels, not just parking lots. When I brought my Cabbage Patch doll, the girls pointed out a lack of Xavier Roberts's signature on her bottom and laughed when I couldn't produce a birth certificate. The next week, I brought the most impressive items I had.

"I have four things to show you: a snake's fang hanging on thread, a rattle, and shed skin." I proceeded to reveal each one like a magician pulling a rabbit out of a hat. The girls in my class recoiled at the items, but the boys leaned forward in their chairs.

"You mean three items?" My teacher suspected I might have a learning disability related to numbers. When I told my mother, she said I'd made it to the fourth grade well enough, so what was the problem? This was also her response to the doctor's revelation that I had a back as crooked as a politician's.

"Scoliosis?" she laughed. "You don't want one of those braces, do you?" Mom didn't reason through problems, she mocked them—daring them to complicate her life, already stretched too thin.

After school, the neighborhood kids and I walked back in the "off hours," where we reigned over the uninhabited playground like feudal lords. The equipment was made of unforgivingly high metal bars, and the hard, dusty ground seemed to leap up at us when we least expected it, knocking the wind out of us. We hung upside down from monkey bars until our faces turned red and we collapsed in fits of laughter. Our falls never broke us, not completely. Our parents figured if we busted our heads open, we wouldn't do it twice. We rode bicycles without shoes—my friend had only nine toes to prove it—and each of the three daughters required a significant emergency room visit: Amy, when she broke her arm falling out of the tree; me, when I busted my head open walking across a wooden plank from car to car; and Mary Kate, when her small body was on my feet playing "airplane" until she fell and hit her head against the corner of a wall.

I felt bad about that one.

"What'd you do to your sister?" Mom ran into the room to find four-year-old Mary Kate covered in blood. During the thirty seconds between the moment her head hit the corner and the time Mom arrived, Amy and I had already negotiated a treaty of silence. We were more afraid of our mother than of a head wound.

"How did this happen?" the doctor asked.

Mom furrowed her brow. Her anger was large and expansive and would strike at any moment. But we were protected by the presence of the medical professionals, so we looked down at our triple-knotted shoes. We'd rather take our chances with the Department of Children's Services than endure Mom's wrath. Even under the inquisitive gaze of the doctors and the withering stare of our mother, Mary Kate didn't snitch for three decades.

I had worms, lice, calloused feet, dented bicycles, and complete freedom. My parents didn't let us back inside our home until the skies turned pink, and porch lights beckoned us to the kitchen table with sloppy joes, spaghetti, or Spam. Then, my sisters and I would reluctantly grab supper, before heading back out to play flashlight tag with neighbors until bedtime.

Dad cruised timber, which meant he checked out the size, volume, and quality of trees on his employer's land to calculate timber sales. He drove a company Bronco, which was covered in mud and always contained cans of OFF! bug spray, tree-flagging tape, and "snake legs," shields to protect from the slithering reptiles. He came home covered in so many seed ticks, he used duct tape to remove them. He smelled of sawdust or Old Spice, depending on whether he was going to work or church.

But in the summer after my fourth-grade year, my dad's paper company transferred him from Kentucky to Tennessee, which meant leaving everything we'd ever known behind.

"Paris, Tennessee." I said—the name of our destination. "Sounds fancy."

"Aww, don't be intimidated." My mother wiped her hands off on a rag. "It'll give you the opportunity to start over. No one knows you there."

This was a strange notion. I'd lived only ten years. I didn't have a long list of regrets to overcome, but the idea captured my imagination. As I packed up my things, I decided I wanted to develop a new personality, maybe walk with a limp or wear a monocle. At the least, I didn't have to be the girl afflicted with pinworms and lice. My imagination ran wild with the opportunity of a fresh slate, with the vigor of a person given a new chance in the federal witness-protection program.

After we got all the boxes packed, we hired movers to put the boxes in the truck—three Black guys chewing tobacco. I was sitting in the living room; at my feet was a Samsonite suitcase stuffed with the now disgraced Cabbage Patch doll, Smurfette, and soiled Jelly shoes.

Suddenly, my mother's face turned white. She dashed so quickly from the room that she knocked over a lamp and it crashed to the floor. Glass from the lightbulb went everywhere.

"I didn't do it!" The voice of one of the movers emanated from a different area of the house.

"It's okay," Mom yelled. "The cat, it . . ."

We didn't have a cat.

She came back a few minutes later with a cardboard box labeled, "Grandfather's KKK Robe."

"Take this," she whispered, shoving the box into my arms. She faced the label toward me so our movers couldn't read it. "Put it in the trunk of the car. Fast."

I walked out of our old home for the last time, realizing there were parts of my family's life we wanted to hide. I also firmly embraced the idea of reinventing myself, but I carried a lot of baggage with me.

In Tennessee, we bought seven acres in the woods. My dad poured a foundation for a house, framed it out, put on a roof, and laid the hardwood floors, plank by backbreaking plank. Since we were doing everything ourselves, we moved in before it was finished and took showers outside with a garden hose. And when we finally had a real bathroom, we had no doors. Dad tacked large brown towels over the openings until we got doors one year for Christmas. It'd be years before we could afford doorknobs, so my friends—who didn't consider bathroom doorknobs a luxury—never wanted to come over. They also raised their noses at our barely running car and my homemade shorts.

Childhood, to me, was a constant war with my clothing: shoes tied too tight, arm holes chafing my arms, and waists either too small or too big. But the people in Tennessee wore more brand-name clothing than the people in Mayfield, and they were also much more interested in the Civil War. My new friends joked that I was a "Yankee"—even though Mayfield was only thirty-five miles north of Paris. Apparently, Tennesseans held a grudge against the commonwealth of Kentucky because it was the birthplace of Abraham Lincoln.

The Civil War seemed to still haunt my new hometown, or at least hover in the background of the most innocent activities. My new church held softball games and picnics at Nathan Bedford Forrest State Park, which was named after a Confederate general and the first Grand Wizard of the KKK. Tennessee also had a state holiday commemorating his birth. The fact that I was born on the mountain in Tennessee didn't cancel out that I'd been living "in the north" for the past eight years of my life, and I was suddenly an outsider on the most minute geographical technicality.

I wanted to belong, but outside forces colluded to make me feel like the lowest rung on the cultural ladder. On television, depictions of hillbillies as slack-jawed yokels infected my sense of identity with shame like an untreated cut. I never saw any positive fictional character "from the mountains," but this was true of southerners in general. Southerners were portrayed as a generic, ignorant, drawling monolith, but in real life there were hillbillies, rednecks, and plain ole hicks. Each category had distinctive characteristics, verbal patterns, and outlooks on life. But we shared one thing in common. Just as the outside world looked down on us, each group managed to find reasons to look down on the other.

My family, for example, looked down on people from West Virginia, people with inside dogs, people who spoke in tongues, and rednecks. Rednecks were posers, after all—people who wore their identities on their sleeves or on bumper stickers in the form of Confederate flags and gun imagery. Hillbillies didn't project any sort of image, because they didn't care what you thought of them. I had enough of that in me to hold my head up high at school.

We had that mountain self-reliance. We built our own house outside the city limits and burned our own trash in that discarded washing-machine drum now that we'd outgrown rolling down the hill in it. The metal drum worked well as a burn pit, and my sisters and I exploded Aqua Net hairspray bottles in it like pipe bombs. I also had a pet squirrel which ate from a medicine dropper and slept in my bed. My dad taught us how to craft toothbrushes out of a sorghum tree, the only type of toothbrush he had until he was a teenager. Though we still drove a land barge, it was much better than the old car we'd sold to our garbage man for fifty dollars. Compared to how my parents grew up, we were wealthy beyond our wildest imaginations. My friends grew up soft in their Camrys and brand-name tennis shoes. Paris, Tennessee, wasn't exactly like George Jefferson movin' on up to the East Side, but as far as I was concerned, we were living the American dream.

Then, junior high. Judging from every movie ever made, the fastest way to achieve popularity was by earning a spot on the cheerleading squad, so my friends and I began flipping, cartwheeling, and spinning our way into the tryouts.

"Not on my watch." My mother narrowed her eyes and looked at me as I was practicing a routine. "You can't shake your bottom in a short skirt in front of a crowd."

"She's right. I want to be an elder at church one day," my dad agreed. "My children must be above reproach."

"Above reproach" was a catchphrase that meant I needed to "avoid the appearance of evil." Church was our Teflon, coating everything to make sure evil slid right off and ensuring we'd never be afflicted with things like poverty or drunkenness. That meant I couldn't be a cheerleader (according to my mom, only sluts did that), couldn't say the word *gosh* (dangerously close to taking the Lord's name in vain), and couldn't watch syndicated reruns of *Laverne and Shirley* (they worked at a beer-bottling factory). I got the feeling Mom was trying to establish a clear line from the way things were done on the mountain.

My grandmother, for example, always had her "face on." Her dedication to cosmetics started when she was playing a riverboat piano, which required a dramatic presence—dyed hair and elaborate makeup. When she played, the bright lights blinding her, she'd hear a *pop-pop-pop* when a poker player was caught cheating before they tossed him into the Tennessee River. Though several pregnancies waylaid her riverboat career, she never lost her dramatic flair and expected all female family members to do the same—no matter our age.

When my cousins entered the first grade, she stopped them at the door and evaluated their unadorned faces.

"A little paint can make an old barn look better." She leaned down and applied rouge, eyebrow pencil, and lipstick on my six-year-old cousins. "Remember, always look your best," she said. "Opportunity will present itself and you need to be prepared to take advantage of the moment." Classmates mocked my cousins for attending school looking like showgirls.

My mother, intending to put a stop to that in *our* family, swung all the way in the opposite direction. While my friends attended Mary Kay parties, she refused to let me learn about skin care and makeup. To blend in with everyone else, I secretly applied drugstore makeup in the bathroom at school. Apparently, my makeup skills were more of the mountain/show-girls variety, because my male science teacher pulled me aside and suggested I take a break from whatever I'd done to myself.

Mom also had no time for the cheerleading squad.

"Try out for the basketball team," my mom suggested. But she never "suggested." She issued orders like a Russian oligarch.

"I've never even dribbled a ball."

My dad, in an attempt to ameliorate my social stunting and preserve my virtue, poured a concrete slab outside our house and erected a goal. We didn't have doorknobs, but we had an impressive basketball court. I became point guard.

Grove Junior High was the Wild West of schools. Fights broke out in the hallways, boys spit tobacco juice on the classroom floors, and teachers smoked in the lounge. Students bullied teachers so relentlessly, some never returned. The ones who stayed were not the type who admonished students to become good citizens or participate in community outreach. They itched for a fight, paddles hanging ominously on classroom walls.

Our principal, Luke Wiggins, was an older man who walked with a limp and couldn't pronounce his L's or R's.

"This is Wuke Wiggins," he said every morning on the intercom. The whole school snickered, but not in his presence. He drilled holes the size of half dollars in his paddle, which made each blow sting.

When my basketball coach was gone for a month, Mr. Wiggins filled in. One afternoon he stood beneath the goal and tossed me the ball at half-court. I dribbled toward the basket, remembering what I'd been taught. Outside foot step (long), inside foot step (high), and always use the back-board. But the ball fell limply on the other side of the goal. Suddenly, Mr. Wiggins's open hand came straight at my face. *Smack!*

"What was that?" he barked near my now-reddened cheek. "Wayups are free points. Nevuh miss 'em."

I looked into the stands at my mom, who was waiting to drive me home after practice. Her expression conveyed, *How are you supposed to beat Puryear if you don't toughen up?* He hit every girl who missed her layup, and no parent raised a voice of concern.

That day, I learned how to hit left-handed layups and that adults could do whatever they wanted to us. No one would intervene. This extended into the classroom.

"Most of you guys won't be attending college, and who's ever gonna use photosynthesis anyway?" My science teacher, Coach Cunningham, showed shocking antipathy toward the subject he was supposed to teach. "How many of y'all have guns in your homes and trucks?"

Every hand went up.

"That's why we're learning about gun safety this semester instead of science." This, to me, seemed like sound reasoning. My dad had dropped out of high school, barely passed his GED, and did not learn to recite his ABCs until his twenties. Yet he was one of the more impressive men I'd ever met—he could fix our constantly breaking car, build a house from scratch, and identify birds based solely on the flapping of their wings. What life skills did he lack by not having an education?

Coach Cunningham went into the back room that held beakers and microscopes and brought out a rifle. We had guns all over the house. They were leaning in corners and lying on the couch cushions. I'd gone deer hunting with my dad and shot Coke cans off logs my whole life. After serving time in Vietnam, my dad's first cousin had been inducted into the Tennessee Hall of Fame and was called "the best pistol-shooter in the US." He held eleven individual national pistol-shooting records, shared in another ten team records, and had been on the Olympic team. Whether or not I was a seer, I hoped I might have the untapped mountain gift of sharp shooting.

But even I had never seen a gun inside a school. The whole class got quiet as Coach Cunningham stood before us, the gun in front of his chest.

"Nancy, come up here and hold this for me." He extended the gun in front of him as I got out of my seat. "Don't worry, it's not loaded." I walked to the front of the class and took the rifle, pointing it toward the ceiling.

"Bang!" he shouted. "You're dead."

The whole class jumped, and I almost dropped the gun.

"What did she do wrong?" he asked. No one stirred. "She didn't check to see if it was loaded. That's the number one rule of firearm safety. Never touch a gun without checking to see if it's loaded."

"You said it wasn't." My voice shook.

"Never trust anyone when it comes to guns."

I handed him the gun and sat back down, my face red.

"By the time this semester is over, all of you will be certified in hunter's safety. This will be much more valuable to you than learning about protozoa, I'll tell you that right now."

Over the course of the semester, I vowed to make up for my first day's lack of gun awareness. I paid special attention when we watched videos of hunters tracking deer and learned when to take a shot by considering what body parts were accessible and the location of an appropriate berm. I learned what soaps to avoid before hunting, the parts of the gun, and the proper cleaning of weapons.

At the end of the class, Coach Cunningham gave all of us students shotguns and lined us up outside.

"Now, we're gonna put what you've learned to the test," he said, walking in front of us like a drill sergeant. This was my moment. I knew that my mountain blood would not allow me to be embarrassed when it came to guns ever again.

We stood in a line, holding our weapons. Someone yelled "pull!" and skeet flew into the air, one after the other. I held my breath and watched the clay disks fly through the sky until I had the first one lined up in my sights.

Bam, bam, bam! All three of my clay disks shattered and their fragments fell to the earth.

"Hate to be a coyote in *your* yard." Coach Cunningham put his hand on my shoulder. "Congratulations, you're the best shot in the seventh grade."

I looked at the ground and shuffled my feet, but my chest swelled with pride.

Though I didn't learn science that year, I figured I wouldn't need that to succeed in the world. After all, I won the seventh-grade spelling bee, dribbled a basketball with my left hand, and—now—made every layup.

But that didn't mean life stopped with all its slapping.

3

VACATION
BIBLE SCHOOL

C an you catch a ride home?" My mother leaned out the car window. It was the summer after my seventh-grade year, and I wasn't old enough to drive. I followed the kids scampering up the church steps for vacation Bible school. "I have to work this afternoon."

"Don't worry," said Conrad, the head of the VBS, who was also in the parking lot greeting the children. In his early twenties, he was too young to be a preacher. But the hiring criteria for country Church of Christ preachers was a car salesman's enthusiasm, a firm handshake, and baptism by immersion. He preached at a rural church down the road but came to our church for midweek or evening services. His dad was an elder at our church, so he was like church royalty. "We'll make sure she gets home."

I loved VBS, a week full of Kool-Aid, sugar cookies, and crafts. Conrad led us in songs like "Father Abraham," "Wandering Jews," and "I Don't Want to be a Goat, Nope."

If the church was family, its old country building was my home. I knew every cranny of the old building. When I made the honor roll, the older ladies mailed me laminated newspaper clippings with a handwritten "proud of you" note. If family members got sick, they showed up at our door and handed over a casserole with a note written in cursive on the aluminum foil top: "Bake at 350 degrees until melted and brown on top." Church was the center of our lives, where they hold a baby shower when you're born, a service when you're baptized, a wedding when you're married, and a funeral when you die. With all that dedication, surely I could find a ride home.

Balloons were tied to the sign outside the building with "Sulphur Well Church of Christ." In the Bible, fire and "brimstone" (the old-fashioned word for sulfur) was evidence of God's wrath. In the Church of Christ, the "fire and brimstone" concept wasn't negative, it was a theological necessity. Warning people that they were going to hell was an act of love, like yelling at someone to run out of a burning building.

The church was named after an old resort community centered around a natural sulfuric well. Sulfur breaks down and releases hydrogen sulfide gas as a result of decay and chemical reactions, making the water smell like rotten eggs. But that old town was flooded years ago. Kentucky Lake soon covered every house, tricycle, church building, and mailbox. Though the old sulfur well was also buried under the lake, locals said it still bubbled up if you knew where to look when you were out on the water.

Attendance fluctuated by season. In the fall, winter, and spring, we had around two hundred congregants, but attendance swelled to three hundred in the summer. After the last "amen," the visitors pulled their boats a couple of miles to get to the loading ramps at Kentucky Lake. I enjoyed the sun-kissed visitors and VBS.

"God, told Noah, there's going to be a floody, floody." Conrad belted out the song, walking back and forth motioning with his hands. After worship, we broke into classes. The younger kids were taught lessons using Bible characters made of flannel, which teachers placed on felt boards to reenact the classics: Noah's ark, Daniel and the lion's den, the parting of the Red Sea. But in middle school, the lessons changed.

"Today, we're doing something different," Conrad announced. "The girls and guys are splitting up for a very special lesson." *Very special lesson* was a phrase usually used for television episodes focusing on issues like Alex P. Keaton's uncle's alcoholism or Nancy Reagan's advice to Arnold and Willis Drummond to "Just say no." In the context of our lives, however, it could mean only one thing.

Sex.

Everything I'd learned about sex so far had come from sneaking glances at *Cosmopolitan* at the drug store, so I was fine with this. The girls arranged chairs in a circle in a separate classroom. Standing in front of the corrugated-bordered bulletin board, our teacher pulled out a flower and held it up. "Isn't it gorgeous?"

The rose was scarlet, prettier than the ones in our yard, the kind I'd imagined someone giving me over a candlelit dinner in the distant future. The teacher handed the rose to my friend. "Go ahead. Feel it."

She hesitantly took the rose, pressed her nose into it, and shoved it to me.

"Don't be shy," the teacher said. "Experience it, touch it, smell it, enjoy it." I took the rose in my hands and examined its velvety petals. A petal fell off, revealing even brighter petals, like they were blushing at being exposed. I hurriedly passed the flower to my friend, who crinkled her nose and passed it to another girl, who ruffled the petals. More fell.

After it made it all the way around the circle, the teacher held it up. "Look at it now." The rose was bruised and torn. "Still beautiful?"

The girls looked uncertain, but I wasn't. It was stunning, even brighter red—the more tender petals having been revealed—and fuller, more open to the world than the tidy rose originally presented.

Miss Yvonne dropped the flower on the floor and stepped on it with her toe. "Still beautiful? Anyone want this now?"

A few girls gasped, but no one moved.

"Your body is this rose. Your purity is a gift to your future husband and God. If you have sex before marriage, men looking for potential wives won't consider you beautiful anymore. Who'd want to marry a girl who's been passed around?"

I nodded in earnest agreement. I wanted to honor God in everything I did. I would not be that trampled rose. Not me.

After VBS, I scanned the adults leaving the building.

"Did you get a lift?" Conrad asked. He patted his truck and told me to climb in.

I was honored. Conrad was young and popular, especially with the kids. Preachers had dedicated their lives to God, and were cut from a different, more holy, cloth. We generally idolized them as being better than us and so I felt special as I climbed into his truck and cranked the window.

We drove down Highway 89 and saw a hitchhiker. "Scoot over," Conrad said. "I'm going to do a good deed."

"What?" This seemed foreign, reckless, and invigorating. I had an appropriate fear of strange men on the side of the road but not for people in the church. There were good guys and bad guys, and the formula for telling which was which was easy: church people were good, everyone else was suspicious.

But Conrad was joking. He sped past the hitchhiker, and I was relieved.

After winding down the long gravel road to my house, he shifted into neutral, pulled the emergency brake, and asked, "Mind if I grab some water?"

I wasn't supposed to bring boys in the house when my parents weren't home, a new rule now that I was no longer in elementary school. But Conrad wasn't a boy. He was twenty-three, eleven years older than me. Plus, he was a preacher.

He picked up on my uncertainty.

"For whosoever shall give you a cup of water to drink in my name, because ye belong to Christ," he said. "Verily I say unto you, he shall not lose his reward."

"You memorized a Bible verse in case you ever needed to ask for a drink?"

He flashed a grin. "Did it work?"

We climbed the stairs and walked past a porch swing my dad made. The door wasn't locked, and the kitchen still smelled of bacon grease. I handed him tap water.

He tossed back the water and thudded the glass on the table. "Gotta go. Catch you tomorrow?" He didn't look at me as he headed out the door. A few seconds later, however, his face appeared through the screen door.

"Forgot my keys." I let him in, and we looked on the countertops, near the sink. Nothing.

"Check your pockets?" I asked. He reached into his front right one and his left. No keys.

"Maybe you left them in the ignition?"

He left the kitchen, and I followed him.

"Your keys won't be in there." He walked into my grandmother's old room we'd repurposed after her recent death. There was a love seat along the wall, and her power-lift chair in the corner. Suddenly, his hand was on my face, and he turned me to him.

He was looking at me in a funny way. At school, we played a staring game, the first one to look away loses. But this was different. I wanted to look away, at the floor or my hands—anywhere but his eyes—but looking away felt like defeat. He held my gaze, then leaned in and hugged me. I awkwardly accepted the embrace. But after I pulled away from him, he kissed me, moved me onto the small sofa, and climbed on top of me.

I froze as his hands slid into the bra I'd only recently started wearing and reached for my zippers and buttons.

A few things happened all at once. First, my sexual purity—vow or not—was shattered. Second, I became "damaged," ruined for all future love interests. He moved on me, his thin lips and pointy tongue on my mouth. It happened so quickly. There was no fumbling, no exploration, just direct and confident motions toward parts of me normally covered in clothing. Parts that had never been touched. He was fast and deliberate, like doing combat maneuvers. Then it was over. He climbed off me, stood up, and smiled.

"Well, look at this." Conrad patted his back pocket and pulled out a key. "If it'd been a snake, it would've bit me."

He smiled, before a sober expression passed over his face. "You can't tell anyone about this. We really shouldn't have done it." He tucked a wisp of hair behind my ears. "If people think a preacher's a hypocrite, they might not believe in God."

And with that one comment, I gained a secret burdened with the weight of other people's eternal salvation. He walked to the door. "Catch ya tomorrow, okay?"

The screen door slammed shut, locking me inside with my shame. What happened on my dead grandmother's love seat was reserved for married people. At the same time, I was conflicted. He was a preacher, and he chose me over his deeply held biblical beliefs because he liked me. I was special.

I was a different person the next day, walking back into vacation Bible school. Older. I didn't need a scarlet letter to know I was a trampled rose now with no chance at getting my life right. I pushed this dread away. For the first time in my life, my real life conflicted with my spiritual life, and I was adrift, and I didn't know how to fix it. It was a dreadful feeling to have ruined your life at such an early age.

For months, Conrad popped by the house to visit my parents, before secretly stealing visits with me on the porch for some variations of the same activity. Preachers weren't inerrant, but they did hold the keys to salvation. Men made the rules—both the patriarchs of the Bible and the church. Conditioned to appreciate any attention men in spiritual authority might give, to obey their teachings, and even alleviate any of their inconveniences, I never even considered putting a stop to this.

All of this must've been okay, I decided, because he'd one day ask me to be his wife. I'd been told this sort of thing should happen only within the confines of a marriage bed. *He'd* said that, and I believed my church's moral instruction.

But the secret I carried was cumbersome, and I spent all of my efforts trying to carry it alone. While Conrad attended Wednesday night services, I sat in the pew stealing glances in his direction. He never met my gaze.

After a few months, he hadn't dropped by the house in a while, and he was keeping his distance from me at church. At first, this seemed like a romantic cat-and-mouse game. It took me a few weeks to realize, with a sinking sensation, that it was just abandonment. He'd ruined me and left.

I'd thought my relationship with Conrad meant I was "in," but it shoved me "out." The warmth and comfort I'd always felt from church was replaced with a cold dread.

At first, I still sat with the youth group on what we called the "amen pew," dropped coins into the collection plate, and volunteered to read the Bible passages. But my innocent, wide-eyed faith was gone, and all of these familiar activities now felt like they were happening on a stage. I was acting.

I'd learned about sin when I'd gotten baptized "for the remission of my sins" the previous summer at camp. I'd emerged from the swimming pool waters spiritually pure and clean. But that evening at church camp, I'd laughed at a joke someone made at another's expense. I was crushed that I hadn't been able to live a full day without sinning, and I didn't know how to tap back into that sensation of purity.

The only way I knew how to achieve this was to "go forward" during the "song of invitation" after every sermon, as preachers asked wayward souls to come forward and either get baptized or confess their sins.

When I got back home after camp, I walked down that long, lonely aisle as the congregation warbled the words of "Just As I Am." The preacher looked surprised to see me, since such public confessions were usually reserved for public sin like an unwed pregnancy or upcoming jail time—something obvious a person couldn't hide. When the preacher handed me a white index card to document the reason for my public confession, I didn't know what to put. I checked the box for "unspoken sin."

My desire for absolution, of course, embarrassed my family, who had been shocked to see me walk down that aisle. I'm sure all the people in the congregation had assumed I'd been caught up in something scandalous. Truth was, I was keenly aware of my own shortcomings and had no idea how to deal with them.

Now that I truly had a scandal, I was too ashamed to go forward. You can't go forward during every service, and I'd already wasted my shot over something trivial. Plus, I couldn't go forward as Conrad sat on the front row glaring at me.

The church convinced me sin would send me straight to hell. Once this was my inevitable eternal destination, I resigned myself to it. I had no recourse. I wanted to be pure again, but I was too damaged for that now.

A hard carapace formed around me, a shell of cynicism to protect me from my newfound lack of hope. I started skipping Wednesday night class and sneaked off with a friend named Henry who was two years older, someone who was already on "the outside" ever since his parents' divorce. Henry and I pretended to go to class but instead walked the long rural road in the dark, learning to smoke cigarettes together and popping mints before we returned to the building. He didn't ask why I was suddenly morose, and I never asked about his parents' divorce. We were malcontents, wondering if any of the church teachings were real.

When I went back to school that fall, my moral standards slipped. Any time my friends and I weren't directly supervised—between classes, in the locker rooms—we played a game in which we held our breath while friends pressed down on our sternums. We passed out in each other's arms, coming groggily back to the harsh reality of school with great reluctance. It was dangerous and terrifying, but I enjoyed the lightheaded, skin-tingling sensation of not being present in my own body. At sleepovers with my school friends, I watched Freddy Krueger movies, smoked Marlboro Lights, and pretended to like beer.

One day, a school counselor conducted a special gathering of eighth graders. She wrote her name on the board in cursive: Ms. Shaw. My cheerleading friends shot me a sideways glance. Nothing screamed "lesbian" more than her short hair and her identifying as a "Ms." I'd never known anyone to identify as a Ms. That was just something we'd learned about in grammar lessons, a question on an elementary school test. The only way it would come up in real life is when we didn't know whether a lady was married and didn't want to offend her. It's a whole different matter when someone chooses it.

"First, I'm going to define sex abuse." Ms. Shaw's speech was the first time anyone had ever introduced the concept of kids having bodily autonomy. While she sat on a stool at the front of the class, I picked at my fingernails. A football player slapped me on the back of the head.

"Listen to the butch, will ya?" He made a V with his fingers and a sexual gesture with his tongue. My friends giggled. My skin grew hot, but I laughed too.

"If you're ever touched in a sexual way by an adult," she continued, "please tell a trusted adult."

My heart pounded, though I didn't believe I was a victim of anything. I had secretly dated a preacher and we'd broken up. If anything, I was responsible, since I'd let him come into the house and caused him to stumble.

A pedophile was a guy behind the wheel of an ice cream truck, not someone who loved me. Conrad had loved me, at least, until I did something to lose that love. What? I didn't know. But I'd never heard we were too young to consent or that adults who pursued us were predatory. If Ms. Shaw explained these concepts on that day, I didn't hear it over the thudding of my heart.

I contemplated making a secret appointment with her and confessing everything, asking for help.

"If you're ever in a bad situation, my door's always open." She climbed down off the stool as my friends made snarky comments behind me. She said all the right things and her office was right down the hall. But I was like a drunk swimmer unable to grab onto the life preserver because I didn't identify that sinking sensation as drowning.

My heart was broken, but that was the cost of what I'd done. Conrad had taken away my innocence, my church community, my relationship with my parents, and my faith. He had also messed up my perspective of other romantic possibilities. When guys my age had an interest in me, I clammed up and expected the worst.

I couldn't go back in time and be casual about romance again. I used to fall in and out of love so innocently that I didn't even identify it as love. I'd taken love for granted as something embedded into the fabric of life, like the fresh smell of rain or the cozy warmth of a nap. Before Conrad, crushes happened and unhappened during the time it took my nail polish to wear off, and they never left an emotional mark. But now I was marked.

One night at church, I sat and listened to Jimmy Credell, a lanky preacher with folksy mannerisms that softened the church's theology. As Jimmy spoke, I tried not to look at the back of Conrad's head, though he was sitting in my direct line of sight. I looked at his sandy hair, the way he tilted his head when Jimmy made various points.

Jimmy ended with a dying-in-a-car-crash scenario which was a staple in Church of Christ sermons.

"Imagine you're driving on the way home tonight when a truck veers into your lane. Before you collide, you have one second before you die. What do you do?" He paused. "It'll be too late to get your soul right then, but you have a chance right now."

It was frighteningly easy to lose our salvation, because any unconfessed sin could send us to hell. If the accident was caused by speeding (a sin) and we died, we lost our salvation. If we saw a truck headed our way, and we cussed (a sin) before dying, we'd go to hell if we didn't have time to repent. If it had been a while since we asked God for forgiveness, there's no telling what sin might send us to the lake of fire.

Though I wasn't sure what was real anymore, a part of me still believed enough to practice confessing fast, just in case. I could say *Dear-God-forgive-me-of-all-my-sins* in one second. I never added "Amen," which seemed like a luxury I might not have with limited breath. Plus, it added a finality to it. I'd never be finished begging for my salvation.

After Jimmy finished trying to scare the hell out of us, someone led us in a "song of invitation," when sinners could give their hearts to God. "Today is the day of salvation," we sang in threatening encouragement. "Tomorrow may be too late."

Conrad shuffled his hymnal from one hand to the other.

We sang *a capella* because we believed the Bible did not permit the use of instruments. This meant people got to know each other on an intimate level as we stood side by side and sang about our most sacred yearnings. Without the forgiving piano accompaniment, our off-key warbling made our singing almost unbearable. But sometimes the harmonies wafted over us and split me wide open, like I'd seen a ghost. Jimmy sometimes spoke of the Holy Ghost being "here in the midst of us," so maybe that's what I felt.

However, these constant threats of hell had limited effect, since I was in hell already. Even the thought of God being in our presence scared me. If he was there, he could see the secrets the baptismal waters were meant to bury.

I sang, side by side with people who were supposed to be family members on our journey toward heaven.

But the sulfur still bubbled up if you knew where to look.

4

THE PHONE CALL

I wanted a guy to change my life. Someone to swoop in and be different enough from me to pull me from the quicksand and take things in a different direction. There was the me "before the glass of water" and the one "after the glass of water." I didn't like the new version, but I couldn't crawl out of my skin. I got it in my head that if only I could find a different man—a better man—we could meet and fall in love and all of the bad would dissipate like dew on the grass in the dawning sun.

I met Jacob when I was a junior. He was a senior who'd moved to town from Arkansas and drove a Toyota Celica GT with a CD player. When he asked me out, I said yes. In a small town, you know most of the guys too well to find them interesting.

A few weeks after we started dating, Jacob's science teacher gave the students in his class an assignment: they were to design and implement a research experiment. Jacob, whose dad was a doctor, decided to determine how much Tylenol would be lethal to mice.

One afternoon, in his garage, he showed me his cage of little white creatures—animals he was slowly poisoning. "They're all going to die?" I peered into the box of little creatures and frowned. "Why are you doing this?"

"Knowing the lethal dose of a drug can prevent unintended deaths." He put the crate on a shelf in his garage. He said it like it was the most logical thing in the world. Obvious.

"Are you at least going to give them a proper burial?" I asked. We were standing in his kitchen, where a box of doughnuts sat on his immaculate counter. Instead of digging one out of the box and popping it into his mouth, he placed the box on the counter, washed his hands, got out a plate, and ate the food slowly with a knife and fork. "Since they're giving their lives for science?"

He looked at me like I'd uttered the most naive sentence ever constructed in English. "Sure, I'll do that." He laughed. "You can even have a funeral for them if you want."

Jacob was liberal and I was conservative, a tension that played out over many meals with his Green Peace–member parents. We went to movies, talked about philosophy, and argued about politics. His senior year, Jacob was unanimously voted "Most Likely to Succeed," probably because his fastidious, deliberate actions made him seem more prepared for life than the rest of us. A man who eats doughnuts with a knife and fork is sure to go places.

After graduation, he went to the University of Tennessee, and we were forced into a long-distance relationship since I still had a year of high school. Without social media, email, or the ability to afford long-distance calls, we wrote each other long letters which we sent through the postal service.

When the postman came, I'd open the envelope and stare at Jacob's block-lettered handwriting detailing his day's events in precise language; he left for class at 8:47 a.m., cleaned his kitchen (again), and was trying to bring his grade up from an 89.3 to an 89.5 to get the round-up. I was more of a sticker-at-the-top-of-the-page, colored-marker, never-have-stamps type of writer. An entire relationship distilled into letters made me see—in black and white—that we couldn't work. But since I couldn't break up with him via the United States Postal Service, I decided to have that conversation the next time I saw him.

In the meantime, I got a job waiting tables at the Huddle House, a restaurant chain in the South similar to, but less sophisticated than, Waffle House. I wore a brown uniform and served coffee to police officers who ate for free, friends from church, and people I knew from school. In small towns, all the drama of life occurs with a regular cast of characters, and you notice anyone new.

One day, a grandfather and his grandson sat in my section. I'd never seen them before. The guy was cute, with his dark hair and green eyes. They ordered scrambled eggs and hash browns, and—as I cleared their plates—the older gentleman stroked his beard.

"My grandson's been working up the courage to ask for your phone number." He picked up the check, and his grandson smiled a lopsided grin.

"I'm Liam." He took a sip from his coffee. "I'm from Seattle, but I'm living here this summer to spend time with this guy"—he shot his grandfather an embarrassed look—"before he kicks the bucket."

His grandfather laughed, slid out of the booth, and walked to the register. I switched the coffee pot from one hand to the other.

"Ever go out on the lake?" He took his ball cap off, ran his fingers through his dark hair, and replaced the cap. "I'm taking the boat out later this week. Maybe you could show me around?"

Liam seemed kind, an outsider who brought knowledge of the Pacific Northwest and other details of life from the wider world.

"Let's go, Romeo," his grandfather said after laying cash on the table.

I had to admit, his grandfather was a great wingman. I wrote my number on a napkin and slid it into Liam's palm.

I'd like to justify this by explaining that Jacob and I weren't exclusive or we'd taken a break when he went to college, but that would all be a lie. When I gave my number to Liam, I was cheating on Jacob. But once I believed a man might be my salvation, they all looked like emergency cords I could pull to stop my downward momentum.

Jacob, I could now tell, was not going to be that cord. Though he was smart and talented, something was off. The way he got into his car and adjusted all the mirrors before we left the driveway every time we got into the car, even if he'd already adjusted it on a previous drive. Or the way he constantly made lists and checked them off throughout the day. Or the way he buckled when his rigid routine was interrupted.

Though I didn't want to break up with him over the phone, the Liam situation made me address the issue more urgently. The next time I talked to Jacob on the phone, I told him I wanted to end things. I didn't reveal I was seeing anyone else, because I'd decided we weren't meant for each other well before I served Liam his coffee that day.

"You can't break up with me over the phone." His voice was both emphatic and emotionless. He was reasoning with me over etiquette, not over the substance of my desire to break things off. "I've not dated anyone else in college because I was waiting for you."

Since I had doubts about ending things this way, I caved. Instead of sticking to my convictions, I promised to have a conversation about our relationship the next time I saw him.

But Liam was right there in my hometown—in person, driving his grandfather's truck, ordering hashbrowns at the Huddle House—so I dated him anyway. I didn't tell Liam about Jacob, and I didn't tell Jacob about Liam. Since Jacob was away at college and Liam was just visiting his grandfather, it was easy to keep everything separate. It didn't matter, because I'd break up with Jacob well before they both were at the University of Tennessee in the fall.

UT was not an option for me. Both of my parents had attended the Church of Christ college named Lipscomb in Nashville, and I was expected to go there as well. Because I wanted to go far away, to escape the aquarium of small-town life, I wasn't keen on the idea of a Nashville college two hours down the road. Church settings made me uncomfortable, and Lipscomb had a daily Bible reading requirement plus Bible classes.

"Are you excited to go to Lipscomb?" I listened to the breathily enthusiastic voices of the admissions volunteers who regularly called.

"Not really." I twirled the phone cord attached to the kitchen wall as I made up a story. "I want to go to a good veterinary school, and you can't get into a good one with a Lipscomb degree."

The next time a different admission staffer called me, so I lied again. "I want to go to a good medical school, and you can't get into a good one with a Lipscomb degree."

The third time, yet another admissions staffer called me so I made up yet another lie. "I want to go to a good law school, and you can't get into a good one with a Lipscomb degree."

But this staffer was ready for me. "My friend David just graduated from Lipscomb, and he's at Harvard Law School. Is that good enough for you?"

In other words, he called my bluff. "Harvard is on my list of possible options," I stammered. "I mean, I'd have to think about it."

"Great, I'll have David call you to answer your questions."

When I hung up the phone, I was paralyzed with anxiety. I had no interest in the law or this David guy. Still I didn't want to embarrass myself. Since we couldn't afford encyclopedias and the internet had not made its way into rural Tennessee homes, I went to the public library and read all I could on Harvard Law School. The articles I found were mostly about how students argued about politics in the classes, and I figured I could make it through a one-hour conversation.

I knew about politics. I enjoyed listening to radio personality Rush Limbaugh and even recorded his television show on our VCR to watch after school. He seemed to care about "the common man." For example, environmentalists were constantly lamenting deforestation, a complaint I took to heart since Dad cruised timber for a paper company.

When Rush defended paper companies and called the liberal environmentalists "tree huggers," things seemed right in the world. Someone somewhere—on television even—understood what it was like living where I lived. And where I lived, there were plenty of trees. No danger of running out.

We slapped a bumper sticker on Dad's vehicle which read "Trees = America's Best Renewable Resource." I imagined this might raise eyebrows in big cities from people who didn't know an oak from a tulip poplar and thought we were a bunch of hicks anyway, but that vehicle never drove one mile into a city. As the sticker adhered to the Bronco, it also seemed to stick conservative principles to me.

When David called the following Tuesday, I pretended to be an ambitious future law student who wanted to one day attend the Ivy League university. I brought up the political turmoil I'd read about, and David explained to me how he was frequently shouted down in class because of his conservative political views. I was mesmerized.

I could tell he was more sophisticated, interesting, and intelligent than I was. And he was quantitatively different from the guys I knew. He was not dating material. First, he was already in law school. Second, he showed no romantic interest at all. He stuck to telling me how great Lipscomb was and suggesting ways to increase my chances of one day getting into law school. As he was talking, however, my heart swooned. While Jacob was unnervingly precise and Liam was a good natured frat guy, David was smart and fascinating. Through the conversation, I was consistently amazed by his kindness, his willingness to help me figure out my educational path. But as soon as I let my mind romantically wander, he mentioned the word *fiancé*. He said he'd met his fiancé at Lipscomb, and my heart sank a little.

I had no realistic hope that I—a high school senior in rural Tennessee—would ever even meet this first-year Harvard Law student living in Boston. But still. After a one-hour conversation, all other guys seemed duller in comparison.

Somehow, talking to him about this improbable, impossible goal made it seem reasonable and attainable. It wasn't, but he treated my ideas and thoughts with respect. During our conversation, I suspended my disbelief long enough to imagine what it would be like to have the world open up before me. I hung up the phone feeling an unfamiliar, dangerous sensation.

Hope.

I wanted a guy to change my life. Someone to swoop in and be different enough from me to pull me from the quicksand. And though I knew I'd never meet him in real life, that's exactly what happened.

5

THE HELICOPTER

Look beside you," the speaker said. "You might be sitting beside your future husband or wife."

On the first day of Lipscomb orientation, incoming college freshmen met for worship and get-to-know-you mixers. I'd rarely been in a place so full of people my age—fresh faced and eager—singing to God about blue skies and rainbows when all I saw were dark, ominous clouds. When I opened my mouth to sing, the words didn't come out, and I was suddenly aware of the veil between my classmates and me.

"Go ahead," the speaker said. "Look around. You'll spend the next four years with these people. Hundreds of Christian marriages have started right here on this campus."

The students giggled and hesitantly introduced themselves. I turned to my right and saw a blonde girl who was six feet tall with piercing blue eyes, a pink blouse, and Wranglers.

"You look like a model," I said.

"I want to be," she laughed. "I only came here because my parents made me."

"Same. The forced-to-be-here part, not the model part," I said. "I already hate this."

"Want to get out of here?"

Her name was Virginia Camille. She scrunched her nose when she told me her middle name, but I thought Camille sounded elegant and sophisticated. It was better than my name—Nancy Jane—which sounded like I was conceived during *Hee Haw*. We blasted Tanya Tucker in her new black Camaro, lowered the windows, and took off into Nashville with the wind whipping our hair.

"Watch out for the curb," I said as she hit it. She was a horrible driver but from that point forward, we were inseparable. Virginia was more concerned about perfecting her strut for the runway than her grades for her classes. I joined the staff of the university newspaper called *The Babbler* and was elected to student government. We had nothing in common. I loved to talk about politics, but she stared in boredom as I spoke about the 1994 Republican Revolution. She tried to teach me about fashion and clothing, but I lacked the money to execute on her advice.

Virginia had been an ugly duckling in high school, but quickly grew out of her awkward phase and was new to the charms of beauty. Now the same people who'd treated her poorly when they were younger suddenly wanted to be friends. As we strolled through Bison Square, we heard the bitter whispers of narrow-eyed girls and felt the appreciative glances of wide-eyed guys. Some guys broke into song when they saw her, usually John Denver's "Take Me Home, Country Roads" because it was the most famous song with the word Virginia in it.

"How's my 'mountain momma'?" some guy said as she walked by him in Bison Square.

She kept walking—no, she was gliding—and laughing at the attention.

"I guess it's better than the other nickname they call me."

"What?"

"Virgin."

"Are you?"

She nodded sheepishly. "Are you?" I hesitated to answer, since many Christians would've wielded this information as a bat, using it to beat me into scriptural submission. I told her I wasn't anyway.

She laughed. "I won't tell anyone, but I do need advice." I turned to listen. "I accidentally told the garbage man I'd go out on a date with him. I didn't know what to do."

"How old is he?" I asked.

"I don't know, like thirty? Or maybe fifty?"

I couldn't help much. In church, we'd been taught to cater to the desires of men while not leading them on in any way. This was like threading a needle in the dark, but I—being a normal-looking person—had more margin for error. Because she hadn't developed the deflection skills that her looks demanded, I worried she'd get herself in real trouble. She plopped down on my twin-size bunk bed and put a pillow over her head.

"He could be a serial killer!" I said. "When's this date?"

She pulled the pillow off her face.

"Tonight?" I asked.

"He's picking me up from here. Six o'clock."

"Cancel it," I insisted, but she didn't have his number. When her date showed up, he was surprised to see me waiting with his date in the lobby of our dorm. He was at least in his late thirties.

"I hope you don't mind," she purred, flipping her hair. "My friend decided to come along!"

He disappointedly bought both of us meals at Shoney's, and afterward we giggled about the whole thing in my dorm room.

"Did you see his face?" she laughed. "When he saw both of us?"

"Where have you ladies been?" My roommate Celeste grabbed her Bible off the mini fridge. It was almost ten o'clock, and the students were gathering in Bison Square to sing. "Are you coming to the devo?"

Celeste, with short dark hair, kept her side of the room tidy and made me brownies. She was the type of person who participated in Bible Bowls and dated Bible majors. Dating was a big deal at college, because finding a husband was an ever-present pressure on Lipscomb's campus. Girls regularly had "candle passings" in dormitory lobbies to reveal who'd gotten engaged that weekend. They'd turn out the lights, sit in a circle, and pass around a lit candle from girl to girl. When it came to the secretly engaged girl, she blew out the candle and everyone celebrated her ensuing MRS degree. As a pauper perceives a billionaire's private jet, I perceived these Lipscomb girls' cheery optimism. They were rich with spiritual and romantic opportunities, unsullied by the world. I was damaged goods.

"We're skipping the devotional," I told Celeste, who pretended to be surprised. "I'm going to break up with Jacob once and for all."

Celeste patted me on the back. She'd overheard multiple telephone "breakup" conversations with Jacob already. Every attempt was met with intense emotion, followed by a half-hearted promise on my part to try and make it work. I needed a stiffer spine.

"Don't back down," Celeste said. "And it's a long-distance call so make it quick."

I was still dating Liam, and both he and Jacob attended UT, an unfortunate coincidence. I had a nagging fear they might bump into each other, but Jacob was a fastidious engineering student and Liam was a business major fraternity guy. Since UT had twenty thousand students, they wouldn't run into each other. Even if they did, I was sure they wouldn't hit it off well enough to compare romantic notes.

In October, Liam invited me to go to Washington, D.C., to meet his parents, where he promised a surprise for me. I was intrigued and touched he'd put so much effort into this weekend away. I agreed to go but privately vowed to break off my relationship with Jacob once and for all. I could end it, and neither of them would find out about the other.

After Virginia and Celeste left, Jacob called.

"Can you come see me this weekend?" he asked.

"Not this weekend." I didn't mention my D.C. trip and I tried to maintain an even tone. "This relationship isn't working for me. We aren't right for each other."

On the other end of the line, I heard nothing.

"Jacob." I watched the minute hand sweep around the clock. "You there?"

"You cannot do this to me." His voice had a more authoritative, almost militant tone. "I won't allow it."

"I have a say in this, too." But years of being taught that women were created to serve men were ingrained in me, and the desire to placate welled within my throat. I swallowed it.

"But you've dated me since high school," he said. "I want to marry you."

I softened my voice. "I love you," I said, "but we're not right for each other long term."

"Is there someone else?" His voice was low and frantic, and a shudder ran down my spine. "If you've been seeing someone behind my back, I swear I'll kill myself."

I immediately denied his accusation, justifying the lie since Liam was not the reason I wanted to break up, but the word *kill* hovered above me. I remembered how he'd determined the lethal dose of Tylenol in mice back in high school ostensibly to prevent human overdoses. Was that more than a classroom science experiment? Was he trying to prevent deaths or cause his own?

The thought chilled me to my bones, but I pushed it from my head. Celeste came back into the room, her Bible in hand. When she saw I was still on the phone, she mouthed, "Jacob?" It had been two hours.

"I have to go." Jacob didn't respond. "Do you hear me?"

Celeste sat on the bed beside me, her eyes as wide as saucers.

"If I can't have you, I don't want anyone or anything," he finally said. "Not anymore. If I'm done with you, I'm done with life."

When I hung up, Celeste put her hand on my shoulder. "Did you break it off?"

I nodded, but my head was full of frenetic thoughts. "He's going to kill himself."

"What?" she asked. "Why?"

We analyzed his last words on the call several times—"If I'm done with you, I'm done with life"—and Celeste helped me find the number for the Knoxville police department. If he attempted suicide, I couldn't get there in time to stop him. My hands were shaking so much I almost couldn't dial the phone.

After I alerted the police, I sat by the phone for two hours as they knocked on his door for a wellness check. What would I do if Jacob was dead? Would I have caused this?

Finally, the phone rang. Jacob.

"I had some visitors," he said. "Courtesy of you, I assume?" Gone was the anger. He sounded perfectly calm.

"I was worried." I whispered, since Celeste had fallen asleep in her bunk and I'd already pulled the blanket to her chin and turned out the lights. "I don't want anything bad to happen."

"If that's the case," he insisted, "let's end this right. Come see me in person. We can eat, drink, and end this like civilized people. One more night. One more date. One more dinner."

I wanted a clean break. But didn't I owe him at least this one request? Didn't he deserve a true ending that didn't involve the police? Plus, I didn't want to upset him more.

"When?"

"Thursday night?"

I sighed, my mouth away from the receiver. On Friday morning, Liam and I were to begin our road trip. This was cutting it close, but I figured I could go one night early, end things with Jacob, and be done with it.

"Please," he insisted. "We can end this. I just want to do it correctly."

I bit my lip and finally acquiesced. I didn't tell Celeste I was going to see Jacob but called Virginia as I headed out.

"If the resident assistant calls, cover for me," I said. "Say I'm staying with you."

I drove to Knoxville clutching the steering wheel and assuring myself that everything would be okay. One more night and everything would go back to the way things were before I met him.

I arrived at his apartment, parked next to his Celica, and knocked on the door. He greeted me wearing an apron, and the aroma of chicken emanated from the oven. He handed me a glass of wine. I heard music from my favorite CD playing inside.

"Welcome." Something was wrong. He motioned for me to come inside. I hesitated.

"May I take your jacket?" He smiled. He was being too formal, too . . . something. My bones seemed to tremble, and the air in his apartment was infused with a current of danger. But I had to do it. I stepped inside.

"I hope your trip was pleasant." Using potholders, he got the chicken out of the oven. "I made your favorite." He placed the dish on his counter, turned, and placed silverware perpendicular from the table's edge, two inches from each dinner plate. He placed two napkins on each plate, repositioned the napkins a couple of times, and left them to get the food. "I want this to be a night you'll never forget."

Chills ran up my arms, and I rubbed them down with my hands.

"You cold?" He looked at my jacket, which was slung over the couch but didn't move toward it. "Please. Have a seat." He motioned to the seat across from him at the small dining room table in the apartment. He took a match and lit two tapered candles on the table. I didn't want this night to be a climax but a denouement. "*Bon appétit*."

The corner of his mouth turned up slightly, like he had a secret. Our conversation was stilted, as if we were strangers at a business meeting.

"Do you need salt? I have salt. I need salt." He got up from the table, retrieved a saltshaker, gave his food two shakes, and thudded the shaker on the table between us.

"Mine is fine, thank you." I continued to chew without tasting anything. Was this poisoned? No. I was being irrational. Everything was fine. Things were awkward only because it's hard to end a relationship. Still, he was watching me.

"How did you say your drive was?"

"It was fine, thank you."

He picked up a glass of wine. "To us."

I didn't move. "To us?"

"Pick up your glass." His glass hovered above a basket of rolls.

"There is no us." The Janet Jackson CD switched from one song to the next. "Not anymore."

He forced a tight smile. "To us," he repeated.

"I came here to break up." I looked at his glass. "We're breaking up."

"I'll die if you leave me."

"Die?"

Was this—the dinner, candles, music—an elaborate attempt to save the relationship? "You mean you'll kill yourself?"

"I can't live without you. You're everything I ever wanted." The chicken grew cool on my plate.

"You're going to kill yourself?"

"It doesn't have to come to that." He chewed as he spoke. "You're driving me to this. It's you. It will always be you."

"Driving you to what?" I asked.

His narrow eyes focused on me. Even though I'd been chilled, beads of perspiration formed on my forehead. My mouth went dry.

"Marrying me wouldn't be so bad," he said. "Unless there's someone else?"

"There's no one else." I repeated the lie.

"Don't worry," he said. "I won't necessarily kill myself, but I won't let us both live in the same world apart." He took a bite of asparagus and smiled as if he had complimented me. I sighed a trembling breath, relieved until I replayed his words in my head. What did it mean that we both couldn't live in the same world? Was he threatening me? He carefully cut his food with a knife into small portions, seemingly relishing each bite. His careful actions and lack of emotion were mesmerizing. Now I couldn't stop watching him.

"If we break up," I said quietly, "we'll *have* to live apart in the same world."

He took his napkin out of his lap and folded it into a neat square. He placed the napkin next to his wine glass and arranged his fork back into the perpendicular position. As I watched him move so slowly, so deliberately, he did something surprising.

He sprang toward me.

His fist hit my cheek first. I was so surprised I fell out of my chair and scrambled not to hit the floor. He caught me, but pushed me over the back of the sofa, his arms flying. I tried to fight back, to wrangle from his grasp, but he pinned me down and hit me over and over and over.

He held my arms, but my legs were free, so I kicked at him until he staggered backward, falling enough away for me to get up and run toward the door. But he grabbed my ankle, and I fell on my face. I tried to crawl to the door, but he pulled me back and I flipped over to see my attacker.

I opened my mouth to scream, but only a small yelp escaped before his hands wrapped around my neck. He squeezed as he looked into my eyes— intimately, almost lovingly. His face was inches from mine.

"Did you think I'd let you live without me?" he whispered. But I couldn't answer. My head throbbed as I struggled for breath. "You die, I die, we both die."

We were lying in the space between the coffee table and the door. He— without releasing his grip—placed his knees on my forearms, straddling me. If I'd been able to talk, I would've begged for my life or agreed to marry him or anything to get out the door. His hands tightened on my throat.

"You're the one for me." He leaned down and pushed my head to the side so he could whisper into my left ear. If I could make it to the door, I might be able to run to the car. I heard a dog barking in the adjacent apartment. If I could make enough noise, I might be able to alert the dog's owners. But I was immobilized and mute, and—for all my straining—I was glued to the floor. "You were my everything."

Were. The past tense verb would've been appropriate in a breakup, but he was referring to death. Mine. When I died here, my parents would think I was hanging out with Virginia. I'd signed out for the week. If anyone asked Virginia where I was, she'd lie and say we were together. No one would notice I was gone.

I struggled against the weight of his body, but he was sinewy strong. I searched his eyes, looking for any trace of compassion or regret, of the relationship we'd had. But I saw only malice. I was his dog, and he pulled the tight leash around my neck just to see me recoil.

Some people, when faced with death, dig deep into their soul and find a ferocity for life that causes them to fight back, to struggle, to survive. Not me. I was tired, terrified, and powerless. My lies, deception, and naivety had put me there, and I knew it. When he pushed down harder on my throat, he pressed out any hope of escape.

Death began to seduce me, and all I had to do to escape was wait. Jacob's breath caressed the side of my face where his fist had landed moments earlier. "You were beautiful. You made me whole."

I quit struggling, which was the only power I possessed, the only decision I could make. He wasn't taking my life, I was giving it up. His knees pressed my arms into the ground, and my heart thudded in my face. The metronome of death. How many beats before the last one? Time was sluggish. His mouth was moving, but I couldn't hear his words. I didn't feel his hands on my throat or the sting on my face or the debilitating shame of getting myself into such a situation. I felt tranquility. Then I began to hallucinate.

It had to be a hallucination, because what I saw before me was impossible. The door burst open and hit the wall. I hadn't heard a knock, so why did it open? Did the neighbor hear the fight and come over? But I didn't see a stranger, I saw Liam.

He stood in the open door wearing a baseball cap, which hid the thick dark hair that had swept into his eyes at the Huddle House. Now they were full of love, regret, and disappointment. All of that in one second.

Was I dying? Was I imagining this? Liam and Jacob didn't know each other.

But he was no mirage. Our eyes locked. In one heartbeat, his face switched from despair to rage. He exploded into the apartment, followed by several fraternity guys.

Liam yanked Jacob off me, and his hand left my throat. As I gasped to take in air, I heard glass shattering, guys yelling, and furniture breaking. Bodies flew. I didn't move as I watched my two worlds collide above me. It took a few seconds for the scene to reach my brain. Liam was there to save me.

While the guys fought, I crawled toward the door. Glass cut into me, and blood covered my hands and arms. Exhausted, I lay in the shards of glass.

Liam punched Jacob, who fell backward over the sofa. From the ground, Jacob saw me and yelled as his eyes flashed with anger. "You can't ever leave. I'll find you."

"Get her out of here!" Liam shouted directions to his friends as he pounced on Jacob and hit him repeatedly in the face. Thick arms scooped me off the floor and into the night air. Liam's friend carried me like a baby across the parking lot and placed me into the back of a Jeep.

"Are you okay?" this stranger asked. He was blond and baby faced. "Can you hear me?"

That's when I knew I was safe. "Should we go to the emergency room?"

Yelling came from the apartment and a door slammed. A few seconds later, the Jeep opened and the guys piled in.

"Go, go, go!" Liam yelled, and we pulled out of the parking lot so quickly the tires screeched. Liam's hands, covered in blood, trembled.

"Is it true?" He looked at the floorboard, his eyes brimming with tears. "Were you dating that guy the whole time?"

I was too ashamed to explain, but I nodded.

We didn't go to the hospital. We didn't want to draw any police attention to Jacob. Liam and his friends feared Jacob might claim he was the victim of a violent crime, and—absent any context—the police might believe him. My injuries would've justified the altercation, but Liam had stayed behind and delivered a beating past the point of necessity.

When we got to Liam's place, we cleaned the glass out of my arms. I felt fine at the time, but in the morning, I felt like I'd been in a car crash. Everything hurt, and I couldn't move without wincing. Still, I gingerly climbed into his old red Acura for our seven-hour road trip to D.C.

I confessed everything as we barreled down Interstate 81. He listened attentively as he drove, his right hand holding a gas-station coffee cup. He, full of lament instead of anger, told me how Jacob had called him out of the blue and explained that they'd been dating the same girl.

"I told him there was no way you'd been cheating on me, but I went anyway to try to figure out what was going on. He sounded unhinged, so I took my friends." Rain fell, and he turned on his wipers. "I was sure he was lying, but then I heard you screaming and saw you on the floor."

The rain, which was slow at first, pounded the windshield. I appreciated how Liam pivoted from betrayal to courage in one second flat. He was better than I was.

When we arrived in D.C. and I met his parents, we acted as if everything was fine. His mother engaged in all the appropriate small talk, before finally bringing up my appearance.

"So, what happened?" she asked hesitantly. "To your face?"

I'd borrowed a turtleneck sweater from one of Liam's fraternity brothers to hide the bruising on my neck, but I couldn't hide my face. We told them I'd been in an automobile accident to explain the cuts, bruises, and why I moved so slowly.

Not sure they bought it.

The next day, Liam drove me to the Capitol Building. The wind blew my hair as we stood on the west side along with tens of thousands of people. The October sun shone brightly against the blue sky but didn't take the edge out of the crisp air. I'd never been to Washington, D.C., but I'd seen this building—this exact spot—when President Ronald Reagan was inaugurated.

"This was the surprise." Liam smiled, but the events in Knoxville overshadowed what was supposed to be a romantic weekend. "They took down the Statue of Freedom from the top of the Capitol to clean and restore it," he explained. Corrosion and deterioration made the statue look light green. "It's the first time she's been off in more than a hundred years. I thought you'd enjoy seeing this. It's historic and all."

That crisp day was the bicentennial commemoration of the date George Washington laid the cornerstone of the Capitol. I didn't have a jacket because I'd left it at Jacob's house two days before. The wind cut through me. Liam wrapped his arms around me to warm me as motorcycles drove by us slowly, followed by police cars with blue lights blazing. A line of cars drove by, including the presidential limousine with small American flags waving in the wind. President Clinton and Vice President Al Gore got out of the car and waved to the crowd.

I heard a rumbling in the sky, when a gigantic orange helicopter carried the twenty-foot-tall statue in the sky above us. The statue had long, flowing hair, wore a helmet of an eagle's head and feathers, and had a fringed toga-like robe. One of her hands rested upon the hilt of a sheathed sword, the other held a shield.

Vietnam-trained pilots carefully lowered the magnificent fifteen-thousand-pound statue directly onto the Capitol Building's dome. Men standing high above us on scaffolding directed her onto the bolts locking her into place for possibly another hundred years. The helicopter hovered as men secured this symbol of freedom. The crowd held their collective breath as we watched this feat of engineering, patriotism, and hope. After about twenty harrowing minutes, they finally released the cords, the helicopter flew away, and the crowd cheered.

After the ceremony, tears brimmed my eyes. Neither of us said it, but we both knew our relationship would not survive this blow of infidelity. We'd break up officially within the month, but we had this day. He'd saved my life and allowed me to see this beautiful moment.

As Liam and I walked back to the car, hand in hand, I knew I was walking away from everything we'd had together. Though we'd had a lovely weekend in spite of the altercation at Jacob's, a river of sadness ran beneath every glance, every word, every moment. This would be the end of us. I took one more look at the Statue of Freedom, who had been restored to her original bronze beauty.

She'd been cleaned, but I could never be.

6

THE CARDBOARD BOX

"We have reason to believe your life is in danger."

A couple of days after I returned from Washington, D.C., two uniformed police officers met me in my dorm lobby. "A student at the University of Tennessee has been telling people he intended to cause you physical harm. According to witnesses, he used the word 'kill.' We believe this is a credible threat." The officer looked at his notebook and back at me. "Do you know this Jacob person?"

Even though I'd promised not to tell the police what happened, in order to protect Liam and his fraternity brothers, I told them everything.

"We're unable to ascertain his location." The officer's monotonous voice indicated he had better things to do than get embroiled in the romantic drama of college students. "When was the last time you saw him?"

"Five days ago," I said.

"Have you spoken since?"

"He left a message on my machine," I said. "He promised to either kill me or himself. Even if it took years." I flinched as I said this. "He said he'd follow me anywhere and I'd never be able to escape him. And if I ever heard he'd died, it would be because of me. Even years from now."

My fellow students meandered by us, trying to eavesdrop.

"He may be in Nashville." The officer looked around the lobby. "Do you have a more private place to stay? Maybe go home while this passes?"

But how could I explain this to my parents? They didn't even know I'd gone to D.C. If they discovered I'd been lying on the dormitory sign-out sheets and traveling for romantic weekends, there's no telling what they'd do. I had to deal with this myself.

I was surprised, a few hours later, when my parents showed up at my dorm. What was this about? They never showed up unannounced.

"We need to talk," my mother said.

We walked to the swing beside the library, where college students carrying backpacks chatted and laughed. Once my mom and I sat on the swing, my dad explained the purpose of their visit. "Jacob visited us today."

I had difficulty processing this information. Jacob, who was dangerous, had been with my parents in our home. My mind reeled with tragic scenarios.

"You let him in?" I asked.

"Of course." My mother spoke in an even yet challenging tone. "Why wouldn't we let him in?"

"He was carrying a cardboard box," my dad explained. "Said you were not the person you pretended to be."

They were onto me.

"What did he want?" I tried to act nonchalant. A couple of students walked by. "What was in the box?"

"Letters," my dad explained. "Ones you wrote in high school."

"Did you *read* them?" I couldn't remember what I'd written. They were undoubtedly full of silly romantic ramblings, with hearts drawn at the top in colored pencil, and included details of my romantic and sexual history. For years, I'd maintained a carefully curated life with a patina of morality and virtue for my parents. My mother didn't answer my question directly, but her stony demeanor told the tale.

As a kid, boyfriends were presented as an inconvenience and any romantic notions ought to be tamped down. If I got too emotional over a boy, Mom might explode in anger. *Snap out of it.* My desire for love was a provocation, and her whole parenting strategy was to crush those inconvenient feelings.

"You were a youth-group leader. Homecoming queen. We were proud of you. And to find out it was all a lie?" My mother opened her arms as if she were attempting to convey—but failing to fully encompass—my lack of character, my unfaithfulness, my duplicity. "To discover you're common trash? A whore?"

For the first time in my life, my mother had truly seen me. And she didn't like what she saw.

"And we read all about Conrad." Her eyes narrowed. "You were carrying on with him while you were in the youth group? And not to mention this Jacob guy."

I didn't recognize this at the time, but "carrying on" was not the right way to characterize an adult sexually targeting a kid. My feet dangled from the swing as my worst nightmare came to life. The barricade of secrecy which held my most humiliating moment had a breach.

"You're no longer welcome in our home," she said. "Don't ever come back."

She turned and walked away. My dad, who'd been standing next to us, sat down. We swung in silence. My face burned and tears rolled down my cheeks. A cardinal flew onto a tree branch in front of us.

"Have I ever told you how I got off the mountain?"

Overcome with shame, I was gratified at the change of subject. I knew his story's broad brushstrokes but it was possible I'd only heard about this story—not from him directly. Family lore was passed down verbally, but not necessarily directly from the source. I waited for him to continue.

"When I was fifteen years old, I filled out an army recruitment form without telling anyone. Momma chased that recruiter off the porch when he showed up a few days later. When I signed up for the air force, she wouldn't even let the recruiter get his mouth open. By the time the marine corps recruiter showed up, she figured she couldn't stop me. 'If you're gonna go,' she said, 'I won't stop ya.'"

He closed his eyes, pulling the memory from the recesses of his brain.

"She kept saying, 'He's only fifteen.' But the recruiter changed my name and my birthday, and I got three years older." He snapped. "Just like that."

"I went to Parris Island and all over the world. To Beirut," he said. "First time I'd been off the mountain."

After serving three years, he was still young enough to go back to high school. By the time he was my age, my dad was already a veteran. I couldn't even properly break up with a boyfriend.

59

"Know what my main fear was?" he asked.

"Getting shot?"

"That I'd forget my new name and fake birthday," he said. "And be outed as an imposter."

Smiling students walked by, hand in hand and backpacks slung over their shoulders.

I knew the feeling of being an imposter. I didn't belong here.

"It hurt Momma to let me go, like it hurt me to send you here. I did it so you could meet a good Christian husband," he said. "We've saved a little of my paycheck for years to give you this opportunity." His voice was thick with lament. "I never graduated from high school, but I worked my whole life to give you the chance for a better life."

The rocking motion lulled me. I thought of all the times he and I had sat on the porch in the swing he'd made when I was a kid. He got up and stretched his legs. Would this be the last time I ever saw my dad? Had I lost two boyfriends and two parents in one week?

"The marine corps was wild," he said. "I'm glad your mother doesn't know half the things I've done. I reckon she'd kick me outta the house too."

―――――

That night, I lay in my dorm and dreamed of going somewhere far away. I wanted to spin a globe, close my eyes, and place my finger anywhere that would provide enough space between me and the home I could no longer go to. This was not a new sensation. This same feeling caused me to seek out guys who were not from my hometown, prompted me to develop long-distance relationships with friends I met at summer camp, and drew me to listen to KQ105 and dream of running away with my true love.

It was crazy how much sway my mother had over me, even though we didn't get along. Maybe because we didn't get along. She had a way of running her eyes up and down me, evaluating my every curve and expressing disapproval with the slightest arch of her brow. And that was best-case scenario. Throughout high school, she kept me under her thumb with overt critiques. *What are you wearing? Those pants make you look fat. Bozo the Clown wears less makeup.* Anytime I tried to better myself—through school, clothing, or grades—she'd laugh and take me down a notch. At first, I cried, and then I didn't.

For my whole life, I steeled myself and dodged her critiques, so negative they chilled almost all communication. As my sisters and I sat around the table, any interaction—from "pass the ketchup" to "can I have five dollars"—could result in a tongue-lashing. Talking wasn't worth the risk. Our home, as silent as a morgue, was full of emotional landmines. I had to watch my step. Eventually I retreated. To my room, to my boyfriends, to myself.

And after all these years, she'd finally moved on from minor putdowns to the big one. Nothing, and I mean nothing, was more eviscerating than for her to shove the label "whore" onto me. As I stood there, mouth agape, terrified at all that had happened, she shoved it into my mouth. The word lodged in my throat and it tasted like a mildewed dishcloth—dirty, suffocating, nauseating. I choked on it but could not spit it out.

If I took all of her insults issued over a lifetime and injected them into my veins, they would be less poisonous than this one epithet. It ran through every part of me until it finally reached my heart.

My church taught sexual purity through various analogies. The rose. Shiny new pennies versus old dingy ones. And, of course, cows. Why would a guy buy the cow if you gave away the milk for free? The lesson was clear, and now I'd been branded a whore. I no longer belonged to God, I belonged to the darkness.

But I didn't have time to dwell on losing my family or my salvation. I had to put this out of my head for now. Jacob was still out there, and I was more exposed than ever. I couldn't go home, and he knew where I lived. When Virginia came over, I told her everything and she hugged me. "Are you safe? Is he? He might be trying to kill himself—or you—right now."

Since Jacob had attacked me, I'd been concerned about my own safety. I never considered he might also be in danger. I decided to call his wealthy, well-connected parents. Maybe they had some way of tracking him down. I dialed the number I memorized in high school. His mother listened silently as I explained what happened. "I'm afraid he might kill himself."

His mother's voice was weak and low. She was concerned, stricken. Not angry. "I'll find him and bring him home."

Jacob was a homicidal maniac, and his mother still loved him. I was only a whore, and I couldn't go home again. Virginia spent the night, curled next to me in the tiny twin bed. "I'm not leaving until this is over."

The next morning, someone did find Jacob—a couple of hikers in Arkansas.

After visiting my parents, he had driven to his hometown to his favorite location. He'd run a hose from the exhaust pipe of his Celica into the car to kill himself with carbon monoxide. The hikers found his nearly lifeless body—he'd passed out but was not dead—and called 911.

"He's recovering in the hospital, and we're driving to bring him home. Please, for the sake of everyone," his mother told me over the phone, "never contact him or us again."

She was acting like I was toxic, that I had pushed him over the edge. I'm not going to lie, I believed her. Going back to college was a challenge after this. Not only had my fellow students seen the police in my dorm lobby, but Jacob might show up and finish what he'd started. I watched my back and saw him everywhere. At the grocery store, on campus, in my large classes. He was an apparition. He was everywhere.

He hadn't broken my bones, but he'd broken me. And I had to deal with it alone. Liam left me after everything had settled down. It was impossible to go back to "dating as normal" after my true self had been revealed. Now I was isolated, once again, because of my decisions. I'd gotten myself into the situation, and I had to get myself out of it. The only problem? There was no way out.

———

"I'm so glad you are a part of our family." Virginia's mother, a former model, smiled at me after serving us spaghetti. "Virginia had a hard time in high school, so I asked God to bring a true friend into her life. You're the answer to prayer."

Virginia beamed at me from across the table, and I felt like I'd stumbled into a Norman Rockwell painting. I marveled at how they interacted with respect and good cheer. How they ate, with cloth napkins in their laps instead of cheap paper towels. Their spaghetti had real sauce, not stretched out with ketchup, and I could ask someone to pass the bread without provoking an argument.

"I have an announcement to make." Virginia cleared her throat. "I got a modeling contract with the Eileen Ford agency."

"What? You're living your dream!" I cried. I jumped up, ran around the table, and embraced her.

"Is Ford a good one?"

"One of the most prestigious agencies in the world," her mother explained. "Candice Bergen, Christie Brinkley, Kim Basinger, Lauren Hutton, and Brooke Shields. All Ford models."

Virginia jumped up from the table with joy.

"Where do you go?" I asked. "New York?"

"Milan first, but eventually New York."

"You'll quit college?" I asked.

Her mother fielded this one. "Yes, Virginia's nineteen years old, which means there's no time to waste. She can finish up later."

"First," Virginia held up a finger, "I have to lose twenty pounds." That's when I noticed her plate was full of salad.

"But . . . you're perfect."

"They want their six-foot models to weigh 120," she said. "I'm at 143." Virginia explained she was going to a spa in Florida where she could work out and have healthy meals prepared for her.

"I was hoping you could come with me?"

"To the spa?" I asked.

"I can't do it without you," she gushed. "Please?"

I had classes but wasn't going to let Virginia down even if it meant expulsion. "When do we leave?"

"Next Thursday," her mom said.

"I'm going to miss you so much," I said.

"We can cry later." She hugged me. "Tonight, we celebrate."

By Tuesday, I had my bags already packed, but the next morning, I jerked awake from a nightmare.

"What's wrong," Celeste asked as she was getting dressed.

"I had a dream." I pulled the covers to my chin. I'd dreamed Virginia died in a car accident, and I was at the funeral home standing next to the casket. Then I got a call from the editor of our student newspaper, *The Babbler*, Erik Tryggestad. He told me he had just heard of Virginia's death, but—since she had quit college to become a model—he wasn't sure whether the paper should cover her death.

I told Celeste, who put her hand on my foot dangling off the bed. "It's nothing. Call her to make sure she's okay."

As I reached for the phone, it rang. But instead of Virginia's voice, I heard my mother's. I was surprised. My mother never bluffed. She meant what she'd said, and she'd said we were done. Something bad had to happen to get her to reach out.

"Your grandmother died." My mother spoke in a tone which dared me to ask any questions. "We're heading to the mountain, and we'll pick you up in two hours."

I ached for my dad losing his mother. And I ached for myself that it took something like this for my mother to deign to talk to me.

After we hung up, I scrambled to change my road-trip plans with Virginia.

"Oh, I'm so sorry," she said. "Come visit after you get back. We'll see each other soon." I was so shocked at the news of my grandmother's death, the dream—as dreams tend to do—receded into my mind. We talked about the logistics of me driving to Florida and she told me where she'd be staying.

"Wait, there was something else I was going to tell you," I said. "But I can't remember what."

"It's okay," she said.

"I promise," I said. "I'll see you as soon as I get back."

———

My aunts, uncles, and cousins stood in the small stone childhood home. They wore black lace dresses and ill-fitting suits instead of overalls. My dad stood next to one of the two pianos.

"Since we're all here," Dad said, "I thought we might could share memories about Mother."

The wood stove emanated enough heat through the house. A few people spoke about her cooking skills. My uncle talked about how she'd worn him out for some childhood shenanigan pertaining to dynamite. My dad told us about how she'd let him join the marines at fifteen years old.

As we left, I passed Aunt Zinnia, sitting in my late grandfather's chair. She grabbed my hand. "According to Indian legend, invisible spirits exist as little go-betweens that speak to the dead." She closed her eyes. "If you want to speak to Momma, call out to them." She squeezed my hand before letting it drop. "And don't forget what I told you when you were a kid. You're one of us. You have the gift of straddling the natural and the spiritual world, too. You'll see it most when you're dealing with matters of life and death."

Death. It was my barnacle. Ever since junior high school, when my friends and I innocently played the pass-out game beneath the bleachers, death attached itself to me. It pressed on me when I was in Jacob's apartment, squeezing itself into me, and then was ever-present. I sensed that if I turned my head, I'd find it sitting there, inviting me to come along. I tried not to look, not to engage, but I could feel it. Its presence tried to pull me down—maybe into the grave. I don't know. But I looked straight ahead and refused to take its hand.

I thought about this as my sisters and I sat in the back seat driving down the mountain in silence. Dad was quiet in his grief, and my mother had a stony silence. In our family we never resolved issues but ignored them until they calcified us. But as we barreled down I-24, Mom casually dropped a bomb.

"Conrad was arrested."

Outside the window, icicles clung to the cracks in the mountain rock.

"For what?" my sister Amy said.

"Rape." Mom said the word bluntly, a slap in the face. "He sneaked into Felicia's basement door, slammed her up against the wall, and now he's in jail."

Her tone indicated I shouldn't ask any follow-up questions. Mom's main power was withholding information. She'd drop one or two facts, refusing to elaborate. But I knew enough.

I thought about the scant information she gave me as my eyelids grew heavy. Felicia was my friend Jason's mother. Conrad had targeted me—a kid—and her—a middle-aged woman? I figured Conrad liked other young girls. What did it mean that he also did this to middle-aged women? I closed my eyes and bit my lip.

Other than a few friends, I'd never told anyone about what happened between Conrad and me. And now my parents knew. I'm not sure what I wanted from them. Maybe to react angrily. Even violently. My uncle Jasper had promised to kill anyone who hurt me, and I figured that inclination would extend to my own family. But it was like nothing happened. They continued to attend church and see him at church potlucks. Their lack of reaction delivered the same message as Jacob's attempt at strangulation: you are nothing; your life is meaningless; we can erase you and your complexities.

I just wanted it all to go away. It never occurred to me he'd strike again. I thought our encounter was unique. An isolated incident. Love.

But I'd been naive. Conrad had used romantic and spiritual language to convince me to stay quiet, and I'd complied. This decision put other women in danger. I felt a second of relief when I heard he was in prison, but my own guilt welled inside me. I should've spoken out.

Not only was I weighed down with the looming threat Jacob might kill himself or me, I also carried the consequences of my silence. I was responsible for this rape.

7

LIVING THE DREAM

Nothing felt real until I could share it with Virginia, but—since she was already in Florida—I carried the information of Conrad's arrest alone. The next morning, I'd drive to her weight-loss spa and tell her everything. She would tilt her head and part her lips slightly the way she did when she was concentrating. We'd cry, and she'd tell me it wasn't my fault. Then we'd jog or do sit-ups and eat lettuce and get skinnier. One day, I'd visit her in Milan and she'd strut the runway wearing expensive clothing and a pouty expression, and she'd break character only after the fashion show and we'd laugh. Somehow, in spite of everything, we'd laugh.

That's the way it was supposed to work out, at least.

When I got to my room, Celeste was standing there, looking at me with big, wet eyes. Something, I didn't know what, had changed. I wanted to turn around and leave and never come back, just to escape the pity on her face. But it was too late.

"What's wrong?" I asked.

"Virginia," she said.

We locked eyes. Hers conveyed despair, sorrow, and lament. Mine held confusion and a flicker of hope that Celeste was overreacting. Three seconds passed. Four.

"Where is she?" I was already crying.

"She's dead," Celeste said. "She's dead."

Virginia had been driving south on I-75 alone in the rain. Her Camaro hydroplaned and slid into the oncoming path of a tractor trailer. The trucker hit her car going seventy-five miles per hour, and that was it.

I should tell Virginia about this, I thought. Celeste embraced me. I was as close to and as far away from a friend as I'd ever been. I could feel her breathing, but I could not receive her comfort. An invisible chasm yawned between me and everyone else in the world. I was alone.

I climbed into bed, and a day passed, and another. At the visitation, the casket was closed, but the funeral director allowed me to see her in the back room before they rolled her out. I peered at my beautiful friend in the box, her hands folded on her chest.

"Who did this to you?" I touched her hair, which had been hot rolled. Her makeup was expertly applied, but her lipstick was the color of Pepto-Bismol, a color she never would have worn. She lay on satin, and someone had left a heart pillow next to her. I kissed her cold face before they shut the casket with a thud.

They rolled her body out into the front room where people formed a line well out into the parking lot. Her friends lugubriously wept and talked about how sweet she was. I slipped away to the foyer. I'd been there for hours, and I was fatigued. When I saw a phone on a small table, I called my dorm to check the messages on my answering machine. Anything to pass the time. Anything to give me space from the grieving.

"Nancy, I hate to bother you, but this is Erik Tryggestad," the message began. Suddenly, I remembered my dream.

"I just heard about Virginia dying, and I'm so sorry. I know she meant a lot to you. I'm calling because I'm trying to decide how to cover this in *The Babbler*. Since she quit Lipscomb, I wasn't sure whether we should write about it. What do you think? Call me back."

Beep.

8

THE SIDEWALK

I overslept on the day of the funeral, so I threw on a black dress and sunglasses. I sat on the row with her family. The mourners packed the sanctuary. The funeral happened. I know it did. But my next memory is walking to the burial site. The rain made the earth soggy, and my heels sank into the earth before Virginia did.

After the funeral, I went back to campus, to a twin-size bed on which she'd never sit again. We'd never paint our nails together, never gossip, never crash each other's dates. But I would somehow have to keep going on with my life.

Every morning, I read Virginia's bubbly handwriting on the whiteboard hanging on my door: "Meet me in the Student Center after Bible class— XOXO—Virgin." Sometimes I allowed myself to think she might show up to grab lunch. Her brush still lay on the shelf where she'd last left it, a few strands of her golden hair still in the bristles.

She never showed. I stopped attending classes, eating, and showering. Friends, in their efforts to comfort me, told me about the deaths of their dogs, speculated Virginia now had angel wings, and told me I'd eventually forget about her.

At our daily mandatory chapel, I looked for answers about the meaning of life and death, but the speakers related lessons about saying no to alcohol, avoiding sexual temptation by obeying curfew, and learning humility after striking out in their high school baseball games. The platitudes, the cheery songs, and the monotone prayers sunk me. I slept around the clock and, in a few weeks, had an F in Chaucer, a D in Calculus, and an F in World Religions. The dean of students summoned me to his office.

He looked at me across his desk. "You're skipping chapel and failing your classes."

I nodded.

"As a student government association class representative, you've got to follow the rules." He had a father's tone of rebuke. "If you don't go back to chapel this next week, I'll remove you from your office and revoke your scholarships."

"Okay."

He paused as if considering how candid to be. "If I was your daddy, I wouldn't look kindly on you giving up all your scholarships because you refused to put your butt in a chair for twenty minutes after lunch."

I was teetering on the edge of an emotional cliff. Every trite spiritual lesson, delivered with a cheery smile, threatened to push me into the abyss. Also being in a church-like setting made me panic. Maybe because of Conrad. Maybe because of the funeral, which was held in a local Nashville church. His condescension didn't cause me to reevaluate my lack of chapel attendance. I couldn't go without it damaging me.

"I'm giving you one more chance," he said. "Don't squander it."

I thanked him, left his office, and walked back to my dorm. When I got back to my room, I was about to open the door when I gasped. Virginia's message was gone. It had been replaced by a Bible verse on my whiteboard. *Blessed are those who mourn, for they will be comforted.*

"Who wrote this?" I demanded, to no one in particular. The hall was empty. I'd never see Virginia's bubbly, childish handwriting again. A student who lived next to my room popped her head out the door and smiled.

"Jesus wrote it. From his Sermon on the Mount?" She edged herself into the hallway.

"Why'd you erase my board?" I yelled. "It was the only thing I had left of her."

"Look, it's depressing to see the handwriting of a dead person hanging there every day." She frowned. "I talked to the RA. It's time for you to move on."

I'd lost everything. Overcome with sorrow, I crawled into bed. But I didn't want to sleep, which held its own dangers. Why had I dreamed in alarming detail of Virginia's death? Did I have a nascent Cherokee gift? Or a gift of the Holy Spirit? One inescapable fact kept thudding in my head: something/someone/the universe had tipped me off about Virginia's death, and I didn't warn her.

The dream alarmed me at the time. Now it terrified me. It was an albatross around my neck, choking me emotionally more than Jacob ever had physically. I lay in bed that night looking at the ceiling. How could I escape my guilt and grief? What would I do if I lost my scholarships?

But I did sleep, and the next morning, my growling stomach awakened me. Since I couldn't remember the last time I'd eaten, I walked out to my car and removed the parking tickets from the windshield. McDonalds was ten minutes from campus. But after driving a while, I noticed an unfamiliar sign as I entered a town I didn't recognize. I pulled over at a gas station.

"Where am I?" My greasy hair stuck to my scalp and I hadn't changed my clothing in a week.

"At a gas station," the older lady at the register said. "Do you need gas? Coffee?"

"No, where am I?" I asked again. "What state?"

"Honey, this here's Alabama." She took off her reading glasses to get a better look at me. "Where are you supposed to be?"

I looked at the back of a man getting a beer from the cooler. Was he Jacob? I watched him select a bottle and turn around. The man wore glasses. Not Jacob. I wasn't thinking clearly.

My mind and my body climbed back into my car at the same time. Before life went bad, my mind and body were connected, one inhabiting the other. But now, they were like an unhappily married couple: they existed independently, were tangentially related, and never seemed to be in the same place at the same time. When I felt discomfort in my body, my mind—like a helium balloon—would just float somewhere more pleasant. Or, in this case, it floated my body and me to Alabama.

I turned over the ignition and drove back to campus. As I sped down the interstate, the chaotic mess of my life pushed against my skull. I'd lost two boyfriends, my parents, and the best friend I'd ever had. As the miles ticked by, death rode shotgun. Death whispered scenarios into my head, and I imagined swerving into the next lane. I saw a tractor trailer in the rearview mirror. I gripped the steering wheel, afraid that my unwanted dark passenger might take the wheel. It wouldn't take much. If I turned into it, the pain would end.

But what about the truck driver? Not telling on Conrad had caused Felicia at church to get raped. Not warning Virginia about my dream had resulted in her death. I couldn't ruin someone else's life. The tractor trailer was approaching me quickly, and I considered my options. I didn't decide *not* to kill myself, but I did decide not to hurt another person in the process. It blew past me doing about eighty miles per hour, and I exhaled in relief. In the passenger seat, death tapped its toes impatiently, biding its time.

The next day, I faced the moment of truth. I stood on the steps and watched as my fellow classmates filed dutifully into the chapel. I'd already missed well over my allotted number of chapels. This was it. Did I hate chapel enough to sacrifice my college degree? If I cared about my future at all, I would force myself to walk in there, sit in my assigned seat, and try to ignore the feckless advice dressed in spiritual language. I was still standing there when the carefree students filed out twenty minutes later.

My fate was sealed. I'd forfeited my scholarships, and my parents wouldn't pay my tuition when they learned I'd wasted my opportunity.

But I had to fortify myself against the onslaught of ostensibly positive theology, which—when I evaluated it—seemed so terribly negative. I wasn't good enough to earn my way into heaven, I knew that. My friends were perplexed over why I was so against a Bible verse on a whiteboard or a chapel talk on humility. But I knew. Somehow, these things were going to kill me.

That sounds dumb. Hyperbolic. But it was true.

Since I couldn't explain my aversion to Christianity, I hardened myself to it. My facade of morality faded, and I stopped trying to preserve any remnants. Instead of going to Bible studies and Wednesday night church services in a caravan of students, I hung out with other malcontents on the edge of campus and smoked clove cigarettes. Though drinking was outlawed, I showed up to class at eight o'clock in the morning, drunk. Professors scolded me, rebuked me, and chastised me, but their admonitions only fueled my desire to antagonize.

Something was wrong about this college, about this theology, about this world. Everyone was going around checking their mailboxes, chatting in the cafeteria, and dating like death didn't exist—like it wasn't breathing down our collective necks—and as if heaven was attainable. At least we could be honest about how terrible everything was, how dire.

"So what about a penis enables a man to be 'the authority'?" I asked in one Bible class, to the groans of my fellow classmates. For some reason, I had decided that this university and its teachings were what was wrong with the world. I was really trying to fight death, but, since I didn't know how to do that, I fought my professors.

My fellow students didn't know what to say to me, so they gossiped about me. One professor confronted me after I'd been caught drinking, saying my behavior was a black eye to our university. He did it with lament instead of anger. The anger was all mine. My fierceness was fake, but people bought it. It was a repellent to the well-behaved students who faithfully attended Bible class and chapel. They left me alone.

During the days, suicide was an ever-present option, and I considered ways to accomplish it without traumatizing the person who'd find me. I came up with nothing. Death, operating on its own inconveniently dramatic terms, infiltrated my musings, my thought experiments, my dreams. When I slept, I let my guard down. Death meandered through the crevices of my mind and came back with reasons my life wasn't worth living. When I'd awaken, I'd go through the same mental pattern. First, I'd remember Virginia was dead. Second, I'd wonder why I was still alive. Then, I'd look down at my fingernails and see they—and my neck and pillows—were bloody. I tried to hide the sheets and the scars from Celeste, but she looked at me with heavy concerned eyes. She didn't say anything as I threw on a turtleneck and darted to class.

How could I decipher Chaucer? I'd forfeited my scholarships for the next semester and tanked my grades. My teachers attempted to meet me halfway, but I was in more trouble than they knew.

"You have to get better grades," they told me. They were kind, but they didn't know I was losing my grasp on life itself.

I decided to cheat.

Lacking the energy to surreptitiously tuck notes in unobserved locations,

I placed borrowed notes on my desk during tests and sat close to friends who put their answers in full view, which caught the attention of our long-suffering professor.

The following week, she stood on stage, teetering on high heels, as she held a stack of our graded exams. "At Lipscomb, we have an honor code. A few years ago, a student named David—you know the one who went on to Harvard Law School—wrote the honor code, because he thought Christian students should conduct themselves with integrity," she said. "But he'd never encountered people like you."

David. He'd been in the back of my mind since he called me three years ago when I was a high school senior. We'd had such a charmed conversation, all others seemed dim and boring in comparison. His photo still hung in the offices of the student government association, and I'd studied it for hours. He had blond hair, blue eyes, and a kind smile. I'd kept my ears open for any gossip about him, which was plenty since people liked to brag about a Lipscomb student getting into Harvard.

Since I enrolled, I met his fiancé Charlotte, who had two sisters. One was in my class. The Platonic form of "Lipscomb female," they believed their outward appearance reflected their inward spiritual condition. They said—inspired by the teachings of Bill Gothard—that pretty women were more godly. Their hair was curled with hot rollers, their faces had expertly applied makeup, and their expensive clothing portrayed a chaste-but-sexy modesty. The bigger the hair bow, the closer to Jesus.

Charlotte gushed about how prestigious David was, what his first salary out of law school would be, and how they were going to have a massive house.

"We believe in courtship," Charlotte said. "It encourages self-restraint and moral purity."

"Sounds fun," I said.

I was disappointed. Not in these women, but in David. Though I knew I'd never meet him, that unforgettable conversation so long ago had given me hope. He'd pried open my expectations about how the world could be, and now to discover he was into vain, vacuous women? Suddenly, he seemed like part of the larger problem. He must've believed all the theology the college shoved down our throat and approved of his fiancé's focus on money and success.

As I sat there in class, the professor placed the stack of papers on her lectern and continued to scold us. "Think about this for one second. You're breaking the honor code and cheating in a class about the Bible. Surely you appreciate the irony?"

As the prof used his name to chastise us, this David became a symbol of all that was wrong with my situation. His enthusiasm made me think this college was a viable option, but it was as horrible as I'd feared. If he wrote this so-called honor code, I was happy I broke it.

A few weeks later, I was shuffling down the sidewalk to attend a literature class.

That's when I saw David. In real life. He was walking toward me, carrying a briefcase and wearing a suit. I recognized him from the SGA office photo, and I wasn't going to let him pass me without giving him a piece of my mind.

"Hello," I said. He stopped and looked at me.

"Do we know each other?" he asked.

I stuck out my hand. "You called me a few years ago to talk to me about going here for college? From Paris, Tennessee?"

"Of course." He placed his briefcase on the sidewalk. "You enrolled?"

"Because of you," I said. "I hate this place. I can't believe you found a wife among the hair-bow coalition."

If he was taken aback by this complete stranger who held all this animosity toward him, he didn't show it.

"Well, I broke it off with her," he laughed. "But she kept the ring."

I knew they'd broken up because I listened to all gossip about this guy. However, I acted surprised.

"I've met her," I said. "No matter how much the diamond cost, you still came out ahead."

He explained he'd graduated from law school and had moved back to Nashville to work at a law firm. David had landed Lipscomb as his first client and was so buoyed by his occupational triumph, he wasn't dissuaded by my terrible attitude. Most Lipscomb students regarded me with a wary eye, but instead of ending the conversation and going to celebrate landing his client, he asked me a question.

"What do you not like about this place?"

The sun shone and the purple violas dotted the flower beds. I complained about the mandatory chapels filled with spiritually suspect lessons, the emphasis on marriage, and my lack of friends. He told me that he, too, had moved on from the Church of Christ theology, that he'd been spiritually transformed through his involvement at his Harvard Law School Christian Fellowship.

"And Charlotte," he began. "What can I say?"

His voice softened in genuine pain. He didn't harden himself against my criticism, he responded to me thoughtfully. Honestly. Transparently.

"She didn't want a husband, she wanted an ATM," he said. "Or at least a husband who could function as an ATM."

Her emphasis on Gothard's teachings and wealth ultimately led to his calling the whole thing off—after she'd already bought an expensive wedding gown, paid the caterers, and broke into tears because his mother's Sears off-the-rack dress wasn't flashy enough.

I softened toward him as my assumption that he was a righteously indignant student forcing others to comply to his much-ballyhooed honor code slipped away. Was it possible he simply had honor?

The professor of my eighteenth-century literature class walked toward us on the sidewalk. I'd missed the whole hour of class.

"It's amazing who you run into on the sidewalk instead of in class," he said. Steve Prewitt was tall, had white hair, wore ill-fitting clothes, and had the manner of an absent-minded professor who might build a time-travel machine out of a DeLorean. But Prewitt didn't shame me for skipping. "You two know each other?" he said. "I'm delighted. Two of my favorite students."

Prewitt's praise of David was important to me, since he was on the theological outskirts of the typical Lipscomb faculty. Instead of shoving answers down the students' throats, he asked questions. Instead of being certain about anything, he questioned everything.

After he scooted away down the sidewalk, David and I sat on a brick half-wall and continued to talk about faith, my experience at Lipscomb, and his experience at Harvard. He told me how devastated he was on his near-marital-miss with Charlotte. I'd first become enamored of David in high school through our one phone call, and all of those same feelings came flooding back. Hope knocked on my door, and I slowly opened it with each turn of the conversation.

Things were different now. They were possible. He wasn't engaged, and our six-year age gap wasn't a deal-breaker. I was twenty years old. He was twenty-six. I'd thought I'd never talk to him again, but there we were. Exchanging anecdotes as the hours rolled by. Our conversation provoked wonder in me. Every turn of phrase was like twisting a doorknob leading into a gigantic house full of many rooms, leisurely strolling through unexpected hallways, discovering treasures. I'd grown accustomed to conversations—all conversations—being little competitions someone needed to win. But he treated them like safaris, explorations into unknown territory.

After four hours, he asked me out.

I said, "Sure," casually, but my heart fluttered in my cheeks.

The next evening, we went out to eat at an Italian restaurant. Though David was open and transparent, I maintained my "interested in law school" head fake which had started it all. He told me how he'd created the first pro-life group at Harvard Law School. He was Republican, Christian, and conservative. By now my affection for Rush Limbaugh and church had disappeared and I considered myself a feminist, atheist, liberal. Our chemistry was palpable. I could talk to this man for the rest of my life and never tire of it.

The next day, while he was working, I couldn't stop thinking about him. I imagined a life with him, which was preposterous, since we'd met on the sidewalk only two days ago. But we spent every possible moment together. And when we weren't together, we talked on the phone until the wee hours of the morning, neither of us wanting to hang up.

That Saturday morning, I tried to take a shower but the water didn't work. I went to call the water company, but my phone had been turned off. Apparently, I'd failed to pay both bills and my service had been terminated, and I had no money.

I heard a knock on the door. David, standing outside my apartment.

"I tried to call," he said. At first, I tried to preserve any trace of dignity, an impossible task. All of my life, I'd tried to project a certain competence, but I couldn't come up with the money or hide any of my dysfunction.

"I can't pay my bills." I didn't tell him I couldn't call my parents for help, but he could tell I had no options by the desperation in my voice.

"We can handle this." David drove me to the water company and to AT&T, where he paid my balances. After we got back to my apartment, he said, "Now you can bathe and talk on the phone in the same day."

He was so full of optimism and cheer, it wrecked me. I began to cry.

"Everything's okay." He had a confused expression. "It's all fixed."

But I wasn't fixed.

"I'm a complete and total mess," I said. "I'd stay away from me if I were you."

I sat down on the floor, and he sat in front of me. We sat cross-legged, knee to knee. He took my hands.

"What do you mean exactly?" His voice was gentle and kind.

I told him how Virginia's death sent me into despair, how I had to cut my fingernails short or I'd claw myself in the night, and how Lipscomb would yank my scholarships the following semester.

"I'm damaged," I sobbed. "Especially romantically. You should leave."

"I don't believe that."

"Ask me anything," I said. "I'll prove it."

"When did you lose your virginity?" he asked.

I answered honestly, telling him an age represented by a number way too small, but he didn't flinch. I also told him about Conrad. Again, he didn't recoil and only offered kindness.

"Do you want children?"

"I never want to be a mother." Again, his face was soft with understanding. He told me he not only wanted kids, he wanted to adopt. Still, this didn't stop the conversation.

"Would you consider yourself a Christian?"

"No." My answer was emphatic, and I didn't pause to consider whether my answers might end everything. He'd caused hope to awaken in my spirit, so foreign and uncomfortable. Better to stave it off now.

"I don't believe in God, marriage, or the patriarchy," I said.

"Well, you can reject Church of Christ theology without rejecting Christianity."

I was taken aback by this because I'd been taught they were one and the same. The Church of Christ was the real, true church. All others were imposters.

David didn't subscribe to this. He told me his Harvard Law School Christian Fellowship was led by a Nigerian named Ruth who believed in the gifts of the Holy Spirit. "Healing, prophecy, dreams, everything," he explained. Everyone in his law school group had experienced the Holy Spirit in a miraculous way.

The dreams part hung in the air because of my prescient dream about Virginia's death. I didn't want him to think I was a mystic. By now I'd had a few more dreams that foretold events, but the events were inconsequential. Nothing as significant as Virginia's death. I had no idea why it kept happening.

"So you're," I struggled for the word. "Pentecostal?" I'd been taught Pentecostals were people given to extreme emotion, led astray by their inability to read the Bible.

"I don't know about the label," he said, "but I experienced God at law school in a way I've never encountered before."

I'd never heard anyone talk about the Holy Spirit without immediately explaining what it wasn't. For the first time since the vacation Bible school incident, hesitant hope and curiosity filled my chest.

"Do you believe in Jesus?" he asked, quietly.

I didn't have any particular feelings about him. "I guess he's fine. He had a lot of good teachings. Turn the other cheek and all."

"Yes, but there's more to him than that." David brought up his respect and admiration for the Christian thinker C. S. Lewis and presented what is known as his philosophical "trilemma." "It's a historical fact he claimed to be the son of God, right?"

"Right," I said.

"Lewis said there are only three possibilities: he was a liar, a lunatic, or the Lord." David stood and grabbed a dog-eared copy of *Mere Christianity* off my shelf and began reading. "I am trying here to prevent anyone saying the really foolish thing that people often say about him: I'm ready to accept Jesus as a great moral teacher, but I don't accept his claim to be God. That is the one thing we must not say."

David sat on the floor beside me. He wiped away a tear and continued reading. "A man who was merely a man and said the sort of things Jesus said would not be a great moral teacher. He would either be a lunatic—on the level with the man who says he is a poached egg—or else he would be the Devil of Hell."

He looked at me to see if I was still tracking him.

"Either this man was, and is, the Son of God, or else a madman or something worse. You can shut him up for a fool, you can spit at him and kill him as a demon or you can fall at his feet and call him Lord and God, but let us not come with any patronizing nonsense about his being a great human teacher. He has not left that open to us. He did not intend to."

This day had taken a surprising twist. "So to sort out your beliefs about Jesus, you can ask yourself if you think he's a liar."

I considered this and didn't think Jesus was deceptive.

"Is he a lunatic?"

Though I'd been burned by religion, I didn't think Jesus was insane.

"That leaves the last possibility. Do you think he's the Lord?" He asked it tenderly, but I struggled against this final option. I felt like I was sitting in a rapidly draining pool of theological antagonism and I'd soon be marooned in empty vastness. The hands on the clock on my bookshelf circled slowly—he had been there for hours—but time had stopped.

David looked at me, awaiting my response. No words came. When I was younger, I believed in Jesus, but now I scorned all religious notions. My disdain was no match for David's robust, authentic, powerful faith.

"I don't know," I said, even as belief was welling within me. For the first time in years, I wondered about Jesus. A silence hung between us as a quiet but tumultuous war was fought in my soul. I'd gone to church my whole life, but it was like walking into a movie theater during the last ten minutes. I never could figure out the plot, or what was going on. This simple conversation had put it all together for me in a decipherable way.

I considered the three categories—was Jesus a lunatic, a liar, or

God?—and couldn't bring myself to say he was either of the first two options. That left only one. Jesus was God.

"Okay," I said, still hesitant to admit my nascent belief. "Yeah. Sure." And with those three words, my ironic spiritual detachment dissipated, replaced by curiosity and openness. "So how does this work?"

"Well, there's no work. You are a Christian." He smiled gently. Coming from him, the word seemed like a warm blanket instead of a slap in the face. He held my hands as we sat on the floor and asked to pray with me. I nodded.

He asked God to send the Holy Spirit to me. I'd become so acquainted with darkness, it threatened to overtake me. But while we prayed, something happened.

I heard a noise: wings flapping loudly all around me. I opened my eyes as David continued to pray. Even though we were inside a small apartment, I half expected to see a flock of crows above me. But there was nothing but an apartment, a plaid couch, and a wooden coffee table.

"Did you hear that?" I asked.

David opened his eyes and listened. Nothing but silence. It was past midnight, and the neighbors were tucked soundly in their beds.

"Hear what?" he whispered.

I didn't want him to think I was crazy, but I'd heard it. "The flapping of wings. Loud, like if you walked up on a group of pigeons and scared them off. Or crows."

Maybe it was some divine angelic melody, maybe it was the sound of darkness taking flight. Maybe it was the sound of a spiritual battle being fought invisibly around me. It could've been the sound of defeat. Or the sound of victory.

For millennia, Christians have described "thin places," where the line between the mundane and the divine is exceedingly narrow. But in that liminal space, you can encounter, or at least perceive, God. Normally, this phenomenon is reserved for holy places—the Wailing Wall in Jerusalem, St. Peter's Basilica in Vatican City. Had God let himself be known momentarily in a Nashville apartment? For me?

This is what I knew.

I heard a noise, and the darkness which had clung to me took flight. It sounded like wings beating furiously, either in triumph or in frantic escape. But there was a sensation accompanying the sound, as if a knife pried a calcified carapace from me, leaving me vulnerable, tender, and exposed. And after the wings stopped beating, I was lighter, hopeful, and joyful. I'd changed. I'd been told I'd done too much, seen too much, and had been damaged too much to ever be redeemed. But there I was, sitting on the floor of my apartment with a guy I'd just met, feeling new.

9

EVEN THOUGH

A woman stood across the counter, clutching her Louis Vuitton bag.
"We encourage an eight-minute initial session to avoid burning."
The lady was as pale as a ghost.

"I'm going to Cabo in a week." She looked through our tanning lotion.
"I need at least twenty minutes."

I knew not to argue with wealthy women. I put her in bed 17, gave her
eye protection, and sold her the lotion which smelled like vacation.

But after she walked back to the bed, the hair on my arms stiffened.
David had traveled to Knoxville to attend a University of Tennessee football
game with friends, and I suddenly felt dread. I couldn't shake the feeling that he'd been injured. I turned on the television in the back room
and found the game. Maybe if there had been any problems in the crowd,
I might see ambulances in the background. Nothing seemed amiss, but
Neyland Stadium held a hundred thousand people. The game cameras
wouldn't catch one individual emergency.

After he'd had enough time to return home, I called him.

"You okay?"

"What do you mean?"

"I don't know," I said. "I sensed something bad happened to you."

"Well, now that you mention it." He ate something that disagreed with
him, but it was minor. I shrugged off my concern and told myself this whole
"seer" thing was mountain hillbilly nonsense.

But the next day, back in Nashville, David called to cancel our plans.

"My stomach's killing me," he said. "I might have E. coli or something." He took off work for a full week, and his acute abdominal pain worsened.

After a doctor ran extensive tests, he delivered the news. Ulcerative colitis. This disease was painful, debilitating, and could cause life-threatening complications. "My body's treating my colon as if it is a foreign body," he said. "It's trying to attack it and expel it."

"Can they treat it?" I asked him.

"It's incurable."

The peace I'd received after praying with David in my apartment shattered. David was—to me—a lifeline to my emotional well-being. I couldn't handle the traumatic breakup with Jacob, my parents shunning me, Virginia's death, and my new boyfriend's incurable disease all in one year. But it was happening. The steroids the doctor prescribed made David's face look like a moon. Even the blandest of foods caused serious pain. In a matter of days, he lost forty pounds off his six-foot frame and weighed only 125.

He faced this diagnosis with courage, even as his hair fell out. When he sat on a chair, he bruised. The doctors hospitalized him, but the IV drugs didn't work. I sat next to him at Vanderbilt University Medical Center, holding his hand while he was in excruciating pain. A top local surgeon came in and drew incision lines on his stomach with a marker. He was preparing to remove David's colon, and he'd be a twenty-six-year-old with a colostomy bag.

It was the only option, but David was in such a weakened state he might not even be able to survive the surgery. I couldn't believe I'd finally met someone I truly loved, and he was dying like Virginia had, just more slowly.

When David got out of the hospital, he was given instructions to rest so he could heal enough to endure the upcoming removal of his colon. This made our dating experience unusual. Instead of going out to dinner, we stayed in and drank broth. Instead of going to movies, we needed to have quick access to the toilet.

Mainly, we talked. In many ways, this disease accelerated our romantic progression. We didn't have time for small talk. We talked about the real issues—as best I could convey at the time—from the onset of our relationship. During the days, I'd go to class, drive him to doctors' appointments, and watch him take his plethora of pills.

But he kept losing weight.

David was dying, and so was my hope. I'd dated a string of guys who never worked out. David seemed to have enough life in him that I could coast on his overflow, but I'd hung my aspirations on a man who didn't seem long for this world, and I was crushed. I felt a certain brightness when I was around David, but it wasn't enough. When we were apart, the darkness returned. And he'd be gone soon anyway.

When I was back in my dorm, I needed to process the new information about David's disease and instinctively reached for the phone to call Virginia. I entered the first three numbers before realizing I couldn't reach her and thudding it back into the receiver. Alone with my thoughts, my mistakes berated me. Might even kill me, if Jacob was out there like he promised. If he attacked again, I wouldn't fight back. Death was all around me. It was coming for me, and I didn't want it to take me by surprise. I'd staved off my despair, but it had come roaring back at me. I grabbed a knife from the kitchen.

I called David and left a message. It was not best to break up in a voicemail but he didn't pick up, and we'd been dating only a few weeks. I wanted him to know I cared about him, but I'd been foolish to think a man could save me. The chasm between someone like him and someone like me was too great to traverse. I'd have to become the kind of person I'd never been to connect with him spiritually like he deserved. I believed in Jesus, yes. But that was the totality of my theological belief, and it wasn't enough to pull me from the morass I'd made of my life. He didn't need to be tethered to such death and despair. I couldn't run away from my problems by uttering a few magic words.

And now that I'd broken up with David, I was utterly alone. This felt right, reflective of my true situation. I went to the bathroom, turned on the water in the shower, and watched it fall. I got into the tub, fully clothed, and sat in it. I held the knife to my chest and moved it to my cheek, the blade wet and alluring.

The water dropped on my hair and body, saturating me. I was calm. I enjoyed the feeling of being in control as I ran the tip of the blade along my skin. After a while, the hot water ran out and a bitter coldness seeped in from my clothes, a familiar coldness, as if it had always been inside me. The knife whispered to me, and I held it to my wrist. There was an internal logic to this moment, to ending things on my terms. I was giving up. I never wanted love again. Whether it was the friendship kind or the romantic kind, I would lose it and it would devastate me. I had no more fight in me, and you have to fight for love.

But as I sat there, the door to my apartment opened. Footsteps. David appeared in the doorway. His eyes widened as he beheld the scene.

"What are you doing?" He slowly reached down and took the blade from me.

"Why are you here?"

"Your message," he said. "It scared me."

Even though I'd had moments of transparency before, only now did he see the mess I was. I couldn't hide it and didn't try.

Still, he extended his hand. I took it and stood. When I got out of the bathtub, I expected him to criticize me, to try to fix me. Instead, he embraced me. My clothing and tears soaked into his suit and tie. Death hovered over us, but we talked. Through the afternoon and into evening, we talked. It was nice, but I figured he'd say soothing words and drop me as soon as it was socially appropriate. How long do you wait to break up with someone who was so emotionally unbalanced? A day? A week?

I waited for it, but he was still there. In my life, in my kitchen. He followed me closely. If I went to make coffee, he'd be right there at my shoulder. If I went to the bathroom, he'd surprise me when I came out of the door. He didn't leave. He stubbornly didn't leave. He was there. Beside me. Even though.

I'd never been with someone who saw my shortcomings but wasn't afraid of them. The talons of death had loosened their grip on me, and it felt miraculous.

Then another miracle happened.

Things normalized. Our conversations weren't dominated by fear or death or knives or stalking exes or predatory preachers or incurable diseases even though he continued to lose weight. We talked about movies, politics, and the news. We laughed.

For Thanksgiving, a week after the bathtub scare, we drove to visit his Nana in Byhalia, Mississippi. After a delicious home-cooked meal, which David could barely eat, we took a slow walk. He was waxing eloquent about his love for me, and he paused to make his points more dramatically. The only problem was that he happened to stop by a sewage pipe.

As he was talking, my eyes fixed on that sewage pipe. Why would he stop by a sewage pipe? But I tuned back into the conversation when he said, "I guess what I'm asking is, would you marry me?"

No romantic movies will be made based on this proposal. There was no friend with a camera lurking to commemorate the moment. Because it was spontaneous, he didn't even have a ring.

I looked at him, mainly to gauge if he was serious.

"I don't know how much time I have left," he said. "But I want to spend the rest of my life with you."

David was a defibrillator: he restarted my heart; after so much trauma, I wasn't sure it'd ever work again.

I didn't hesitate.

"Sure, I'll marry you." He was a man of courage and honor, and he'd proven he'd stick by me no matter how many times I warned him off. Baffling, perplexing, and amazing. Suddenly, that hope swelled in my chest again—the one I first felt in high school when we talked—that everything could be better. The world opened for me, once again, but this time I knew we could be together every step of the way. I smiled and we embraced.

"But," I pulled away, "I do have two conditions."

"Conditions on a proposal?" He laughed. "Okay, what are they?"

"I want to get married in Paris," I said. "The real Paris." I'd never been to France, but the city loomed large in my mind since my hometown had its own miniature Eiffel Tower. Plus, I didn't want a church wedding since Virginia could not be my maid of honor.

"Second, I want to live in an apartment with a view of the Empire State Building." I'd never been to New York, but I'd recently watched *Sleepless in Seattle*, and this felt reasonable and romantic to me.

These two conditions were as spontaneous as the proposal, but they sounded like the type of thing a recent Harvard Law graduate might expect in a future wife. David outclassed me and was smarter than me, but we were both dreamers. Leaving all of my turmoil in the rearview mirror was intoxicating. Plus, living in New York would provide a buffer between Jacob—wherever he was—and me. But the main reason I wanted to get away from our lives in Nashville was much more hopeful and defiant. Planning for a fun, adventurous future in spite of his incurable disease seemed like a way to fight back against death.

"A wedding in France and an apartment in Manhattan?" He smiled. "Looks like we're getting married."

10

THE FRIENDS

David's eyes widened and he pressed the phone into his cheek. He was talking to my uncle Jasper. When the conversation was over, he turned to me.

"What happened?"

"He told me—and I quote—'If you ever lay a hand on my niece, I'll kill ya.'"

He laughed, but I didn't smile. "He wasn't joking," I said. "That was a real threat."

But Uncle Jasper wasn't the only one who had misgivings about my upcoming marriage. Our former professors, who reprimanded me for showing up drunk to class, expressed concern. A deacon from my hometown church wrote me a letter admonishing me not to marry some guy I'd met weeks ago. And David's best friends had concerns.

One evening, he invited me to his apartment to meet them. I appreciated this opportunity to spend time with them, because I was confident I could win them over. So I put on my prettiest dress and sat beside David in his living room as they peppered us with questions. I explained how we met, that we were getting married in France, and were moving to Manhattan.

"Wait." One of his friends leaned forward in her chair. "How long ago was all this? When did you meet each other on the sidewalk?"

I hesitated because I knew my answer would alarm them. "Three weeks."

One of his friends whispered, "Three weeks?" They were smiling that tight-lipped kind of smile, the kind you give when you pity someone. But I didn't have the capacity to explain how we'd gotten to know each other so intimately and quickly, that we'd packed a lot into those three weeks. I couldn't possibly explain that David introduced me to Jesus and the Holy Spirit, that his arrival in my life—in my bathroom—had saved my life. That wasn't their business anyway. All of his friends were Lipscomb alumni, and I didn't respect their theological or romantic hot takes.

"And how old are you?" the wife of his friend asked.

"I'm twenty."

The whole room was silent as they looked at me. I could tell they were trying to gauge how to respond to this news. Finally one of his friends spoke what perhaps everyone was thinking.

"Normally twenty-year-olds don't marry someone they met three weeks ago." She had an edge to her voice. "You guys don't even know each other," another said. "Instead of dropping out of college and moving to New York, maybe you should graduate? Or get premarital counseling?"

I squeezed David's hand.

"I do not believe in premarital counseling," I said. "I believe in love." That sounded good, but the truth was that I didn't want anyone to talk us out of it. Any professional would look at the differences between David and me and immediately tell us to call it off.

His friends didn't understand the urgency. I searched their faces, hoping to find one ounce of support, but saw only disapproval. That's when I realized. This was not a normal get-to-know-you conversation. This was an intervention.

"You're about to have a life-altering surgery in two weeks," David's friend said to him. "This is not a time to make such a momentous decision." A few of the friends began to cry.

That's when one leaned forward on his chair and blurted, "Be honest. Are you pregnant?"

Everyone looked at me. I could tell this was the only logical explanation for such a radical life choice, but they didn't know me. I could tell they didn't want to know me.

"I'm not pregnant." I smiled, hoping to find one ounce of support etched on their faces, but I saw only incredulity. His friends thought we were nuts. My friends weren't too happy either. When I told my mom I was going to marry David, she said, "Why would you marry a rank stranger?"

None of this dissuaded me, not in the least. David was the best thing that had ever happened to me. I'd already lost Virginia to death, and his health was deteriorating so quickly there was no time to waste. By now he was facing this surgery the doctor feared he was too weak to survive. Almost all of our efforts were geared toward him keeping his food down, getting rest, and preparing for a life with a colostomy bag. This was not a typical engagement, and there was no reason to pretend otherwise.

One night, we were about to watch a movie when David's phone rang. It was Ruth, the leader of his law school Christian fellowship. I was eager to find out what they were discussing, but he spoke to her in another room. After an hour, David hung up, and he came out of a back room with his face red.

"How is everything?" I assumed she had heard of our engagement and was calling to urge him to break it off.

"She said she'd been praying for me for the last few hours, and God told her that I was healed." He waved his hand. "That it's over."

I wasn't expecting that. I sat down on the couch.

"God told her? Like they chatted?" I asked. I'd never prayed for myself for hours, and I'd definitely not prayed for someone else that long. His body was thin and frail, his face puffed like a balloon. I expected him to be elated at this news, but I wasn't sure a person's intuition qualified as "news."

"How dare she." He eased himself into a chair and winced at the pain. "Right as I'm about to have to gear up for the surgery."

We skipped the movie and ended our evening early because David was so upset at this turn of events. David respected his friends in the Harvard Law School Christian Fellowship, but assuring a sick person that they were not sick was wrong. Cruel, even.

However, the next morning, he felt better. "For the first time in weeks, my stomach feels fine."

"No pain?"

"None."

And the next day, he continued to improve. Slowly, he ate some rice.

After another twenty-four hours, he added chicken. We waited, but nothing bad happened.

The third day after Ruth's call, David ate one of his mother's chocolate chip cookies. And again, he was fine. Like completely okay. A few hours later, he ate another.

The doctor was perplexed by this but decided to delay the surgery while David continued to eat. He made up for lost time. His diet consisted of cookies, bland chicken, and plain rice. Within three weeks, he'd gained back all forty lost pounds, was weaned almost entirely off steroids, and the doctor proclaimed he was in remission.

"What? You're healed?" I asked.

"Remission can happen with ulcerative colitis patients," he said. I could tell he was hesitant to call it miraculous, but I'd seen this transformation with my own eyes. But it *looked* like he'd been healed of an incurable disease.

The doctor did a colonoscopy to compare it to one at the onset of his diagnosis. In the first, his colon resembled hamburger meat. The second showed a colon as new as a baby's.

"You don't have chronic ulcerative colitis," the doctor told David. "Not anymore."

He stayed in remission. Every day that passed, he grew stronger. He gained weight. He wasn't in pain. David's health continued to improve so much that—three months after we got engaged—we were ready to get married. In spite of his disease, David was determined to give me that wedding in France.

This was so far outside our experience that it took a while for my dad to understand.

"We're getting married in Paris," David had told him.

"I assumed so." David was talking to my dad in his basement wood-working shop. My older sister had recently gotten married at Sulphur Well, and he thought David was talking about Paris, Tennessee.

"No, I mean Paris, France," David said.

My dad looked up from his miter saw. "We're going to France?"

David and I planned a small ceremony on a *bateaux mouche* on the Seine River with a small collection of people—my family, David's family, my friend who was maid of honor, David's friend from law school as best man, and a Lipscomb professor of rhetoric (the officiant) and his wife (a professor of French).

We were a motley crew, unused to travel in general, let alone international travel.

My dad wore his "good shoes," his steel-toe boots, which set off the metal detectors at the airports. When we finally arrived in France, the airline had lost David's luggage, which meant he had no clothing in which to get married. To complicate matters more, the owner of the *bateaux mouche* called and told David the boat we were to get married on had run into the dock and sunk.

"It sank?" I asked him.

"It's gone."

I laughed. I didn't care about such complications. I was thankful that I was alive. I was thankful that David was alive. Drunk with love, we thought this was funny, not some cosmic clue. Undeterred, we walked around Paris, going into restaurants and asking if they could accommodate a wedding. On Rue de Charonne, near Notre Dame, we saw a cute little restaurant called Chez Paul. David's best man—who also spoke French—inquired about their availability. The *maître d'* seemed enthusiastic about the idea. He must've asked when we wanted to get married. David's best man responded that we needed a place to marry the following day.

"*Demain?*" the manager asked.

"What does that mean?" I asked him.

The best man laughed. "He's surprised you want to get married tomorrow. He asks what the hurry is."

The restaurateur was asking the same question as everyone else, but I had no interest in convincing anyone of the urgency. The next evening, I wore a dress I'd bought off the rack, carried flowers bought off the street, and climbed the stairs into a room they'd prepared for us in that restaurant. David wore borrowed khaki pants as well as shoes that were two sizes too small. We'd ordered a last-minute traditional French wedding cake called a *croquembouche* from a local bakery and were surprised to discover it was not a cake at all but a pyramid of caramel-crusted cream puffs with candied ribbons spiraling down from the top.

The restaurant served us a seven-course meal, and our Christian teetotaling families baffled the servers when they eschewed the champagne offered for the celebration. The actual ceremony was conducted at least partially in French, and I wasn't sure what vows I was taking.

Still, we kissed, and it was official. We were husband and wife.

David's healing and our French wedding shook me, because—though I believed in God—I never expected him to be involved in my actual life. I imagined him as the divine clockmaker who wound up my life and watched it tick away into nothingness. But through this experience, God expanded, spilled over, and hit me in the gut. God was real, not only in an intellectual "I believe this" sort of way, but as an active character in my life. His healing and our wedding were practical and life-changing.

Our boat sank, but I—maybe for the first time—was buoyant.

11

GRAMERCY

David nudged me awake, and it took me a second to realize I was in a plane. "Look!" he said. "We're home." I looked out the window and saw the skyline of New York City glittering in the morning sun. The city's mystery, potential, and excitement emanated from the buildings like heat waves. I swallowed hard.[1]

My family, landing in Tennessee about now, did not usually fly in airplanes, go to France, or live in a town with buildings tall enough to require elevators. We were more of the dirt-under-fingernails, catfish-eating, smelling-of-Deep-Woods-OFF! kind of people. Yet Manhattan gleamed beneath me, and I squeezed David's hand in excitement.

When we landed, we jumped in a taxi. I pressed my face to the dirty glass trying to see the tops of the skyscrapers. Just being in a yellow cab was exotically exhilarating. I gawked at the people waiting at traffic lights—women wearing business suits paired with tennis shoes, bicyclists carrying messenger bags, and couples walking well-coiffed dogs.

The cab stopped at our post-war apartment at Third Avenue and Eighteenth Street, and—after talking to the landlord—we got keys to our five-hundred-square-foot apartment. The postage stamp–sized kitchen had an oven that almost hit the sink when opened, but it had hardwood floors and a curved wall at the entrance that gave it a certain elegance. Plus, I could see the Empire State Building, when I crawled out onto the rickety fire escape. I'd seen it countless times in movies like *King Kong, Sleepless in*

Seattle, and *The Muppets Take Manhattan*, but now it was a towering part of my own life. When it was illuminated at night, it lit up my world—my real world.

After our furniture arrived from Tennessee, we created a cozy home in our little Gramercy Park apartment. We had a few weeks before David started to work and I started at New York University, so we explored the subways, delis, and the areas around our apartment. The first time I went to the grocery store at the foot of our building, I was astonished at the scant selection. The aisles were narrow and dark, and the products were just whatever came in on the truck that week. When I couldn't find a chocolate cake mix, I asked the cashier.

"We have strawberry mix this week," she said. "And lots of Pepsi."

Normal tasks were difficult, expensive, and inconvenient, and the hard-nosed negotiating required to buy groceries, hail a cab, and get a table at a restaurant assaulted my southern acquiescence. I had to assert myself, to force people to make space for me, just to walk down the street.

Pedestrians jostled each other in an unacknowledged way that would've resulted in constant fist fights in the South. The avenues (north/south) and the streets (east/west) had a soundtrack of constant honking and colorful invectives yelled out of cab windows. Doormen opened doors of darkly tinted town cars for well-heeled tenants, orange and white pipes belched subterranean steam, and people on rollerblades danced dangerously close to cars at intersections. As I walked by soaring apartment buildings, I considered the eight million people stacked atop each other in little rectangle boxes—picking fights, having sex, and putting up groceries just feet away from people urinating on the sidewalks, bodegas peddling adult magazines, and hospitals saving lives.

It was chaos, and I loved it all.

The streets, however, were empty on Sunday mornings—a stark contrast to Tennessee, where police had to direct the massive traffic in front of church buildings. Our new church met in an old theater in Times Square, a true sanctuary amid the neon decadence surrounding it. The faithful crowded the stage, raising their hands in prayer. Men in ties sat next to men with hair so greasy it stained their already soiled shirts. Though the churches I'd attended had been largely segregated, this church was full of so many ethnicities they handed out headsets for live translation of the sermon in six different languages. And on our first Sunday, I watched an elderly Black man stand on the floor to the left of the podium yelling, "Jesus! Jesus! Jesus!" over and over until the service began.

When Pastor David Wilkerson got the podium, he said, "Ladies, when we stand to sing, please don't leave your purses on the ground. Some thieves are in the sanctuary, so keep an eye out on your belongings. And for those of you who came here to steal," he said, "we welcome you. You came here to get a few bucks, but you'll get the life-changing love of God."

This church didn't overlook sin to maintain the appearance of godliness. It was after the real thing. If Jesus was the Great Physician, this church was the hospital, filled with hurting people staggering under the weight of their problems.

When I was growing up, nothing deserved more contempt in the church than emotionalism—a catchall term to describe anything that deviated from the standard two hymns, a prayer, another hymn, and a twenty-two-minute sermon. You could be thankful Jesus died for your sins as long as you didn't show it in any way other than a furrowed brow during communion. But after all the years of feeling discomfort in church, I loved sitting in my red velvet seat in the uncomfortable, dynamic presence of God. I closed my eyes during "Amazing Grace," heard people singing in their native tongues, and knew exactly what heaven would sound like.

I fell in love with New York with the same alacrity and abandonment with which I'd fallen for David. With all the wild promise, mystery, and energy emanating from the hot pavement, what choice did I have? Even though everyone was opposed to our getting engaged after three weeks and moving a thousand miles away, we'd made the right decision.

David and I got to know each other during long, lazy summer days, until he started at the law firm a few weeks later. Friends warned me about his upcoming heavy workload, but I could not fully be prepared for the number of hours he was at the office. He left early in the morning and didn't come home until after midnight. On some days, he'd work through until the next day. He kept an extra suit, shirts, and ties in his office and had two secretaries—one for the day and one for the night—so he could work sometimes twenty-four hours a day. While he toiled away in midtown,

I read novels in Central Park, bought cheap theater tickets from the TKTS booth, and cheered in the audience of *Live with Regis and Kathie Lee*.

In the fall, I was both excited and nervous about my philosophy classes. On my first day of classes, I walked from our place to New York University's campus comprising buildings dotting Washington Square Park. Though I was intimidated by NYU, I was thankful to be able to salvage my college life after my Lipscomb experience. Finally, I could attend college at a place that would welcome me, a southern feminist refugee, into the feminist fold. I looked forward to making new friends with people who accepted me the way I was.

I walked into my first class, a philosophical exploration in women's studies, and sat in the back row. The professor asked us to go around the room and describe our backgrounds and reasons for taking the class. Most came from private and boarding schools and were either women's studies or philosophy majors. When it was my turn, I explained I had dropped out of a Christian college in Nashville, got married, and was now pursuing my education while my husband worked. I explained I'd taken this women's studies class because I had never been able to truly explore feminism at my previous college. Though I feared I'd sound boring compared to people with more sophisticated backgrounds, my classmates sat in rapt attention.

"Wait, you've never studied feminism? How old are you?" a girl asked, leaning forward in her chair.

"You're *married*?" a guy with Amnesty International stickers on his folder asked. "Did you take his last name? Does he make you wash dishes?"

As I answered their questions, I was keenly aware of my pronounced southern accent—mainly because they snickered when I opened my mouth.

"No one can make a lifelong decision to get married when they're twenty years old," Mr. Amnesty International said. "You could date for years and not know someone well enough. Did this man pressure you into this? Did he knock you up?"

I shook my head, and he sighed in relief.

"I don't mean to meddle," he said. "But maybe you should get out of this while you still can."

"Leave her alone." A girl who was dressed like Pippi Longstocking chirped from the front row. "She probably married her cousin."

I waited a beat while everyone chuckled, unsure what was most amusing to them: my accent, my young marriage, or my lack of feminist knowledge.

"Nice one, but he's not my cousin." I tried to be good-natured. "And, yes, southerners tend to get married earlier than northerners."

I'd hoped this might cause my classmates to let up, since I'd heard liberals were all about respecting people's cultural heritage. But this deference must've stopped at the Mason-Dixon Line.

Mr. Amnesty International turned fully around in his seat and looked at me with kind, concerned eyes. "Look, you may not know it, but you've been victimized by the patriarchy. It's not your fault. But you're trapped in a birdcage of missed opportunities—a cage you can't see because you've never known freedom."

"Yeah, shouldn't you have gotten a college degree before getting married?" Pippi asked.

The professor, sensing she'd lost control of the class, cleared her throat. "We welcome you here," she said. "There's no better place to study the philosophy of sex and gender than this classroom."

I survived the day. But over the next weeks, walking into class was like jumping headfirst into an aquarium—and my classmates were constantly tapping on the glass looking at me with wide-eyed curiosity.

Everything about me was unacceptable. My nascent Christianity was offensive because I used male pronouns for God. They surmised my dyed hair was because of my subservience to men. And my pro-life beliefs caused a male student to burst into tears and run out of the class. On his way out, he said class was no longer safe with me in it.

"I know you're new to this, but feminism isn't a salad bar, where you can have a little of this and a little of that," a classmate explained once he left. "You can't be a feminist and oppose abortion."

As I walked through Greenwich Village on my way home, I mulled over my situation. I was considered liberal at Lipscomb, but a feminist apostate at NYU; I'd switched from one monolithically religious school to another. I'd never be accepted, because people saw me as a project, someone to change.

I meandered down Third Avenue, looking at friends eating casually outside at pizzerias, and felt a lump in my throat. I'd never be able to authentically connect with my classmates. I was lonely. Plus, I saw Jacob everywhere—in Washington Square Park, at the coffee shop, in the line of Empire State Building tourists. He had wider shoulders than his lean cyclist body, and he walked in a sort of hunched-over way that was distinctive. I saw him tossing a ball with a dog, reading a book in Central Park, or riding the subway. It wasn't him, but I braced myself for the possibility that one day, it might be.

When I finally arrived at home, I dropped my backpack on the floor, took off my jacket, and heard my phone ringing from its cradle in the kitchen. This was back before caller ID, so I answered the landline.

"May I speak to David?" The caller was a woman with a cigarette-sexy voice. I explained he wasn't there, and she abruptly hung up without leaving a message.

Who was that woman? I forgot about it until the next day when the phone rang again. "Hey there, is David around?"

I bit my lip. This was not the same woman, I knew that much. While the first woman's voice was cigarette-low, this woman sounded like she'd inhaled helium. This was the rare weekend when David was home, so I reluctantly passed him the phone. He grabbed it and walked around, so I hovered near to listen in on their conversation.

"I'm sorry," I heard him say—very formally. "You have the wrong number."

When he plopped back down on the sofa, I tried to push it out of my mind, but the phone rang at three in the morning, and four o'clock—more women asking for David, both times David claiming they were wrong numbers.

I rolled over and tried to go back to sleep, but what was happening?

The calls became more regular. After a long day at school, I dreaded coming home to see the red flashing light on my answering machine. I heard from Jill, Michelle, and Tiffany. Most were short—"Hey, David. Call me."—but one lady said she enjoyed meeting him and said his lips "tasted like butter."

When I answered the ringing phone, some women were testy. One woman cried. "What do you mean, he's at work? We were together yesterday, and he said he'd be home today."

I paused, before asking—in a shaky voice—"Yesterday?" He'd told me he was at work preparing for a trial. For fifteen straight days, he didn't come home until after two o'clock in the morning.

"Where did you see him? Exactly?"

"In SoHo," she cried. "At a club."

David worked in midtown. I sat down and rubbed my hand over my face. "Are we talking about the same David?" I cradled the receiver on my neck. "Tall, blond?"

"Yes, and handsome. We danced, and he wrote down his number on a cocktail napkin." She read the number aloud.

I listened as she rattled off the number, which was our phone number, before she ended the call. I began to sweat.

David seemed so Christian during our short time of dating and engagement, but I'd been burned by that religious act before. Was he leading a whole different life I didn't know about? Were my fellow students—and everyone else—right about us?

One night, David came home from work after midnight, plopped his briefcase on the floor, and sank into the couch. Whatever he was doing all day and night must've been exhausting.

"You missed some calls." I shoved a list of first names and numbers I'd collected that day into his lap. He scanned it and tossed it aside. "That's weird." He picked up the remote and turned on the television. "I don't even know a Desiree."

He acted like it was a slightly confusing phenomenon—not a sign that I'd made the biggest mistake of my life. And that was saying something.

"Wrong numbers usually don't ask for you *by name*," I said quietly, but he—exhausted—was already watching NBA highlights. I'd seen him for only a few hours in the past two weeks because of his workload, and it was usually in the middle of the night as he fell into bed after a long day at work. Who did I marry?

One afternoon after class, a man called asking for David.

"Sorry, he's at work." I sighed heavily, expecting him to hang up hurriedly like everyone else. But he didn't.

"What?" His voice was laced with indignation. "I don't know anything about a job today."

"He works every day."

"Since when?"

"For a few months, I guess."

"But all work should go through me." I was woefully unfamiliar with the machinations of law firm life. Perhaps the firm was misallocating cases to David—who was a new attorney—which should've gone to more senior lawyers.

"I'd be happy to take a message," I said. "What's your name?"

"What's my name?" He laughed. "Oh you've got a lot of nerve. I've known David for years," he shot back. "The real question is who are you?"

There was something about the question that embarrassed me. Who was I? I was the spontaneous twenty-year-old who'd watched so many romantic movies that marrying a stranger and moving to New York was a legitimate life plan. Finally, I muttered, "I'm his wife."

"His *what*?" His voice was raised and full of anger. "Why didn't he tell me about you?"

Unprepared for this explosion, I began explaining. "The wedding was spontaneous. I'm sure he would've invited you, but it was in France," I stammered before launching into a defense of getting married quickly, but with less confidence than in previous conversations.

"Okay, I'm coming over. We have to fix this," he said. "Don't talk to anyone, don't leave the apartment, and don't answer the phone." He lowered his voice. "Level with me. Are you pregnant?"

I felt strange about this angry man coming over to my place to discuss the status of my uterus. But, once again, I declared, "I'm *not* pregnant."

A heard a massive sigh on the other end of the line. "Okay, okay," he said, more slowly. "We can work with this."

I walked to the window and looked onto the fire escape. It was hard to see the Empire State Building in the day, when it wasn't lit up against the night sky.

"Look, I'm not trying to be a jerk, but a little David Lee would really hurt our comeback. You understand, right?"

"David Lee?"

He laughed, and I imagined him rolling his eyes. "You don't even know him, do you?"

Well, he had me there.

"I mean, David's middle name is Austin. Are you calling for the attorney, David French?"

"No. I'm calling for the singer, David Lee Roth."

At this I slid down the wall next to the window and sat on the floor. "Did you say, 'David Lee Roth'?" I waited, but my question had apparently rendered him speechless. "The lead singer of Van Halen?"

Even though I'd spent the 1980s trying to figure out the Rubik's Cube, even I was aware of Van Halen, global phenomenon. Roth had a long mane of golden hair, acrobatic stage moves, and brightly colored spandex. My David wore glasses and suits and sometimes dressed up for *Star Wars* and *Lord of the Rings* movie premieres.

"Yes, David Lee Roth the rock star. I'm his agent." He said the words slowly and a little sarcastically. "Wait. That's right. He got a new number," he said. "So you're not . . . He's not . . ." His voice trailed off. "I called his old number."

That's when I realized. We had David Lee Roth's old phone number, and he was still using it. Apparently, the rock star had changed his number right before we moved to Manhattan but still gave out his old number to women he met but wanted to let down easily. We happened to randomly be assigned his old one, which would've been a simple, easy-to-fix mix-up had my new husband not had the same first name.

When David came home that night, I explained the big, confusing, almost-marriage-killing coincidence as soon as he came in the door.

"You thought I was out clubbing this whole time?" He put his briefcase on the table. "Have you ever met me?"

"I met you like five minutes ago."

We laughed and—just then—the phone rang. This time, David answered it and explained to the disappointed woman that regrettably David Lee Roth had given her the wrong number. She paused and seemed to swallow tears. In a soft voice, she asked, "Do a lot of other women call here?"

"Yeah, I'm afraid so," he said gently before hanging up. Afterward, he turned to me and frowned. "I think I just broke that woman's heart."

I grabbed his hand and smiled, happy that David French—the attorney—had not broken mine.

12

THE PROPHET

A prophet?" I asked. "What do you mean? Like a psychic?"
Two years after we married, David and I traveled to Atlanta to attend a reunion of the Harvard Law School Christian Fellowship. I knew some of the attendees well, since we'd lived in Manhattan together—but the others I'd only heard of through tales of spiritual greatness like when they prayed David's ulcerative colitis away. I was intimidated, especially when I heard they'd invited a prophet to the gathering.

Apparently, prophets were still a thing—an idea that both invigorated and terrified me. If this guy was for real, he'd see my spiritual inadequacy. *You need to read your Bible more*, he'd say. And *you are a whore*. Though I'd now been a Christian for more than two years, I felt I'd never truly feel forgiven for my rebellion against God. I'd been branded, and I couldn't get rid of the scarlet W even if I tried.

Still, I was curious about someone who called himself a prophet. When we arrived, I spotted him immediately and smiled.

"I'm Gary." He stuck out his hand—short, Vienna sausage–like fingers—for me to shake. I figured he'd have a name like Ezekiel or Jeremiah, not the same name as my plumber. The buttons on his Hawaiian shirt strained against his protruding belly. He had a stubborn patch of wispy hair on the front of his head.

I sat in the back next to David and crossed my arms. I figured this guy would make some sweeping generalizations that anyone with common sense would make to HLS alumni. *I see wealth in your future; you're a perfectionist; you focus too much on your accomplishments and should focus on God.*

"Just a quick word." The leader of the Christian fellowship stood at the front of the room with a handheld tape recorder. "I want you to know I'll be recording every word of this. If Gary's a true prophet, his words will be true now and years later." She held up the recorder. "This will hold him accountable."

"Yeah, she asked if she could record me." Gary spoke confidently, with the air of someone used to being doubted. "And I insisted."

He called on our friends Jeff and Shaunti first. I'd gotten to know them in New York, where they had hosted a weekly Bible study but now lived in Atlanta. I watched as they stood awkwardly in front of Gary as if he were about to officiate a renewing of their vows. But this was much more interesting.

Gary closed his eyes and waited a moment. The room had the silent eagerness of children waiting for a magician to pull something cool out of his hat. I expected Bible verses, admonitions, or flat-out rebukes, but not what actually came out of his mouth.

"God wants to speak to you about that jalopy you drive," Gary said.

Everyone in the room had been holding their breath, but—at this—they laughed. Jeff and Shaunti really did drive a clunker. At one point or another, since in New York they were the only ones who had a car, we'd all been in the back seat hoping their old Isuzu would make it home.

Shaunti nudged Jeff on the shoulder. "I was just saying that, wasn't I? That we need to get a newer car?" She looked to Gary, whom she now considered an ally. "It's getting too bad to drive, but Jeff wants to hang onto it."

"She's right," Jeff admitted. "We couldn't agree, so we said we'd pray about it, and . . ." His voice trailed off. "Now this."

I figured Gary was about to make a divine proclamation that Jeff was, in fact, a cheapskate and Shaunti would take a victory lap around the room. But Gary shook his head and said, "No."

Jeff looked up in surprise.

"Like the shoes of the children of Israel in the desert, your car will not wear out. You will experience great financial hardship and great financial prosperity over the next few years. Prepare for both."

Jeff and Shaunti seemed genuinely moved and sobered by this word.

A nervous, hopeful anticipation settled over everyone one in the room, but not me. That seemed more like a parlor trick than a prophetic word. Maybe Gary had overheard Jeff and Shaunti discussing it as they walked in, but I seriously doubted God cared so much about the minutiae of our lives.

The next woman stood up, a meek and kind attorney who lived in Manhattan.

"I want to talk to you about your poetry," he said. "The stuff you've been writing in secret."

This woman had been in our small group Bible study in New York, at least when she could get off work to make our eight o'clock meetings. She loved her law firm and—because of her dedication to her job—frequently had to miss. No way she was secretly a tortured poet. Her friends looked incredulous. But to our surprise, the woman's shoulders slumped, she breathed a huge sigh, and tears formed in her eyes.

"How'd you know that?" she asked.

"What?" Shaunti interrupted. "You write poetry?"

"When I'm not working," she admitted. "It's my secret passion. Well, not so secret now."

"It's time to share your work with people," Gary said.

I imagined encountering a real-life prophet would be like seeing an angel. It would result in sobbing and repentance, not vehicular and literary advice. But each and every person stood before Gary, and every time he surprised them with secret information to which no one else was privy.

"Okay, your turn." Gary pointed at me, and the hair on my arms stood on end. I felt like I had when I was gazing into my aunt's crystal ball, and electricity shot through me. David and I walked up together.

Gary smiled at me as our friends sat around us. The lady with the recorder turned it on and stuck it next to the prophet's mouth, a signal for him to begin. But he didn't. He looked at me for a few moments, closed his eyes, and opened them again.

"You're in despair?" He tilted his head and studied my face, on to which I pasted a look of incredulity. I had no interest in my deep-seated anguish being on full display. "You have so much shame that you've injured yourself during the night. Am I right? You've hurt yourself?"

Only David and my roommate Celeste knew—in the wake of Virginia's death—I'd mauled myself with my fingernails in my sleep so much that I slept with socks on my hands. No way Gary was referring to that. No, he was fishing, waiting to see my reaction, but I'd give him nothing. This was a spiritual poker game, and I—straight-faced—would call his bluff. I returned his gaze, daring him to continue without any emotional feedback.

"A blood-stained pillow. That's what I see." He raised his eyebrows ever so slightly at me and he touched his own neck, covered in stubble. "Yes." Now his voice was full of sober confidence, as if he'd read my dossier and had the evidence before him. "That's right. You bleed from your throat in the night."

Someone scooted their chair, leaning forward to hear my response. But I was speechless. He, in a few sentences, had opened me up and showed everyone what was inside. I opened my mouth to speak, but I could only muster a nod.

"Because of your sin, you secretly believe you will be unable to have children." He paused. "And you believe God will punish you."

I was holding a pair, and he just laid down a royal flush. My poker face disappeared. He was right. After all I'd been through, I didn't feel like I'd be a good mother. Every night, as I drifted off to sleep, I was distracted by this fear, like a dripping water faucet constantly drawing my attention. I'd never articulated this to another person, even David—who was looking at me with wide eyes, along with Gary and everyone else.

My throat tightened. Perspiration formed below my hairline. He had the manner of a Secret Service agent, receiving classified information in his earpiece and relaying only enough to convince me not to lie to him. He saw right through me. I feared he'd admonish me for my lack of spiritual devotion, but this was worse.

"But there is no condemnation for those who are in Christ Jesus." His eyes were full of gentle compassion, but his words fell on me like cartoon pianos plummeting out of a high-rise. "I have some Bible verses for you." At this, he spat staccato Scripture citations out of his mouth, one after the other. Bible verses that applied to me? It seemed improbable.

He could tell by my blank face that I had no idea what these verses said. "Look them up later. These verses are messages from God for you. God is not unhappy with you. He is not punishing you by withholding children. He will bless you."

My trepidation quickly lifted as his words wrapped around me like a quilt. But all of that dissipated at his next sentence.

"In fact, you're pregnant now."

At this, the whole room gasped. So did I. Though I'd heard about mothers-to-be revealing their pregnancies to loved ones in creative and unusual ways, I'd never heard of a random stranger revealing a pregnancy to the mother herself. That's not how it works. Pregnancy is determined by double-lined tests, and hormone spikes, and cravings for pickles and ice cream. But pregnancy is ruled out by one incontrovertible sign: a menstrual period. And since I'd gotten my period that very morning, the only craving I had was for truth.

This guy was a con. The spell was broken.

"This is not possible." I didn't want to reveal this intimate information to this room of attorneys, but I was the one who brought it up. He should have been embarrassed. Not me. And so I cleared the emotion from my throat and declared, "I'm on my period."

The four words did not land the intended punch, because Gary chuckled. "With God," he assured me, "all things are possible."

This was religious hysteria. Even though I was a college dropout, I knew a con man when I saw one—and all of these Harvard grads were going along with it. Sure, Gary knew about the jalopy, the poetry, my pillow, and my motherhood apprehensions. But either you're pregnant or you're not. And I was not. Prophets have been stoned for less.

"But listen." He proceeded as if I'd said nothing. I knew he'd heard me. Everyone in the room heard me, and he was two feet from me. "You need to know some things about this pregnancy."

I frowned.

"God is speaking." He said it so authoritatively, so confidently, that a chill ran through me.

"Your baby is a girl." Emotion welled inside me, but I pushed it down. This guy knew that I wanted to be pregnant and was manipulating me for a dramatic moment. "She'll be delivered this year. But." He slowed down.

"The doctors will tell you that you will miscarry. You will not. By the end of this year, you will have a healthy baby girl."

It was late March, but I could not do the math in my head with everyone looking at me. After this prophecy, Gary continued with the rest of our friends, who were not dissuaded by incredulity and received personalized divine messages with gratitude. I went home dejected and embarrassed.

No doubt, this is why my period stopped the evening Gary had prophesied about this fictional pregnancy. A week passed. Another.

Every time I went to the bathroom, I thought of Gary and his extreme confidence. He'd gotten under my skin. Was that why my period had stopped? Extreme spiritual agitation? I resented the idea that he would toy with my deepest fears in front of a room full of people I'd just met.

Still more days passed, and I decided to find out once and for all. I secretly went to the drugstore and bought three pregnancy tests. The box instructed to wait two minutes, but I held it in my hand and watched the little window from the first second. I wasn't nervous, I was angry. Angry that I'd gone to the retreat. Angry that Gary had gotten my hopes up.

To my surprise, two faint lines appeared.

I sat on the edge of the bathtub and stared at it as if I expected it to speak to me. Since it offered no more information, I took another one. And the next. All positive.

Apparently, my "period" was "implantation bleeding," when a fertilized egg attaches to the lining of the uterus, which sometimes causes light spotting. That night, I wrapped up a baby bottle and gave it to David as a present. He was overjoyed.

The doctors gave me a due date in January. But I knew—as Gary had said—that I'd deliver "by the end of the year." The prophecy also took all of the drama out of the ultrasound that revealed the gender—it was, as predicted, a girl—but there would be plenty of drama. About six months later, the phone rang.

"There are complications," my doctor said. "Call off the celebrations, because you are aborting."

I politely asked a few questions and thanked him for the information.

"I want to make sure you heard me correctly? Are you alone? Do you understand?" he asked. "Your baby is not going to make it." But I hung up the phone without any sort of shock or grief. Not after everything I'd seen. Gary had warned me this would happen and told me not to worry.

I found an ob-gyn who specialized in complicated pregnancies, rested, and went into labor on a Sunday evening, December 21, 1998.

I named her Camille.

In the past, God felt amorphous, like a fog. If I reached up to him and tried to touch him, my hand would come back empty. But in the past few years, he had become real to me. After David's healing and our wedding, I could feel him. I could perceive him.

But now he seemed as solid as concrete. As soft as a wool rug. I planted both feet on him and wiggled my toes.

I could stand here.

13

BUZZED

Six months after Camille was born, David was offered a teaching position at Cornell Law School so we headed to upstate New York, where the annual snowfall was seventy inches. Cornell sits on a hill in Ithaca overlooking Cayuga Lake and is surrounded by deep gorges, rolling hills, and Riesling vineyards.

I loved holding and fussing over my new baby. Holding her was like holding hope. Purity. The darkness I'd felt before marriage seemed to have left. I was given things I never thought I'd have—a husband, a baby, a life. I breastfed Camille, which stunted my periods, so I didn't realize I was pregnant again until after the first trimester. Once again, I was overwhelmed with joy.

But giving birth in Ithaca would be quite different from my previous experience giving birth. My new friends in Ithaca had hired midwives for birthing at home or had given birth in the hospital in underwater tanks through hypnosis. My doctor told me he didn't administer epidurals but used a variety of other, more healthful pain-alleviation strategies. Also, I would have only one ultrasound, which they believed were societally overused. The hospital provided only cloth diapers to prevent climate change.

During our time in Ithaca, Tennessee's own Al Gore faced George W. Bush in the 2000 presidential election. After my experience at NYU, I realized I wasn't truly a Democrat, so I was pulling for Bush. But when the election-night results were so close, a winner was not revealed for weeks. In this confusion, doctors and nurses kept coming in to ask David about Florida election law.

My doctor asked David about hanging chads as my contractions grew more intense. Several nurses and hospital staff members stopped in to hear David's opinion as a lawyer specializing in Constitutional law.

I gave birth to a wonderful baby boy that December day, minutes after the Supreme Court decided on a technical argument to give Bush the victory by the narrowest of margins. I was gratified at the results of the election, but thrilled over having a new baby boy.

But my son—Austin—wasn't nursing and was making a purring noise when he breathed. The nurses whisked him away, and we sat in our room alone, waiting to hear what was wrong.

"As you know, there is no God." This is how the doctor explained our son had pneumonia and would not be able to leave the hospital any time soon. The juxtaposition of Camille's birthing experience, where the doctor laid hands on her and prayed, with Austin's was jolting.

For days, the baby was encased in a plastic bubble in the neonatal intensive care unit. Going to great lengths to ensure he didn't experience an unnatural feeding (in other words, a bottle), the nurses nourished him by injecting milk into a nasal tube leading to his stomach. Not only could I not breastfeed him, I couldn't even hold him. Realizing I wasn't able to comfort my new son—who was crying when he wasn't panting for air—I broke down and asked for what was perfectly acceptable in the South but considered anathema in Ithaca: a pacifier. The nurse refused.

She explained that this was a "breast-friendly" hospital, which encouraged breastfeeding exclusively. It did not use bottles or pacifiers that could potentially cause "nipple confusion," which prevents babies from latching on during breastfeeding. But this was more than a nursing complication.

David was frustrated.

"In our family, we don't believe in nipple confusion," he said. "We practice nipple diversity!"

She relented and sold us a pacifier from a stash she kept in her locker. For ten days, we waited in the neonatal intensive care unit and spent the late nights with the nurses. Austin was put in one of those incubators, with white sheets under a clear plastic bubble. He had so many pokes and prods they eventually had to use the vein in his forehead for his IV. Though our black-market pacifier was worth every dime, it kept falling out of his tiny mouth and he didn't have the ability to put it back into his mouth. So we sat outside his bubble and watched him unable to retrieve this basic comfort.

We couldn't stay all night with him in the NICU, so we came back to the room and asked David's parents—who'd driven up from Kentucky—to pray. David's parents were Pentecostals, so they prayed differently than other people I knew. Specifically, they prayed that since we couldn't be in the NICU around the clock that God would send an angel to watch over the baby.

This wasn't a metaphorical prayer. They believed God would literally send an angel with wings, flapping and hovering over little Austin to protect and comfort him. That sounded sentimental and improbable, but they prayed like they were making a divine personnel request they fully expected to be fulfilled. Though I appreciated the sentiment, I was mildly annoyed. I wanted a normal prayer—healing, comfort, perseverance. Not a request for an angel.

The days turned into nights, which turned into a week. I perched myself on an uncomfortable stool next to his little incubator. Slowly, the baby got better.

After ten days, we brought Austin home. Our family was—finally—all together. And the baby grew strong. The memories of his difficult birth receded into the background, and we almost never spoke of it. He grew into a kid who loved garbage trucks and Buzz Lightyear and Spider-Man.

Three years later, he woke up from a nap.

"I had a dream," he told me. Though this is a common utterance, a shudder ran through me. Ever since my dreams had turned out to have a prescient quality, I took them more seriously than most.

"Want to tell me about it?" I asked.

"I was in a bubble. Lying on white cloth. And I saw my pacifier but I couldn't reach it. And you were looking at me through the bubble."

I sat down at the kitchen table. We'd never told him he had birth complications. Could he possibly be talking about his NICU stay?

"What else?"

"And this woman poked a needle into my forehead." I'd forgotten the nurse had used an IV in his forehead. But his description of the dream reminded me, and I felt a prickling in my eyes.

"I was all alone," he said. The days after his birth were filled with so much sadness and despair, mainly because we couldn't be physically with him. Why would God reveal all of this sadness to him in a dream?

"But then I wasn't."

"Who was with you?" I asked. I hoped he remembered we were trying desperately to be with him.

"Buzz Lightyear," he said.

I laughed, which punctured the moment. I'd gotten so engrossed into this tale that seemed so uncannily like his birth. But there's no way a premature baby could remember his NICU experience.

Austin was serious as he tried to convey his dream, and I could tell he was frustrated he didn't have the right words to express himself.

"No, it wasn't Buzz Lightyear, but there was a man and he was big like Buzz Lightyear and he had wings like Buzz Lightyear and he stood right there beside me."

I remembered my in-laws' prayers and my heart constricted.

"Did the winged creature speak?" I asked, gently.

"He only said one thing." Austin closed his eyes to go back to sleep. "He told me not to be afraid."

14

THE QUESTION

In 2002, we moved to Philadelphia when David got the opportunity to lead the Foundation for Individual Rights and Expression (FIRE), defending free speech for all Americans in our courtrooms, on our campuses, and in our culture. We settled into this new urban life with kids in a two-level apartment which overlooked the Eagles stadium.

David wrote for *National Review*, a conservative magazine founded by William F. Buckley Jr. in 1955. Because we were interested in politics, we paid attention to up-and-coming possible GOP leaders, and particularly to a former governor of Massachusetts named Mitt Romney. I dreamed of one day becoming a political writer, but—without a college degree or training—I had limited options. I started off answering writing ads in Craigslist and was paid precisely $0 for all of my work.

Instead, I wrote about what I knew. I submitted a column for the Philadelphia *City Paper* detailing my life being a southern conservative in a liberal city. The editor accepted the piece, paid me $100, and eventually offered me a column called "The Liberty Belle." For the first time in my life, I had a regular writing gig, and I wrote about my conservative political thoughts, much to the dismay of the paper's more liberal readers. Once I was standing in line at the post office as a guy read one of my articles. He leaned over to his friend and said, "Can you believe this girl?"

We enrolled Camille in a school near the Liberty Bell, and after school we hung out in the park near Independence Hall. One day, the kids played with a ball, which bounced against the stone statues of historical figures.

"Who are these people?" Austin, now four years old, stood at the base of a statue and gazed up at it.

"That's George Washington." I pointed to the large carved letters and the smaller identifiers below, which stipulated that he was a planter, a lawyer, a soldier, a commander, and a president.

"Some people just can't keep a job, I guess." My friend's quip punctured my teachable moment.

"And who is this one?" Austin meandered to a different statue.

"John Barry." I read his statue, which explained that he had been a farmer, a soldier, and the creator of the modern navy.

"Farmers get statues?" I could see his wheels turning, trying to figure out how to get his own statue one day and hoping he could fit it into his room next to his LEGO table. "Who *were* they?"

I paused a second, figuring out the string that tied all of these men together. "They were patriots."

"What's a *patriot*?"

My friends were amused by our conversation, but I wasn't sure how to answer. It was a tough question, but I finally settled on a suitable answer. "Someone who loves America so much that he does something about it."

"Are we patriots?" He looked at me with wide eyes, and the question struck me to the core. But something about it unnerved me. I had a feeling in my blood that everything was about to change, electrified and melancholy.

"Yes, we are." When I said these words, my voice cracked with emotion. It seemed important. A few of the other mothers smiled, the way they might after hearing another mom reassure their kid that the tooth fairy is real.

The kids played for a couple of hours. When we got home, David had an earnest look on his face as he stood in the doorway to the kitchen. I was about to tell him about our day, when he stopped me cold.

"I want to join the army." The afternoon sun poured through the windows and an ambulance passed by our building eighteen floors below us. "I'm not in great shape, but I'm going to start jogging every day."

He had changed careers several times since we had gotten married, but I wasn't expecting this. He'd practiced energy law in Kentucky and taught at Cornell Law School in New York. Since he also was a Constitutional lawyer, we'd moved to Philly so he could be the president of this nonprofit free-speech organization. From our little enclave in Philadelphia, David protected the Constitution right next to the Pennsylvania State House, where it was originally written.

He held up a copy of the *New York Times* and pointed to a story about a soldier who'd been wounded in Iraq. "This guy has two kids and a wife, but he fought anyway. And it dawned on me. He loves his kids just as much as I love Camille and Austin. He loves his wife just as I love you."

I took the newspaper and my eyes glanced over the photo accompanying the article, but I didn't try to process the words.

"The difference between this guy and me is that he's already done his duty for his country. I haven't."

During this moment of the war, the military had announced they were experiencing a recruitment shortfall. Over the course of the past few weeks, David had worried that our nation was losing its resolve.

"But America hasn't lost its resolve," he said. "I lost mine."

"But you're an attorney."

"The army needs good lawyers. Lawyers could've stopped Abu Ghraib from happening."

"But you're . . ." David was thirty-six. He didn't seem like the type of guy who would just up and join the army. "Old."

"I *was* too old, but they just raised the maximum age limit to deal with the recruitment shortfalls."

He was prepared for this conversation, but I was not. Why would anyone with a Harvard Law degree do something so dangerous? After the 9/11 attacks, people gave blood, stuck God Bless America magnets on their minivans, and hung flags in windows and from front porches. Republicans and Democrats sang "My Country 'Tis of Thee" on the steps of the Capitol. However, by the time I was sitting at the kitchen table that afternoon, years had passed and so had our collective surge of unity.

"What about a will?" I asked. "Do you even have one?"

"When you enlist, they help you write one," he reassured me. "But I'll be fine. I'll be in the green zone somewhere doing boring office work, probably."

Green zone? It had taken me a while to truly understand what he was saying. My lawyer husband wanted to join the army and be deployed. "You plan to go to Iraq?"

"Joining the army during a time of war," he said gently. "I want to do my part."

He'd been thinking of this for a while. His answers flowed out reasonably though we both were crying. "But isn't that scary to even think about?"

He moved closer to me and we wrapped our arms around each other tightly. We'd been married nine years, but I never needed him more than I did at that moment. Ever since that conversation in my Nashville apartment, he'd been my rock of stability and a source of spiritual strength. Could I do this alone?

"People have always pointed out that I switch jobs every few years," he said. "I've been an attorney, a professor, and now I want to be an army lawyer." My mind went back to the statues near the Liberty Bell and how the statues showed that our Founding Fathers had all done various jobs.

"I practice Constitutional law because I love America. When you take the military oath of office, you don't vow to protect the country." Now his voice was full of emotion, and he paused to collect himself. "Instead you vow to protect the Constitution, from enemies without and within. It only seems natural, after all I've done to fight for the Constitution, to do this too. I've done all kinds of jobs, I've been a lawyer, a lecturer, and an activist. But mostly I feel like . . ."

He paused, and I didn't rush him. This conversation, I could tell, would change the course of our lives. I wasn't sure I wanted him to continue.

"This probably sounds dumb, but I've always felt that the theme of my life has always been that I am a patriot."

He'd never told me that, and the word *patriot*, which I'd said at the park hours before, echoed in my ears.

That's when I knew that my husband was going to war.

15

THE OTHER SIDE OF
THE MOUNTAIN

After David's decision to join the military, we moved to a rural Tennessee community to be near family. From there, he could do drill weekends, exercise more regularly, and prepare for the eventuality of a deployment. We traded our Philadelphia penthouse for a two-story home with room for dogs and chickens in the back. The soundtrack of our lives switched from police sirens and jackhammers to mules eerily braying in the distance.[2]

David joined a Christian organization called Alliance Defending Freedom, which specialized in religious-freedom cases, where he created a legal arm to defend the rights of Christian students. Our new friends in Columbia loved that David fought for religious freedom and wrote for *National Review* about issues they cared about in ways that aligned with their beliefs.

When the 2008 presidential primaries heated up, our support of former Governor Mitt Romney put us at odds with other southerners more apt to support Mike Huckabee from Arkansas, Fred Thompson from Tennessee, or Rudy Giuliani, America's favorite mayor. Southern conservatives didn't rally around Mitt because, though he governed relatively conservatively, he was perceived to be a liberal flip-flopper. However, I sensed the main sticking point was the fact that he was a member of the Church of Jesus Christ of Latter-day Saints.

"Don't Mormons believe that Jesus and the devil are brothers?"[3] Baptist preacher Huckabee asked, attempting to reinforce the idea that Romney should not get a seat at the political equivalent of the high-school cafeteria table. He told evangelical voters they should support a candidate who speaks "the language of Zion as a mother tongue."

Robert Jeffress, pastor of a Dallas megachurch, asked, "Do we want a candidate who is a good, moral person, or one who is a born-again follower of the Lord Jesus Christ?" He said it was "imperative to vote for a Christian" and that voting for Romney would give credibility to a "cult."[4] Televangelist Bill Keller said a Romney victory would help ensure "at least 1 million souls will burn in hell."[5]

To addresss the evangelical hesitance about Romney, David, some friends, and I created a blog about the intersection of faith and politics called "Evangelicals for Mitt." Mitt had been our candidate of choice since 2005, before Mitt had even decided to run, and we'd since gotten to know Mitt and Ann through David's friends from law school.

As a part of our efforts, we attended conferences, worked straw polls, and met with evangelical leaders about how faith should—and should not—inform our politics. We did our best to assuage them of their apprehensions about supporting a Mormon and became experts on Mitt and Ann.

When Ann asked me to help her write a book, I immediately responded, "Yes, I can do that." I was not dissuaded by the fact that I'd never ghost-written before in my life and didn't even know how to record or transcribe a conversation. I'd do anything to help voters to get to know the Romneys, because—in my experience—to know them was to love them.

Soon, I was on a large, plush bus, barreling through South Carolina with Mrs. Romney from one campaign stop to another. I'd interview Ann on the road on the way. Though it was fascinating to see a presidential campaign up close, the pace was grueling. One afternoon, I pointed out that Ann had a stain on her blouse.

"Oh, that's from breakfast." She dabbed it off. "From Tuesday."

When we weren't on the bus, reporters were always nearby, their boom mics floating overhead, picking up every stray comment. I knew reporters could turn even the most innocuous comment into a disparaging news article. Pundits mocked Mitt's virtue by calling him a Boy Scout and casually insulted his character by accusing him of misogyny and racism. When those boom mics were around, I kept my mouth shut until we got safely back on the bus. Even then, the media chased us down the interstate attempting to film us through their open windows. In my life as a ghostwriter, I went from sitting in the car line at school one day to dodging reporters on a presidential campaign the next.

Politics became all-encompassing, a sort of marital pastime for David and me the way some couples play tennis or binge television series. Because he had a way of cutting to the chase of complex geopolitical issues, I developed a crush on "political David." The 2008 campaign helped us connect in new ways, and I loved working side by side with him on these important cultural issues.

In the fall of 2007, the day I feared finally arrived. David received orders to go to war. Mitt and Ann gave us a compass engraved with "may your journeys always lead you back home." We got our house in order, drew up a will, and prepared the children emotionally.

"Will he come back?" Austin, who was only eight years old at the time, asked, his eyes wide and wet. I've never been able to lie to my children, even about Santa Claus and the tooth fairy. I couldn't promise David's safe return. Instead of offering platitudes and wishful thinking, I explained that war was dangerous and hard, but that we felt called to this journey. God alone controlled the number of our days.

I'm not sure whether radical, unflinching honesty was the right way to deal with children so young, but that's what I did. Though I thought the army would use his legal skills in a green zone, on November 22, 2007, David flew in a Chinook transport helicopter to Forward Operating Base Caldwell, in eastern Diyala province, Iraq, with the 2d Squadron, 3d Armored Cavalry Regiment. Right into the teeth of the Iraqi insurgency. He lived within sight of the Iranian border. For the first time in eleven years, after meeting on that sidewalk, our lives diverged.

"Don't you have kids?" a woman asked me when she heard of David's deployment. "What about your children?"

"Wars are complicated," I said. "We need adults over there to run things. Frequently, officers have kids."

"Well, his priority should be his family."

In a culture that defines good parenting as being at every piano recital and basketball game, this was a common objection. But David and I believed it was more important to demonstrate to our children how to live out their values rather than being present every second. If no parents served in the armed forces, we couldn't have won the Revolutionary War, triumphed in the battle of Gettysburg, or stormed the beaches of Normandy. However, the day-to-day fear made it hard for me to communicate this notion with conviction.

The church rallied around me. Busybodies called when I missed the sermons, a deacon pulled my son's tooth for me when I was too anxious, and an elder fixed my car.

Previously, al-Qaeda terrorists were processed by JAG officers in safer spaces called green zones, but David's commander decided it would be more effective to process them at the point of capture. That meant he had to go "outside the wire," meaning he had to leave the safety of the operating base. Between early February and early April 2008, David's squadron took about 20 percent of the total coalition casualties in Iraq.

Because of the conditions of his deployment, David and I couldn't have long phone or even text conversations. The only way we communicated was through glitchy instant-messenger conversations. We often went several days without any communication, sometimes weeks. During those blackout times, I knew someone had been killed (and they were notifying family members) or he was on a mission (and we had to be kept in the dark). When David went silent, I watched the news, hoping not to hear any horrible developments.

When we could talk, our conversations were stilted and incomplete. What to say? His friends were being killed, but we could hardly process this trauma through five-minute iChat communication once a week. I relayed information about the kids' lives, but I couldn't add to his burden by telling him how hard the deployment was on them.

Instead, we talked about politics. This was safer than talking about our real lives.

I kept up the "Evangelicals for Mitt" blog in David's absence and got real-time updates on all the standings in the vital battlegrounds. My friends were surprised when I'd say, "Well, David thinks this new Hillary development is . . ."

"Wait," they would interrupt. "With as little time as you have to talk, you spend that time discussing Hillary Clinton?"

But we did. It was perhaps the one thing about our relationship that didn't change, and it was comfortably familiar to discuss the Iowa caucuses.

While David was gone, I became an adult. I'd been known to get my phone and my water turned off in one day and had bounced tithe checks. But I didn't have the luxury of carelessness.

My writing opportunities were sporadic and sparse, and I'd written a novel I couldn't sell. And so when it came time to get Mitt Romney on the Tennessee ballot, I took my first and only paid campaign gig getting hundreds of signatures from each of my state's nine congressional districts.

Turns out, Tennesseans were not eager to sign on that line. Had I worked for Giuliani, Huckabee, or Thompson (whose supporters dubbed themselves "Frednecks"), I would've had an easy time getting signatures. But many Christians refused to sign because of their "deeply held biblical beliefs." My Romney support took a toll on my relationships at church. Angry evangelicals would send letters to my church asking our elders to discipline us and claiming we were closeted Mormons—even though we repeatedly said we did not believe LDS theology to be orthodox Christian theology.

It wasn't enough.

One Sunday morning, a man accosted me after Sunday school. "Why do you have a bumper sticker that says 'Evangelicals for Mitt' on it? You can't speak for me!" One elder constantly picked fights. "I'll never support a heretic," he said as we walked back from the communion table.

The lesson I'd heard since childhood never wavered: orthodox Christians were good, all others were bad. But by now I'd lived in New York and Philadelphia and had gotten to know a lot of these so-called bad people—people outside the church—and they weren't so terrible.

Though my church friends weren't too keen about the LDS Romneys representing their much-beloved GOP, some approved. "It's a wonderful opportunity for the Romneys to be exposed to true Christianity," they explained. I could be God's chosen vessel, the face of Christianity to them, the spiritual equivalent of Vanna White turning over the letters of *grace* instead of the works-based theology LDS people seemed to espouse.

Since our home was located one mile from church and school, and most of my life happened in the agricultural community, I no longer traveled, because—with David gone—I vowed to tuck the kids into bed every night. They deserved that. I worked around the clock getting Romney on the Tennessee ballot, then continued to keep up our political writing and worked on the book.

In February 2008, a Romney campaign staffer invited me to the Conservative Political Action Conference (CPAC) in Washington, D.C., the largest annual gathering of conservatives in America. I declined. I could attend other speeches and events later when David was back home. Hopefully with Mitt as president. However, I'd vowed not to leave the kids during David's deployment, and I couldn't break it for CPAC.

"Can't you come?" the staffer asked. "It's going to be a big speech."

But I didn't want to leave the kids. A few days later, I drove down a rural road listening to Rush Limbaugh's radio show, trying not to get frustrated at the tractor blowing hay or at Rush's callers blowing smoke.

"Word just in from CPAC. Romney dropped out of the presidential race moments ago," Rush said. "I gotta cut to commercial break."

It was that sudden, that final—months and years of work evaporated like rain on the scorched land. From my driveway, I texted David, "WMR's out," and pulled up the Drudge Report on my phone.

"In this time of war," Gov. Romney's voice came through the radio, "I have to stand aside for our party and our country. . . . If this were only about me, I'd go on, but it's never been all about me." Since we were at war, Mitt didn't want to weaken the GOP's chances by staying in the race too long.

Just like that, the political chapter of our lives came to a close.

I reeled with the implications of this news. This upended the entire routine of my life—waking up, drinking coffee, and reading the Drudge Report, The Fix, *National Review*, and POLITICO. And when David and I talked, we talked about news of the campaign. Now that we no longer had this to conversationally bind us across the globe and our lives had grown so different, would it be even harder to find things to talk about?

And I'd missed everything. Had I gone to D.C., I could've heard his speech, seen my Romney-campaign friends, and wiped away the tears. Though I wasn't able to articulate this, I resented how narrow my life had become without David there to share the load.

A month later, people who'd worked on the Romney campaign decided to meet in Salt Lake City. I needed closure, so I broke my vow to stay home with the kids, dropped them off with their grandparents, and said a teary goodbye.

When I arrived, I was stunned by Utah's beauty. While writing Ann's book, I had the opportunity to listen to her stories and imagine her life— some of which took place in Michigan, Massachusetts, and Utah, where Mitt ran the 2002 Winter Olympics. Ghostwriting allowed me to inhabit someone else's world, writing words like "my brother Rod and I used to ski down the hill in our back yard . . ." or "when I was First Lady of Massachusetts . . ."

Because my imagination has always been so vibrant, it was like I'd lived several lives. At parties, people would mention riding horses, and I'd have to fight the urge to say that I was into dressage—as Ann Romney had participated in the Grand Prix. Or if someone mentioned they had gone to Michigan, my first thought was, "Oh, that's where I grew up in Bloomfield Hills."

Of course, I've never been to Michigan and the only horse I'd ever ridden was a worn-out old mare on our family farm. But I'd immersed myself into the story of Ann's life so thoroughly, part of me believed I had lived a much more glamorous life.

Although I'd never seen the Utah mountains, they were familiar the way the Eiffel Tower is when, after seeing it in movies your entire life, you finally see it up close. Being a ghostwriter gave me the sense that completely unrelated events were somehow familiar and a part of my realm of experience.

At the weekend event I met with former staffers and consultants, gratified to be near the only people I knew who understood what it was like to be a part of a failed presidential campaign. We discussed what we did right and what we did wrong. And when it was time to part ways, I'd gained some emotional closure on the campaign loss.

"You gonna ski before you leave?" a friend asked.

"Flight leaves at four." I had planned a short visit, to make sure I could get back to the children. I'd brought only one change of clothing.

"Oh, you can't leave without experiencing the skiing. Utah has the best slopes," another man added amiably. "That's one reason they chose this place to host the winter Olympics."

Of course I was all too familiar with the fact that the 2002 Winter Olympics were held right there in Salt Lake City. This is where Mitt took over the event and saved it from certain disaster and where Ann kept her horses. I'd had the Utah experience, in a ghost-writing way, but not in a real way. I kept thinking about Mitt and Ann, whom I hadn't spoken to since Mitt's withdrawal—they weren't at the meeting—and texted Ann. To my surprise, she immediately texted back. She was flying in to Utah the next day to their Deer Valley home.

"Come see us," she suggested.

"I'm heading to the airport."

"Switch your flight and stay with us! Are you a skier?"

"I love to ski." Tired of missing everything and intoxicated by the idea of hanging out with the Romneys, I forgot about my resolution to be at home with the children. I also forgot that I technically couldn't ski. In seventh grade, I'd gone on a Baptist youth ski trip to Paoli Peaks, Indiana, where a tug line pulled me up the three-hundred-foot hill, but that was about it.

"Come to the slopes with us," she texted. "We've got gear."

She sent directions to her Deer Valley house, instructions on getting the key from her brother and sister-in-law, and a request for me to buy groceries for the fridge.

I didn't pause to consider my lack of skiing prowess. I wasn't going to miss another opportunity, and my lack of snowplowing ability wasn't going to stop me. I figured it'd work out. And since Ann was a great skier, I'd *written* about skiing. That might be good enough.

I climbed in her brother and sister-in-law's vehicle, which creeped up the nine-thousand-foot mountain. Monteagle Mountain was a mere two thousand feet, and I'd never seen moose meandering beside the steep roads.

When Mitt and Ann arrived late that night, we settled on their living room sofa and drank hot chocolate. I'd only known them during the campaign season, when aides and staffers hovered near them with phones and laptops in hand. But this was quiet and calm and—amid the worry of the deployment—perfect.

"Do you ski?" Gov. Romney asked me the next morning as we ate breakfast and made plans to hit the slopes. This was God giving me the opportunity to come clean about my skiing ability, but I was too obtuse to take advantage of the moment.

"I'm about as good as Jean-Claude Killy," I said. Killy was the only skier's name I knew. This kind of exaggeration would've worked back home with normal, noncelebrity people who hang around other normal, noncelebrity people. They would've recognized my hyperbole and gotten the clue that I was not as good as I'd let on.

"I know Jean-Claude," Mitt said, "from my days running the Olympics."

I began to panic, but I had a plan. I would politely excuse myself while they headed off down the steep slopes and maybe I could secretly join the kids' classes.

After breakfast, Mitt took me to a gigantic closet full of gear, then he looked me up and down, sizing me up. He bit his lip when he saw my feet. "I'm guessing you wear a size eight?"

This is exactly when my plan started to go awry. Snow was so rare in the South, we never had proper gear. If we wanted to go outside and enjoy it, we'd make do with multiple layers of socks, multiple sweatshirts, pantyhose for a base layer, and plastic bags cinched to keep the water out.

Mitt, having run the Olympics, had everything you could imagine: jackets, goggles, actual ski pants, thermal underwear, and multiple hats all embroidered with the five Olympic rings. Though I was trying to avoid attention, I was completely clad in official 2002 Winter Olympic gear.

When we got to the lodge, I walked behind Mitt in his daughter-in-law's boots. I didn't realize you weren't supposed to buckle them up until you arrived on the slopes and were ready to ski. While Mitt was gliding like a gazelle through the lodge, down the stairs, and through crowded halls of people, I waddled like a duck.

However, my vantage point allowed me to see the reactions on people's faces when they unexpectedly encountered the former GOP contender. They all went through the same cycle: recognition, disbelief, nervousness, then enough courage to make jokes like, "Hey, Governor! I hope these slopes aren't as hard on you as that last debate."

I rode with Ann in the ski lift, talking about how they can't go anywhere without people snapping photos and asking for selfies. Somehow I managed to get off the lift without killing myself. And then, the moment of truth. By the time we got to the top of the mountain, I was shaking in their daughter-in-law's boots. Nothing prepared me for that moment of looking down the ski slope. I didn't even know whether I had my new military insurance card if I needed emergency medical care.

"Go on without me," I encouraged Mitt and Ann. "I haven't skied in a while, so I might need a little time to familiarize myself." I was standing atop a death-defying slope, surrounded by snowcapped mountains.

"We don't mind. Let's stay together as a group." Ann skied off, looking stylish and elegant in her perfectly matching gear. The rest of the group—her brother Rod, her sister-in-law Cindy, and Mitt—all followed her.

It was my turn to go, but I felt like a soldier about to jump from an airplane for the first time. There I stood, looking down the steep slope. The last thing I wanted to do was to take off down that hill, but that was my only way out of this. The Romneys had already darted down the slope, and if I didn't go, I'd be stranded at the top. I had no choice.

I took a deep breath, prayed, and regretted the deceptive bravado that had landed me in this situation. Because of a weird combination of hubris and cowardice, my life was hanging on precariously to the side of the mountain. It was time.

Maybe because I'd watched too many inspirational sports segments on television, I hoped through the power of positive thinking I'd catch up with the Romneys and make my way down the mountain with panache. I'd realize I was a natural-born skier, and Bob Costas would hear about my story and make a segment about how I didn't realize I had this innate ability until I learned to believe in myself.

Hesitantly at first, I began my descent. Quite quickly, however, I started gaining speed. Too much speed. I shot down the mountain, a barely managed free fall. My arms flailed, I lost a pole, and I realized I had no idea how to slow down. It was a beautiful, sunny day, but I couldn't enjoy the mountain scenes as I flew down fast as a bullet. I kept getting faster and faster, not knowing how to stop. Since I no longer had one of my poles, I decided the best course of action was to simply fall. But when I did that, my momentum caused me to flip, lose control of my Olympic-clad body, and—unfortunately—I absolutely took out another skier who'd been beside me in my free fall.

I hit him so hard that it took me a second to realize that I'd collided with Mitt Romney. Had he won the GOP primaries—the Secret Service would've taken me out with a single shot through my official Olympic snowcap. Our bodies were entangled, and we were precariously close to the edge of a cliff. Laboriously, Mitt and I disentangled from each other. The former governor of Massachusetts and GOP presidential candidate had to disentangle my body from his. What had I become?

When I opened my eyes, the sun shining in my face, the Romneys were looking at me in disbelief. A skier passed by slowly and stopped to snap a photo. I imagined her later explaining to her family that she saw Mitt on the slopes accompanied by—since I wore gear emblazoned with the Olympic rings from head to toe—an apparently drunk former Olympian.

When I tried to get up, I slid toward the side of the cliff. I took Mitt's hand, and tried valiantly to get up but, once again, I brought him down with me. There we were, in the middle of a run, unable to get to the bottom of the slopes and paralyzed by my utter and complete inability to ski.

"I'm sorry," I gasped. "I wanted to hang out with you guys after the whole campaign thing and I felt I missed out on everything. I lied about being able to ski."

Ann's sister-in-law, in a sober voice, said, "Yes, we can see that." Then she looked around at the steep mountain, me clinging precariously on the side, and mustered a suggestion. "Maybe we should stop right here to pray?"

Ann readily agreed. "It's possible that you are in more physical danger right now than David."

We stood in silence on the side of the mountain, no one daring to say a word. First I heard Cindy giggle, then Rod. Finally, Mitt and Ann started laughing before the "amen" was even uttered.

My fellow Christians believed my relationship with the Romneys was a great opportunity for them to be exposed to true faith. After all, they explained, I could represent the true face of Christianity. I could teach them about grace.

However, the idea that anyone outside traditional, orthodox Christianity would be drawn to God after hanging around me was absurd. If anything, my deceptive bravado could've been used as proof that my virtue was much shallower than that of any of the young Mormon missionaries who have knocked on my door with pamphlets and earnest smiles.

I'd like to use David's deployment as an excuse, that I was under emotional duress and not really myself. Or maybe I could've blamed ghost-writing for my assuming that I had more experiences than I had actually had. After all, Ann was a great skier, and I'd written her book. But the sad truth of the matter was that nothing about me changed when David left for Iraq or when I wrote other people's books. I still carried the same selfish limitations with me, just in more melodramatic circumstances.

But the Romneys thought it was a moment to laugh, not condemn. Instead of shaming me for putting them in this position—getting down was memorably dangerous—they encouraged me. And then, to my amazement, they took me to the other side of the mountain where there were less-treacherous slopes. For the rest of the day, Mitt and Ann gave me skiing lessons and helped me get over my problems through kindness, patience, and snowplowing. Instead of pointing out my inadequacies, they showed me love.

The next time I thought about how my fellow evangelicals told me Mormons don't have a doctrine of grace, I remembered this moment—infused with such kindness—and I laughed.

16

COMING HOME

In 2008, I drove to Fort Benning in Georgia to pick up David. We'd made it through the year, and every day I'd imagined the tearful embrace, the unmitigated joy.

But in the days before his arrival, he expressed a palpable, nagging, persistent, acute sort of dread. "I can't shake it," he said. "I don't think I should leave."

Yet orders are orders. And staying in a war zone where terrorists were blowing people up didn't seem wise. So he obeyed his order and began his journey back home. On the drive to pick him up, my phone rang.

"Nancy, this is Major Cantlon." The voice on the other end of the line sounded distant. He was calling from Iraq. "Have you picked up David yet? Tell him to call me as soon as you see him. I'll try the base."

Something was wrong.

I kept driving. When I arrived at the army base, I pulled over on the side of the road. There he was. David was wearing a sand-covered uniform, his bag on the ground beside him. He was skinny. Dirty. Shaken.

We tearfully embraced, but these were not the tears of joy I anticipated. "What happened?"

David's dear friend Mike had just been killed when their team attempted to detain an al-Qaeda suicide bomber. He had been out ahead—leading from the front.

"I shouldn't have left."

"His death is not your fault."

"He didn't die," David snapped. "He was killed."

Since David was the JAG officer, he was the one whom the soldiers asked for permission to engage, detain, or kill. He made the shoot-or-don't-shoot calls on the ground, often making this difficult decision based on grainy surveillance footage in the middle of the night. Were the two guys farmers digging at night to avoid the hot sun? Or were they terrorists planting an explosive device? David knew every decision he made could end in the loss of life—for us or them. Because Mike was killed as he moved to detain the terrorists, he would've called David had he been there. Maybe David would have told him it was okay to shoot. Maybe not. But Mike didn't shoot, and now he was dead.

"I shouldn't have left," he said.

We went out to eat. As he ordered, he still had Iraqi soil on his boots. That was not all that clung to him.

David had always been the life of the party, but now he had an edge to him. Before he left, he'd been patient, slow to anger. But now my formerly carefree husband was foul tempered and anxious. Many of his friends had been killed, but war did not provide him time to process the trauma. After someone was killed, he had to focus on the next thing and the next and the next. But now he was swallowed up by grief.

Plus, his faith had taken a hit. And since he was the one who'd introduced me to Christianity, it was unnerving. One night, when we settled into bed, he explained his feelings.

"After I left here, I went to Balad. I knew nothing about war."

I got still. If I moved, I might break the spell.

"I stood on the tarmac when huge Chinook helicopters came out of the sky. It was about three o'clock in the morning. I could barely carry my weapon, body armor, a backpack, and duffel bag, but I was one of the first guys on so I took a position behind one of the gunners. I could see over his left shoulder. When we took off, the noise was unbelievable, even through my ear protection. We flew across the Iraqi countryside, low and fast. I could see the fires from distant fights. I prayed. I asked God for some assurance—a sense of peace, maybe—that I'd come home, that I'd see my family again. I felt no peace. I felt no assurance. It was like God wasn't there. Or if he was there, he wasn't listening to me."

I nodded.

"And I hoped I'd be protected, but I saw many men—much better Christians than I'll ever be—get killed. Where was God? During my whole deployment, I prayed, went to chapel, read my Bible. But I never—not once—felt a sense from God I'd ever make it home."

"But you are home," I said, though we both knew he wasn't.

When we turned off the lights, he tossed and turned. The lack of sleep exacerbated his grief.

"What's for dinner?" he asked me one afternoon as we drove home.

I shrugged. I hadn't decided whether to cook or go out, but he snapped. He was used to people saluting him and obeying him and was frustrated I didn't have a ready answer. But I'd grown accustomed to calling the shots as the only adult in the house, and—sleep or no sleep—I didn't like his response.

When we came to a stop sign, I jumped out of the car and walked.

"Get in the car," he yelled through the open window.

He was driving three miles per hour on an old country road.

"No." I kept walking.

"Get in the car."

I didn't have the tools to deal with the trauma he'd been through, and I knew only a fraction of it. He'd seen genocide, he'd almost been blown up in a canal, and he'd seen his friends die in horrific ways—these details came out sporadically and without notice over the next few years. After being married thirteen years, I was living with a stranger.

"Get in this car," he said in a softer voice. I was about three miles from home, but I kept walking until finally I decided I didn't want the neighbors to see this slow-motion marital explosion. I got in the car. We had spaghetti.

David had gone through the most intense year of his life—full of death, friendship, and purpose—and now was suddenly attending parent-teacher conferences, washing dishes, and lying awake at night in rural Tennessee.

After a few months, he learned how to sleep again. That helped. But this was not the man I married, and he'd never be again. It was hard, but I began to love this new man even more than I loved the original. I saw before me a man who didn't shrink from doing the right thing, a man who obeyed God, a man of courage. This new David was damaged, to be sure, but he was in the process of becoming the man God intended him to be.

Over the years, he'd witnessed me transform from one thing into another, and now I had the honor to be beside him as he transformed, out of the ashes, into something new.

17

BEAUTIFUL

About a year after the deployment, we continued to adjust to a new post-war normal—more complicated, sad, and untidy than before. David went back to work, I continued to write, and the children adjusted to life with a dad. We were more regulated, more stable than we had been in a long time. One day, the kids came up to me, grinning, holding a piece of paper.

"What's that?" Camille and Austin handed over the paper, which was labeled—in their childish handwriting—"Ten Reasons Why We Should Adopt."

They'd gotten to know our neighbors who had adopted and thought we should too. I read their list and smiled. Adoption had been on David's mind ever since we were dating, but with everything else going on, it hadn't come up again.

Experts advise against making any dramatic decisions after a soldier returns from war. Still, the kids' note caused us to think seriously about it. I wasn't sold on the idea. Adding a complete stranger to the mix would affect our family dynamic. Adoption was hard. I knew that much. James 1:27 said that Christians should "look after orphans in their distress," and I figured if it were easy, God wouldn't have had to command us to do it.

Later that evening, I brought their adoption treatise to David and we discussed it for the first time since we were dating.

"The kids are well behaved." I settled down beside him to explain my apprehension. "They make good grades. Our marriage is stable. Adding someone else to the mix might mess all this up."

David smiled. "Yes, our marriage is stable and the kids are fine. So what kind of family should adopt? Couples who don't get along with problematic kids?"

The question hit me in the gut. I didn't know how to answer him, because I knew he was right. At the same time, I was right. Adding a complete stranger to our family unit was unpredictable and scary, but we also had the type of family that might be able to withstand the ups and downs of the process. Of course, I didn't know what "the process" involved. But still. We had a good family, and 150 million children had been orphaned and needed someone to love them.

"Look, I don't want to pressure you," he said. "You've got to consider how this would affect your work and life."

He was being generous. "My work" had gone nowhere fast. After getting the gig at the Philadelphia *City Paper*, few people read my work. I'd written a novel my agent couldn't give away. Even Ann's book got canceled after Mitt dropped out of the race. I'd given writing my best shot, and I'd failed. Sure, I could continue in the writing hustle, but I wouldn't choose a mediocre, uncertain career over the well-being of a child.

Before that conversation had even concluded, my heart had changed on the matter. I would stop writing and focus on our family—but our family would grow through adoption.

David and I went back to the kids, holding the piece of paper.

"We want to talk to you about this," I said. "Adoption is hard and unpredictable. Kids who have lost their families are going through enormous loss. So we would be adding someone who has experienced great trauma into our home."

They looked up at me with gigantic, wet eyes. "So there's no way to predict how this might turn out, but your dad and I have decided. We think it's the right thing to do."

The kids immediately hugged us, and the four of us would soon be five. My heart was full of trepidation and love, both fighting for preeminence. But after a few days, another emotion emerged: hope.

I perused adoption websites, and—with every photo—my heart lifted.

It seemed that boys were harder to place than girls, and we didn't want to compete with other families for children. I plunged headfirst into adoption preparation—researching, planning, dreaming. The process was a litany of forms, home inspections, medical tests, notarization, and interviews. Not only do you have to provide financial information, you also have to prove to social workers that your home can accommodate more children—so I'd heard it was like being audited by the IRS while also trying out for HGTV.

We selected a reputable agency, one that focused on keeping children in their own families and communities if it was possible, and selected a country. We chose the most expedient country, Ethiopia at the time. Countries wax and wane on the ease of adoption because of the enormous amount of red tape and cultural pressures. Also, we decided to adopt a sibling group, since they seemed to be more difficult to place in families. What would it be like for these children to grow up in the South? I wasn't sure but figured love would be enough.

Eight months later, I got an email from the adoption agency with our match. Sometimes, parents request another based on looks or gut instinct, but David and I decided to accept whoever the agency referred. I was terrified to open the email, so I called David instead.

"Did you get the email from the adoption agency?" I was at the kitchen table. "The subject line says 'referral.'"

"Yes, let's open it at the same time." David was excited, without one ounce of fear. "Three, two, one."

I clicked and he clicked. The image emerged on both of our screens. Though we'd requested two boys, we saw one girl. Gigantic brown eyes, no hair, dressed in camouflage.

"Beautiful," David said.

And he was right. Literally. The photo was labeled "Konjit," Amharic for "beautiful."

We learned few details about her history, but the ones we learned were grim. The baby was born to a young, unwed mother, who gave the baby to her mother and father before disappearing. Konjit's grandparents were subsistence farmers and had a tough time providing for the baby. After the death of her grandfather, the grandmother and Konjit couldn't afford to buy food. When she was two years old, Konjit weighed only fourteen pounds, and her grandmother lacked the resources to feed herself and the baby.

We were overwhelmed with a desire to get to our daughter, who was more than seven thousand miles away.

Camille, who was twelve years old at the time, decided on a name. "What about Naomi?"

I said it aloud. "Why Naomi?"

"Because in the Bible, I read about my own middle name, Ruth. In that story, Naomi came from a place of famine. And God used people 'who were not her people'—including Ruth—to be her family."

And so our daughter had a new name, and Naomi Konjit felt more a part of our family even though she was eight thousand miles away.

For six months, we prepared a bedroom, had baby showers at church, and bought new diapers, bibs, and onesies we thought we'd never need again. Finally, in June of 2010, it was time to travel to Addis Ababa.

The journey on Ethiopian Airlines was long and arduous. Cramped leg space, sitcoms in Amharic playing on the screens in front of us. When we finally made it to Ethiopia, we were exhausted, jet-lagged, and excited. The baby in our photos and hearts was just a couple miles from us, but the adoption agency had strict protocols. They wanted us to stay in Ethiopia a day before we met her, and we could meet her only at the orphanage—without taking her outside the walls of the building. Apparently, Ethiopians were sensitive about Americans coming in and adopting "their children," so we had to make sure to respect that dynamic.

For one day, we hung out with other American families in a hotel and compared notes about our feelings, hopes, and expectations. We ate Ethiopian food and saw sites while our expectation grew to almost intolerable levels.

On the second day, we were allowed to meet our new family member. All of the American families traveled in a caravan to the orphanage, where they'd set up an "American" party—complete with balloons and, oddly, a man dressed as Santa Claus. Since it was the summer, I wasn't sure what to make of this, other than perhaps they considered America as a place of gifts and strange superstitions.

After a tour of the orphanage—which was brightly colored and comfortable—workers came out with a slew of children. Babies were held by nannies, toddlers clung to staffers' legs. Some babies cried at seeing us. Had they ever seen White people before? I quickly scanned all of the babies' faces, trying to find Naomi. One of these children was mine, and I had no idea which one. The photos we'd seen in the referral email did not seem to correlate with the healthier looking babies before me. I began to panic. Surely, a mother would be able to recognize her own child, but—as my eyes darted from one child to another—I could not.

The orphanage leader made this sacred, beautiful, terrifying moment into a game.

"Okay, so now we're going to see if you can pick your own family member," she said in broken English. She was smiling, and I was sweating. I would fail this test, which might indicate that I was not up for this task.

But then, Camille and Austin looked at me with wide eyes.

"Can we go to her?"

"Sure," I said hesitantly. Though I wasn't sure which child was Naomi, my kids knew her immediately. I watched as they ran to a little baby on the hip of a caretaker, and I followed them. The caretaker gently handed her over to me. She was a cuddly, pudgy ball of a baby. She'd gained weight since arriving at the orphanage. As I held her, I tried to pull her into me while also admiring her, beholding her. I quickly saw that she lived up to her Amharic name Konjit (which means "beautiful") and her biblical name Naomi (which means "pleasant").

The whole room erupted into a cacophony of crying, cooing, and laughter.

After we got a chance to meet the babies, they ushered us into the lunchroom, so we could see the type of foods the kids were used to eating. On Naomi's plate was injera, a soft spongy bread, and chicken. I crouched down beside her, holding her hand. The other kids ate heartily, but Naomi sat quietly. She seemed serious and sad. What had I done during my five minutes of parenting to make her unwilling to eat? She was only two and a half. But did she understand what was going on? Maybe she didn't want to go with us.

Finally, a caretaker came over and pointed to me.

"No hand," she said, waving toward my hand holding Naomi's. That's when I learned that Ethiopians don't use utensils but eat with their right hands. As soon as I let go of her hand, she was free to devour her food.

After eating, she still sat there quietly looking at her plate. My son, Austin, had gotten behind her and made faces and, to my delight, her eyes lit up. That's when this cute little toddler broke out into full-throated laughter. I closed my eyes and listened to the sound—a toddler's laughter in an Ethiopian orphanage—enjoying her silly brother for the first time. That is when I knew—in spite of this difficult, emotional moment—everything might be okay.

We walked out of that orphanage, red-eyed, hearts full, a family of five.

Naomi slept on the flight from Ethiopia to Rome, where the plane refueled, and slept all the way to Washington, D.C. On our layover there, we gave her fast food—undoubtedly the first chicken nuggets she'd ever consumed—and she ate every single one of them. Apparently, D.C. is full of Ethiopian immigrants, because many of the airport workers walked by and said, "Hello, Konjo."

"How did you know her name?" I asked the first person.

"Konjo," she smiled. "It's a nickname meaning 'beautiful.'"

I basked in the airport workers' admiration of our new child, and finally it was time to get on the plane and take this baby home. Our friends and family were gathering at the Nashville airport to meet her, and we dressed her in the Ethiopian dress the orphanage had given her.

As soon as we got on the plane, however, she screamed. A full-throated, hands-over-your-ears type scream. No matter what I did, I could not console her. She didn't understand English and I didn't know Amharic. All she knew was that she had been yanked from everything she had ever known and—though she was unfamiliar with cars—she was now on a plane with a group of strangers.

"Give me that baby," an older Black woman said to me halfway through the flight. The entire plane looked at me expectantly. Everyone wanted Naomi to stop crying. No one more than me. But I'd read in adoption books that it was important to hold and nurture your child, not to pass her around. The books said that passing the baby around might impede bonding.

The lady had her hands out, palms up—she was ready to help. But

I only shook my head no, and the entire plane groaned at my stubborn response.

But something painful, something miraculous was happening on this flight. Naomi got on the plane in Ethiopia as a little girl who came from a village with no written language. She would get off the plane with parents who wrote for a living. Her earthly possessions, which fit into one plastic bag, were traveling to a newly decorated room in a new home with a trampoline in the back yard. The baby who was all alone in the world was getting a brother and sister who couldn't stop admiring her. The girl who almost died from starvation would have a full refrigerator. Her destiny was being shaped, expanded, but it came at great cost—as the country of her birth was receding with every passing mile. I promised to teach her about her home country while hoping she would grow to love her new one.

We finally made it home and walked into the loving embrace of family members and friends who'd made signs and carried balloons and were anxiously waiting for us on the other side of the security line. We were jet-lagged and emotionally fragile and ready to get home. When we put Naomi in her new car seat, she screamed and cried—because she'd never been restrained in a car seat in her entire life. But on the way home, she fell fast asleep and we noticed a rainbow in the sky.

The next few months were challenging and delightful. We got to know this little toddler, who seemed younger since she was so tiny. We marveled at her strength of will, her tenacity, and her quick smile. Finally, it came time to sign the official adoption papers. This would be our last bit of paperwork, and I was ready to get it done. David and I sat at our kitchen table, documents spread out before us, my pen hovering in the air ready to sign.

That's when David gasped.

"What is it?"

He pointed to the birth date listed on Naomi's forms: November 22, 2007.

"What about it?"

"I just realized." He swallowed.

"Naomi was born the day I flew off to war," he said. "The day I was filled with so much doubt and fear."

It was the moment David was in the Chinook helicopter, scanning the horizon for distant firefights. That's when he asked God to give him assurances of his future, that he'd one day be home with his family.

He thought God hadn't answered him.

But God was answering David's prayers. He didn't let David in on the plan, maybe because he wouldn't have believed it anyway. God was planning for our family's future in a way we never could've imagined.

Because at that moment on that night somewhere—in a small village on a continent we'd never seen—our daughter was born.

18

THE FIRE ON A
FROZEN LAKE

I gave your number to my publisher. Hope that's okay?" My friend—a celebrity ghostwriter—had just written a bestselling book for an NFL player and was getting several requests to write more books. For years, I'd desperately had been trying to get the attention of editors—I'd written a novel I never could sell—so this was news. "They need a ghost, and I thought of you because of the Romney book."

"Who's the client?"

"No idea," he said. "You know how it is with celebrities."

I didn't know how it was with celebrities, because I didn't know any celebrities. I'd been busy with diapers, sippy cups, and teaching Naomi English.

"It's a quick turnaround, so if you have stuff going on, it might not work out."

I talked to David about whether it was even possible, because this job would require me to travel with the client. Naomi had been in our family for only seven months. Though I thought my writing was over, this opportunity fell in my lap and I wanted to find out more.

"You should go!" David's enthusiasm surprised me. "When I was at war, you stepped up on the domestic front, and now—if you get the job—it'll be my turn."

My agent fielded the initial scheduling requests; my phone rang a week later. I was on the phone with one of the most high-powered editors in the industry. She interviewed me about my skills, strategies, and speed. "This needs to be done fast."

I'd always written more quickly than anyone I knew, and—after tapping out chapters on a campaign bus—I could write anywhere.

"And I mean fast," she repeated. "You don't have kids, do you?"

"No." I answered quickly, emphatically, irrationally. The kids were watching television and Camille and Austin were tugging at the bowl. Naomi let out a cry. I ran out of the house and climbed in my Jeep so the editor wouldn't hear my nonexistent kids.

"Good, because—if you get this job—I need you on a plane in three days," she said. "The client is Bristol Palin. Sarah Palin's daughter?"

That was a surprise. I'd paid such close attention to politics for years until Mitt dropped out of his presidential campaign. But everyone in America had heard about Bristol's pregnancy. She was the daughter of Sarah Palin, who was the first female Republican vice-presidential candidate in American history. After John McCain selected Sarah as his running mate, Bristol revealed that she was a pregnant teenager. She had to deal with a pregnancy while the nation gawked and pundits laughed.

"You know her story?" she asked.

"The basics."

"Okay, please hold." The phone went silent, and I tapped my fingernails on the dashboard. After a click, the editor's voice.

"Bristol, meet Nancy. Nancy, meet Bristol."

I didn't expect to be on the phone with the actual client without a chance to research or prepare. But this was happening. We exchanged pleasantries, while noise, commotion, and the sound of a child dominated the background.

"Sorry it's loud," Bristol said. "I'm at Walmart."

There I was huddled in a Jeep, sweating over every syllable, while she was in an Alaskan Walmart, baby on her hip, multitasking like a she-boss. I liked her.

"Since you live in Tennessee," the editor asked me, "How can you capture the voice of a twenty-year-old Alaskan?"

I didn't know I could, so I said the first thing that came to mind.

"Ann Romney trusted me with her voice, and she's a Mormon multi-millionaire former First Lady of Massachusetts, while I'm," I let my voice trail off. "Not. If I could capture Ann's voice, I can capture Bristol's."

"Why is that?" the editor asked.

"Well, I've never been a Mormon or a millionaire or a First Lady, but I have been a twenty-year-old woman," I said. "Plus, Bristol, you're an Alaska redneck and I'm a Tennessee redneck, so we'd have a lot in common."

I regretted this as soon as it came out of my mouth, but Bristol laughed. "I like you. Let's do it."

The editor interrupted. "Now let's not get ahead of ourselves." She proceeded to ask me more questions. I didn't have the kind of track record that would commend me—especially for a book the press would scrutinize so heavily. But the editor relented. "Job starts Friday. Pack warm. It's February in Alaska, after all."

I didn't even have a jacket, and the stores in Tennessee didn't carry gear effective in the cold Alaskan climate. Still, I confidently replied. "I'll be there."

Four days later, I landed in Anchorage, rented a car (which had tire chains in the trunk), and drove to the address the publisher had given me. I was surprised to find myself in Wasilla at a gate covered with multicolored Christmas lights. A group of people stood around the gate holding cameras. This wasn't a hotel. When I stopped and rolled down my window to push the gate code, they snapped photographs.

"Is that one of the daughters?" A lady in a puffy jacket lowered her camera to look at me. "That's Willow!"

Willow was one of the Palin kids. Cameras clicked.

I followed the instructions to let myself into the gate, wound down the icy drive, and pulled up to a russet-colored house on the right and a tan house on the left. A moose antler was nailed to a tree. On it was written one word: Palin.

I placed my feet on the icy path. The door flung open and there stood Sarah Palin, wearing a black fleece pullover, jeans, and boots.

"Hey, I'm Sarah." She shook my hand. "Hope you like moose hot dogs." The house was full. The entire Palin family was there, plus Sarah's parents, Todd's parents, Sarah's sister, and several cousins. And of course, Bristol.

I shook her hand. "Thanks for picking me." The room was two stories tall with gigantic windows that overlooked Lake Lucille. Snowcapped mountains towered behind the frozen water. The aroma of melted cheese wafted from the oven.

"Salmon casserole," Sarah said. "Family recipe. I hope you don't mind piling in. The Best Western's booked, so you can stay here until the book is written."

Until the book is written. Writers labored over books for months. Years, even. I'd parked my car in the airport's short-term lot.

"Show her around," Sarah said. "Show her where to put her bags."

Bristol had long dark hair, pulled into a ponytail, this person whose pregnancy sent a thousand pundits to their laptops.

We got my luggage out of the car and walked across the ice to the separate tan building with tall double garage doors.

"This is where Dad keeps his Piper Cub and snow *machines*. That's what we call snowmobiles here." Bristol led me into the attached home, which had an apartment, a studio, and an office.

"Put your stuff in here." She motioned toward the bedroom. "There's coffee in the kitchen."

After a delicious meal with the entire family, I retired to my area and turned on my laptop. News of Bristol's book had broken. I had to write and fast. In the mornings, I interviewed. In the evenings, I wrote. In the afternoons, we drove to Mocha Moose coffee shack and drank "chocolate mooseachinos." Seeing where she went, drinking what she drank, and seeing what she saw gave me insight into her life.

Once, I held her little brother Trig as we prepared to go bowling.

"His middle name is 'Van.'" Sarah handed me a diaper bag. "Say it."

"Say what?"

"His full name."

"Trig Van Palin," I said. The pun slowly dawned on me. "Oh, like Van Halen?"

She laughed. "I love their music." I thought of the David Lee Roth telephone mix-up. I'd never escape that guy.

The days turned into weeks, and I missed my family. The sun never really rose, so I was encompassed by darkness, punctuated by the sun coming up over Lake Lucille, briefly, following a little eyebrow path across the horizon. Blink, and you'd miss it.

One morning, Sarah asked me to get their mail. I was prepared to see the gaggle of camera-toting tourists at the gate but was not prepared for a strange sound coming from behind the trees. Something between a honk and a growl, low and grumbly. A moose—towering in the darkness—stood five feet from me. I dropped their mail in the snow.

When I came back to the house—panting, holding wet mail—the Palins were on the couch laughing.

"Did you see a ghost?" Bristol asked.

"Looks like she saw a moose." Sarah laughed.

One morning, I walked out of my bedroom, bleary eyed, wearing my pajamas. My head was down, because by now I could find the coffee maker in the perpetual Alaska darkness. But I stopped when I saw brown leather shoes.

Governors, politicians, and friends frequently showed up while I stayed there, but I was surprised to wake up and come face to face with Steve Bannon.

At the time, I knew him as the founder of Breitbart News. But he would later become the White House's chief strategist under President Donald Trump. I introduced myself and made him breakfast every day when he and his crew showed up in the morning. For a week, I made them coffee and served bagels before the day's interviews.

"Tell me about your baby shower." I thought I'd ask Bristol about something easy to start the session.

"Never had one." Bristol folded her legs under her.

I was stumped. In my research for the book on the plane, I'd found a description of her baby shower, a list of the attendees, and seen a photo of Bristol holding a camouflage onesie.

"Really?" I pulled up the article, and she took my phone to examine it more closely.

"Nope." She pointed at the image. "See what looks like a crease in the photo?"

I enlarged the photo. Though I would've testified under oath Bristol had a baby shower, the image was photoshopped. In spite of my certainty, the truth turned out to be much more complicated than I'd thought.

"So you want to talk about the pregnancy?" I made my voice low and nonthreatening. She'd been through so much public scrutiny, I wanted her to tell her side of things. "You know, how it happened?" I was expecting a story of a momentary lapse of judgment or a devil-may-care attitude that went awry, but what I heard was much different. Bristol told me she had told her mom she was going to a friend's house. Instead, they sneaked out to a campground, where she was plied with alcohol. When she awakened the next morning, she could tell that something had happened.

"That's how you lost your virginity?" I asked.

"More like stolen."

As her words sunk in, I blinked back tears.

"If I hadn't told Mom I was spending the night with my friend, everything would be different." She took a sip of her soda. "I love being a mom, but it's funny how your whole life can change like that."

The opening scene of a book is always a big decision. It has to be important. Significant. I felt this was where the whole story needed to start, and Bristol was on board. We weren't going to spin, defend, or apologize for this situation. We were going to be candid and transparent, so I took the opening sentence straight from our interview.

"I lied to my mother."

I wrote around the clock. Because the sun's trajectory was so different up there, I lost track of time and found myself working until four in the morning—making decaf, snuggling under a blanket, and watching moose walk on a frozen lake. February turned to March, and I was still in Alaska. After twenty-eight days of living with the Palins, we wrote the last lines. When I got home, I paid an exorbitant amount to get my car out of short-term parking.

The book was an instant *New York Times* bestseller. I braced myself for the rippling news of Bristol's opening chapter. I imagined this would cause a huge stir among the writing class, that opinion columnists and journalists would bend over backward to apologize for their previous writings.

One *Washington Post* headline showed promise: "Is Bristol Palin's New Memoir the Story of a Rape Survivor Speaking Out?"[6] I hoped the article, which was written by a woman, would provide a thoughtful analysis of consent, but the opening paragraphs went through a litany of insults. "It can be hard to take Bristol Palin seriously," it began. "The young mother turned reality TV star is a bundle of contradictions—or hypocrisies, depending on whom you talk to."

Another female writer urged people not to take her seriously, calling her "a mini-queen of publicity stunts." She wrote that characterizing her as a victim was "an insult to women who have truly suffered." The *National Journal* claimed she was capitalizing on the incident to keep her name in the headlines.[7] One popular liberal blogger described her account as "self-exonerating bullshit" before putting it bluntly: "I don't believe Bristol."[8]

When Bristol appeared on *Good Morning America*, I curled up on the couch to watch the interview. GMA host Robin Roberts cut right to the heart of the matter.

"You open the book, and you talk about, not that your virginity, that you lost it, but you used the word 'stolen.'"[9] Robin's voice was kind. There was no condemnation, no mockery, just curiosity and concern. "Can you clarify that at all?"

"That's what it felt like. I'm not accusing Levi of date rape or rape at all. But I am looking back with adult eyes and thinking that was a foolish decision. I should have never been underage drinking and I should have never gotten myself into a situation like that."

Robin told her co-host that Sarah supported Bristol, but "could've gone without that first chapter [of the book]."

As the show went to commercial break, I felt like someone had punched me in the stomach.

I floated on an ocean of ignorance. I didn't know women sometimes don't use the word *rape* to describe an encounter which might meet the legal definition. I didn't know their shame and society's brutal reaction makes them hesitant to use the word. I didn't grasp that when the victim trusts the abuser, their sense of betrayal and self-blame is compounded. I didn't predict that when victims don't act like society thinks they should, people don't believe them. I didn't understand why or how many victims don't report the crimes of sexual violence, don't reveal it quickly, and feel bound to their perpetrator.

I'd experienced all of this with Conrad back when I was younger, but I'd filed that away as my dropping the ball, as my being uniquely weak. I sealed my disappointment into an emotional sarcophagus and buried it so far down I wasn't even aware of it. While I watched Bristol's interview, however, I didn't think of my own abuse because I was ignorant of the ways it had affected me, how it made me feel heavy and fatigued to be dragging it around.

But on the surface of that vast ocean of ignorance, I felt a wave wash over me: this wasn't right. I'd thought that people of both parties would rally around Bristol and show her compassion. That's not what happened. It slowly dawned on me that when the Democrats loudly proclaimed "believe all women," they really meant "the right kind of women"—meaning not "right" on the political spectrum at all. I shouldn't have been surprised. They had embraced Ted Kennedy, even though he flipped his car, sent his female passenger careening into a pond, and left her there to die. They revered Bill Clinton, even though he was credibly accused of rape by multiple women.

Bristol was well spoken and the book was clear. However, a nuanced, trauma-informed conversation did not arise from her revelations. Bristol told the truth, and Democrats laughed. After seeing how people mocked this young mother, I was fully confident the Democrats were not only wrong on the issue of women, they were callously wrong. They harbored and protected abusers of women, and Republicans alone would stand against sexual injustice.

In spite of my certainty, the truth turned out to be much more complicated than I thought.

19

THE LAST DANCE

Thank God, you made it." The man breathed a sigh of relief and ushered me into a Washington, D.C., hotel suite filled with cameras, a film crew, and room service. I was about to appear on a reality television show.

"The girls are in the next room," he explained. I looked at a screen and saw Bristol and her sister Willow hanging out on the other side of the hotel wall eating chicken fingers.

"On our cue," he said, "leave this room, go out into the hall, and knock on the other door like you are just arriving. Since you haven't seen each other since Alaska, catch up."

"Be natural," said the producer, "but it'd help the plotline if you could bring up the following five topics." I memorized the list as we waited and chatted with the camera guys, who'd filmed *Real Housewives* and *Hoarders*.

"So how many chickens can live in a bedroom?" I sat in rapt attention as he regaled me with stories of shooting that show, trying to forget I was about to have to go on camera. I was nervous about appearing on camera but more nervous about how long this might take. David, the kids, and I had come to D.C. for the 2012 Conservative Political Action Conference (CPAC), where thousands of activists, authors, pundits, and officials had gathered to celebrate the best of the GOP.

Earlier that day, event organizers told me they were going to award David the prestigious Ronald Reagan Award that evening at a banquet. They swore me to secrecy, wanting David to be surprised, but I had already planned on filming with Bristol and would be late. I let the older kids in on the secret—I told them to brush their hair, dress as well as they could, and try to act casual if cameras were filming their table. I knew they could make sure David got there on time. However, I didn't want to miss the actual award ceremony.

"You're up." The producer ducked his head into our room, pointed at me, and called me into action. "Try to ignore the cameras."

I walked out into the hall and knocked on the door of the suite next door. Bristol answered the door and hugged me. A man crouched at my feet, filming up at me. I maneuvered around the cameraman, conscious of my appearance. I hated my smile, teeth as big as tombstones, and tried to arrange my face in an appropriately casual manner. Walking suddenly felt unnatural, but I made it to a chair with the grace of a three-legged race participant.

I tried to remember the producer's conversational goals. How has she been since I last saw her? How are things going with the family? Was she nervous about the book signing? We hit all our marks. After a few minutes, this portion of the filming was over. Next we loaded into black SUVs, along with security guards, and drove across town. Outside the bookstore, a line of fans and protesters snaked out the door and onto the street.

I was anxious. When Bristol filmed a different episode at a bar, a man yelled obscenities while she was on a mechanical bull. "Your mother's a whore," he yelled. Would a confrontation break out at the bookstore? I sat at a long table, Bristol to my right next to a pile of books. She signed a book and slid it over to me for my signature.

"So nice of you to come out." I smiled as I signed Bristol's book.

The customer frowned. "Who are you?"

I pointed to my name on the cover. Ghosts are supposed to be invisible. When we appear, people are surprised, shocked, and unnerved. When I handed the man his book, now marred with my signature, I uttered a quiet, "I'm sorry." This was repeated with almost every customer. A few worked up the courage to simply grab their books before my pen touched the page. Other than that, everything went smoothly. No protests or confrontations. People smiled, got their book, and left.

After an hour, the producer gave a signal. Willow, Bristol, and I were ushered to an SUV outside. At the hotel, I ran through the hotel toward the banquet hall where politicians were still delivering speeches.

When I got to our table, everyone was in a fine mood, and David was oblivious. My heart raced, but I caught Camille and Austin's eyes and breathed a sigh of relief. I'd made it.

Naomi was already tired of sitting for two hours. Camille had packed a book, crayons, and an iPad, but four-year-old Naomi was antsy. I found a first aid kit in my purse, and she unwrapped each bandage and tenderly applied them to imaginary wounds. I pretended to have injuries on my hands and fingers.

David smiled at me across the table as he listened politely. I noticed the camera crew was closing in on our table, but he didn't.

"This year, we're giving the award to someone who has fought tirelessly for conservative values in many different battlefields," Al Cardenas, the chairman of the American Conservative Union, said. I didn't look at David, afraid a wayward glance would give away the secret. He could be talking about anybody.

"Hey, we might go up there." I whispered into Naomi's ear to prepare her for an abrupt transition. "Want to see the lights?"

"From American college campuses and federal courtrooms to the front lines of Iraq," Cardenas continued. "He's come under fire both from liberals in America to terrorists overseas."

Should I have told him? Would he have wanted to prepare a speech, since he was about to be on television unprepared?

"This individual represented conservative values while he was a student at Harvard, where he was a pro-life activist in the early 1990s."

That alone should have clued him in, but he didn't catch on.

"In 2004, he became president of FIRE, the Foundation for Individual Rights and Education."

Finally, Cardenas had reached a level of specificity that could only be referring to David. He looked at me across the table, eyes wide, gobsmacked.

"He felt the call of military service following the attacks of September 11th." Cardenas's voice was full of emotion. "He was awarded the Bronze Star. We need more people like him—in our movement and in our country."

David sat up straight in his chair as the words of praise washed over him.

"Because he defends the US Constitution in the courtroom, fighting for freedom on the battlefield, and living out conservative values. I'm proud to present David French with the Ronald Reagan Award."

The crowd rose to their feet and we followed him onstage. When Cardenas shook my hand, he looked at my fingers covered in Band-Aids.

David began his impromptu speech by quoting James 1:17: "Every good and perfect gift is from above." He turned to Mr. Cardenas. "And this might be a perfect gift." Naomi reached for Mr. Cardenas, and he gave her a high five like a proud grandfather.

"I battle in court so you can spread your message," said David. "A message of hope for the hopeless, lifting people up, defending the engine of free enterprise that's lifted more people out of poverty than any other human system that's ever existed, by defending the defenseless, protecting unborn children in the womb, and protecting innocent victims of jihad abroad." In a few words, he encapsulated why we'd always been Republicans. "And by being fathers to the fatherless, through adoption."

When Naomi leaned over and kissed her brother, the crowd cheered. Suddenly, she saw herself on the jumbo screen and waved at the crowd like a homecoming queen atop a convertible.

David's voice cracked when he mentioned his brothers in the army who'd died. Cardenas fought tears. Nothing could cause a tear in the eye of a conservative like a soldier. David ended his speech by honoring "the people in this room, the giants of this movement who represent these values, the beating heart of America."

The crowd rose in unison. They loved, appreciated, and admired us. I'd never felt more Republican than that day. I'd filmed a show with the Palins and now I was standing on stage with my veteran husband being honored for his conservative values. If CPAC was the "prom of conservatism," David and I were 2012's prom king and queen.

I had no idea it was the last night anyone in that room would ever applaud us, and we'd never be welcomed there again.

20

MY DOUBLE LIFE

I was on the trampoline with the kids when my agent called.

"Hey, good news! Your collaboration made the *New York Times* best-sellers list!" Austin jumped over me. One year ago, I'd considered giving up my writing altogether to raise the kids, and now I was a bestselling author. Naomi caught a bounce wrong, but Camille caught her. "Congratulations," my agent said. "Enjoy this."

Pretty soon, the effects of having a *New York Times* bestseller became apparent as conservative pundits, leaders, organizations, and politicians contacted me for books, speeches, blogs, and newspaper articles. I took on more clients, doing most of this work from my home in rural Tennessee, sandwiched between school pickup and grocery runs. None of my friends in real life were ghostwriters, or even writers. My friends and I ate lunch on the square in downtown Columbia, took the kids to the park, and went to church potlucks on Wednesday nights.

While the kids were at school, however, I'd brainstorm political takes for my clients that might resonate on the national level. Once, I suggested my client write an article about a policy change by President Barack Obama. We worked out the language, and I published the piece before heading out to the dentist.

Twenty minutes later, I walked into the waiting room and saw a television in the corner tuned to Fox News. My client's photo flashed on the television screen. What had happened in the past twenty minutes? We'd just talked. Had there been an accident? A scandal?

I walked over to the television and turned up the volume. The other patients rolled their eyes, yet—in spite of themselves—everyone looked at the screen.

Sean Hannity was reading the article I'd published moments ago, verbatim. After he finished, he said, "The White House should respond to this." On the lefthand side of the screen was a graphic of my client's words—the words I'd just written—and then he went to commercial break.

The other people in the waiting room went back to their phones and magazines, and I turned the volume down and sat back in my seat. This attention meant other bloggers, pundits, and politicos would cover the same issue in the coming days. Though the White House did not respond to this article, other publications—including *E!*, *Today*, *Us Weekly*, *Entertainment Weekly*, and CBS—reported on the article. Celebrities also weighed in on the piece. I felt like a criminal at the scene of the crime—watching the police arrive and observing the chaos I'd created, blending into the crowd.

Because I had so many different clients by this time, I could generate buzz over a topic by getting all of them to write slightly different takes on the same topic. News articles would appear about whatever topic I'd ginned up interest in, and they'd cite my words coming from several different clients. I could create a groundswell of attention for conservative positions without changing out of my pajamas. Once, when I heard about an American citizen who'd been wrongly imprisoned in Iran, some of my celebrity clients spoke out. In response, US Secretary of State John Kerry made a statement expressing concern and demanding his release.[10] Eventually, with the attention of the White House firmly on Iran, the American was set free.

Occasionally, I'd travel to help in real time. When one client invited me to the Fox News building to help prepare hot takes to use on air, I sat outside the shot and listened as my eviscerating lines unfurled. Ghostwriting was empowering because my likeminded clients and I could accomplish so much.

But in the summer of 2015, everything changed.

That's when Donald Trump came down the escalator and declared his candidacy for president of the United States. It was a spectacle—Melania slowly descending into the building, followed by her husband. It was the kind of moment that would've fit into *Celebrity Apprentice*, except that it was a real presidential announcement. Not many people took him seriously, but—as soon as he announced—all eyes were on him. From that point forward, every controversial statement was played over and over on the news in inflammatory soundbites.

I was not against inflammatory soundbites per se. I'd written my fair share of them. However, I criticized liberals, not my fellow Republicans. Plus, I was writing on behalf of people who—in my opinion—held solidly conservative positions. People within the mainstream of normal Ronald Reagan–style conservative thoughts. Trump was making statements that wouldn't even be permissible if a middle school kid uttered them—and his hot takes were in direct contradiction to the values we Republicans said we held.

In 2015, I was standing at church after Sunday school scrolling through Twitter when I read an article about how the GOP hopeful had mocked John McCain.

"He's not a war hero," said candidate Trump. "He was a war hero because he was captured. I like people who weren't captured." I couldn't believe that Trump, who'd dodged the draft because of "bone spurs," mocked a man who'd spent more than five years as a prisoner of the North Vietnamese.

Showing contempt for American heroes? Well, this is not what conservatives did.

"You're not going to believe this." I read the quote to my friends who were pouring coffee into Styrofoam cups. These people supported the troops. They'd prayed for David's safe return. They sang patriotic hymns at Fourth of July services. But when I read them the quote, they laughed.

"I wouldn't say that about McCain," a guy standing next to me said. "But I'm happy someone had the guts to say it."

I'd had the "conservative talking points" down to a science. I could write about American military strength, "family values," and personal responsibility in eight hundred words or less, and know exactly how the articles would be received among other conservatives. But as I stood in that church in Columbia, I felt a rumbling beneath my feet. I was standing where I'd always stood—in this case, in support of McCain's military service—but the ground was quaking.

If I laughed—along with Trump, along with my church friends—I'd be turning against my father, a United States Marine at age fifteen. I would be turning against my husband, a US Army JAG officer in Iraq. I would be turning against values like self-sacrifice and courage. I'd be turning against America.

It was appropriate this conversation was happening at church. My entire life, Sunday school teachers presented scenarios designed to make us stick to our values, usually about resisting peer pressure at high school parties. But today the peer pressure scenario was not an imagined scenario at all. It was real, and the temptation was coming from Christians themselves. My fellow churchgoers were passing around the red Solo cup of bitterness and contempt, laughing, and eventually the cup stopped in front of me. But I'd paid attention to a lifetime of Sunday school lessons. I would not drink out of that cup.

That evening a client I'll call Ethan asked me to write about the comment. "McCain deserves to be called out," he said.

I suggested various issues my client could write about, "but not this, since we value the sacrifice of our veterans, right?"

I waited for him to respond. We'd worked together for a while now, and I knew him so well I normally didn't even have to confer with him on his political positions. No matter the issue, I knew what he'd say, and he told me he trusted me with his brand and messaging. But we were coming at Trump's McCain comment from different angles. It was a strange feeling, to suddenly be so thoroughly surprised by someone. Ethan was a salt-of-the-earth, patriotic Christian who—in 2007—was furious that Obama didn't wear an American flag lapel pin, which he interpreted as disrespectful of "the troops." I would've predicted righteous indignation over mockery of a war hero. Instead, he was amused.

I wasn't a pundit, I was a ghostwriter. But still, I felt a moral responsibility to my clients. We had give-and-take relationships that allowed us to discuss and haggle over any position, dialogue which allowed us to produce better articles than we would've individually. Though my clients and I could disagree on issues, we normally didn't have significant space between us. But the chasm between us got larger and larger.

However, I had a sinking realization. If conservatives were going offtrack—I was the little engine pushing them in the wrong direction. Or at least, I was watching them career down the wrong hill. That was my realization, my confession, my shame. My own "sharp elbows" approach had contributed to a no-holds-barred discourse that was hurting our nation. I had been the "hired gun"—or more accurately the "hired pen" or "hired laptop"—of many pundits and politicians. I knew how to eviscerate perceived political enemies, and I did.

Part of that approach was "nutpicking," which is finding one liberal in Madison, Wisconsin, and extrapolating from his odd behavior that "this is the way liberals are." I looked for the worst of Democrats and elevated them, even though the outliers can't possibly represent the whole of a political party.

I "owned the libs," but I thought the political barbs were delivered with a *wink-wink*. I'd grown up reading about Republican President Ronald Reagan and Democratic Speaker of the House Tip O'Neill, who were ideological rivals during the day. Reagan famously said O'Neill was like Pac-Man—"a round thing that gobbles up money." O'Neill said Reagan was "a cheerleader for selfishness." But after six o'clock, they enjoyed each other's company. When Reagan was shot, O'Neill was one of the first visitors Reagan allowed at his bedside. His old rival took the president's hand, got on his knees, and recited the Twenty-third Psalm.

Politics felt like a battleground—where political barbs were warranted, expected, and part of the fun. Though I eschewed my family of origin's pugilism and violence on the mountain, combativeness was in my blood. I was prone to feistiness in my approach to politics because the stakes always seemed high. I wasn't about to let my deeply held beliefs be watered down by civility. But wasn't I making the problem worse? This wasn't fun.

This conversation with my client was even worse because I felt like I'd been guilty of mischaracterizing my fellow Americans. Who was I to now take a principled stand?

However, Trump's comment about McCain—so clearly wrong and mean—caused me to try to apply the brakes to this cultural locomotive. As I was talking to Ethan, I got the feeling I was like the person at a party discouraging alcohol. A scold.

"We could criticize McCain for any disagreement you have over policy,"

I suggested. "Or if you really wanted to take a stand, you could even criticize Trump for this mockery?"

He paused. "Nah, but let's skip it."

In the early stages, my clients typically agreed with my pushback. They hadn't fully jumped on the Trump train yet (though eventually they all supported the GOP front-runner and some joined his campaign). Eventually, when they were "all in," they grew impatient with me.

"I hired you to write *my* beliefs," one client told me, in exasperation. "Not yours."

He was right. But God hadn't given me a writing talent to present mean takes as persuasively as possible, so I doubled down on trying to convince people to think differently.

A few months later, I was at a political conference with Ethan's organization. After a long day of meetings, we were winding down for the evening with Ethan's friends chatting about politics.

"I don't get your opposition to Trump." Ethan shrugged. "He's not my favorite, but he'll surround himself with good people."

"Yeah, he's the lesser of two evils," added one of Ethan's friends.

"But when you're presented with a choice between the lesser of two evils, choose neither," I said, paraphrasing Charles Spurgeon.

This friction had been building between us for months, and we'd reached a peaceful solution: I would push back and Ethan would consider my pushback. Most of the time, he saw my point of view. Sometimes, he did not. Overall, however, Ethan was a good man who tried to be open to my opinions and treated me with respect in spite of our growing disagreement.

"Can't we at least listen to the women who are accusing Trump?" I asked. Though this was early in Trump's rise, several accusers of Trump had spoken out and more women would come forward. The few who had accused him, however, were enough to give me pause.

"I've checked out their stories," my client said, "and they aren't credible. They're lying."

Suddenly, this casual conversation in the lobby of a hotel took a turn.

Ethan was not targeting me specifically, because he didn't know I was a victim of abuse. But couldn't we at least listen to these women and evaluate their credibility instead of dismissing them? Ethan was talking of Trump's accusers, but what I heard was, *I've checked out your story, and you aren't credible. You're lying.*

This wasn't fair. Ethan had never been disrespectful to me at all, but his posture toward possible sex-abuse victims reflected a calloused disregard for those who were hurting and an inherent privilege toward the predatory powerful. I opened my mouth to push back on this statement. "Really?" I said. "You've looked into the victims' accounts and found them . . ."

To my horror, I couldn't finish my sentence. I wanted to say the word *unconvincing*, and I wanted it to drip with incredulity and sarcasm. I wanted him to feel the rhetorical punch of my disregard. But I couldn't form the word. Instead, I burst into tears.

My whole life, I'd seen people ignore the sexual actions of men if they were valuable enough to the organization. My hometown church did this, of course, but this troubling trend was emerging in the Republican party. I thought only Bill Clinton– and Ted Kennedy–loving Democrats were afflicted with this tendency. It was late—too late—and I left Ethan and his friends in the lobby, wondering what this exchange would do to our relationships.

I'd been emotional with my boss, which I never did. I knew more about my clients than they knew about me, which is the proper balance of information for a ghost to maintain. My momentary lapse embarrassed me, but I could feel it in my bones. I couldn't keep an emotional distance from these issues. Honest lament and grief over Trump's deception, bullying, and predation felt warranted.

I couldn't defend this man or make fun of his critics. I had become his critic.

The next morning, I pressed further into this discomfort. I decided to write Ethan and his friends an email explaining more about my opposition to Trump in a less emotional way. Though this would jeopardize my job, I wouldn't be able to work for Ethan anyway if we diverged so dramatically.

"As Republicans, we've always believed 'character counts.' With the nomination of Trump, we have to deal with these things honestly," I began my letter.

I listed more than a dozen sexually questionable or clearly terrible things Trump had done, including how he had a public extramarital affair;

how he described his one-year-old daughter's breasts to a reporter; how he told Howard Stern he didn't treat women with respect; how he told *People* magazine, "If Ivanka weren't my daughter, perhaps I would be dating her"; how he said no one should vote for Republican Carly Fiorina because her face was ugly; how he told *Esquire* magazine, "It doesn't matter what [they] write as long as you've got a young and beautiful piece of ass"; how he said Rosie O'Donnell had a "fat, ugly face" and insulted her weight; how he told a *New York Times* writer she had "the face of a dog"; how he said Bill Clinton's sexual indiscretions were because Hillary couldn't "satisfy" him; and how he had described Jeffrey Epstein as a "terrific guy" who was "fun to be with" even though his romantic partners were "on the younger side."

I also made a list of other nonsexual issues on which he didn't have a conservative—or even coherent—stance, including entitlement reform, NATO, NAFTA, the Iraq war (which I took personally), ISIS, the Second Amendment, the First Amendment, and Russia.

I hinted at my own abuse, without explaining it.

"My entire life, I've been victimized not only by the men with degrading views on women but also by the people who refuse to hold these men accountable because they're culturally and socially important. Frequently, their indiscretions are couched in religious language and now they are couched with political language. Also for my entire life, I've fought liberals against the accusation that Republicans are sexist. If we support Trump, how can we deny this?"

I didn't care whether I was fired. "He's a sexually questionable guy who donated to Hillary Clinton back when all of us were fighting her," I wrote. I needed this income but added one final thought. "I want you guys to be the type of men who refuse to cooperate with a man who treats women the way he does."

I pressed *send* and waited.

One day passed. Two.

Finally, Ethan emailed me back. He said I was judgmental and self-righteous. He said he wanted me to be the type of woman who refuses to let my own experience of abuse mischaracterize others. I paused as I read his email.

Was I mischaracterizing Trump? Was it possible that these women were all making up these allegations for their own personal gain? Ethan was convinced of that, but what did they have to gain other than public humiliation? I'd read the stories and they seemed credible, independent of my own story. My own abuse didn't rob me of the ability to evaluate facts. But after seeing the heaps of public contempt lavished on these women, I knew I'd never have the guts to ever discuss abuse in a public way.

To my surprise, Ethan didn't fire me. The trouble between us was brewing and bubbling, so we had to come to an agreement. Ethan wanted to continue our partnership, so he offered a compromise. I'd write general, conservative articles for him but he would not ask me to praise Trump.

That sounded like a plan that might work. In my mind, however, I made a vow: I would not bear false witness against my liberal neighbor.

That one decision was the beginning of the end of my political ghostwriting career.

21

ALT WRONG

R emember Steve Bannon?" David asked me.
"Only how he took his bagels." I couldn't get over the fact that I had made him breakfast when I stayed at the Palins' house. "But I haven't kept up with him. Is he still running Breitbart?"

Breitbart was a popular conservative website that received more traffic than any site other than Fox News.

"Yeah, but he's now embracing the alt right. He's even calling Breitbart the 'platform for the alt right.'"

The "alt right" was a group of White nationalists who rebranded regular ole racism under a new name. They wanted to fundamentally change the way we thought about immigration and ethnicity, claiming immigrants were not able to assimilate into our culture and would ultimately destroy our nation. They believed America was facing a "White genocide" and characterized Black and Brown immigrants as dirty, violent, and sick.

Bannon elevated that toxic philosophy and allowed it to proliferate throughout conservatism. He denied the "alt right" was racist. Instead he claimed the movement was "nationalist" and the fact that racists were drawn to the movement was coincidental.[11]

Then the alt right got the biggest advocate of all. Donald Trump appointed Bannon to run his presidential campaign, which skyrocketed the "alt right" platform to the highest levels of cultural prominence. Words like *cuckservative* entered the mainstream conversation. This is a combination of *cuckold* and *conservative* and referred to a genre of porn in which silent White husbands watched their wives have sex with Black men.[12]

Cuck was their ultimate insult. Why was their favorite insult related to sex even though the disagreements might have to do with policies like immigration? The alt right is not about ideas. It's about stigmatizing perceived enemies and making them regret ever speaking out. It's about control.

In my first conversation with David, when I was in high school, he explained how his liberal law school classmates had shouted him down, unwilling to even hear conservative arguments. I'd always thought liberals were intolerant. But now I realized "our side" sexualized criticism and racialized critique. The main tactic of their rhetorical playbook was cruelty. They were sexually weaponizing their insults to hit, so to speak, below the belt.

In September of 2015, David wrote an article criticizing this movement. I wasn't surprised White nationalists were not pleased with this article, but they didn't attack David's arguments. They attacked him because we have a Black daughter. They claimed we were "raising the enemy."

The enemy? Sweet Naomi, now seven years old, who wore her hair in braids? I couldn't think of her as anything but my daughter, but these White nationalists believed all Black people were "invaders." I scrolled, absorbing this online hatred. When a certain image filled my screen, I gasped.

"David?" I called out to him, since he was on the other side of the house writing. "Come here. There's a photo of Naomi online." My eyes focused on the image. It was Naomi in a gas chamber, with Donald Trump—wearing a Nazi uniform—pulling a lethal gas lever.

David called through the house. "I just now saw it." A few seconds later, he appeared in the doorway. "Did you see the photo?"

I nodded.

"I can't believe they called her enslaved."

I looked at him in confusion, and we exchanged worried glances. We were talking about two different photos. He handed me his phone and I showed him my laptop. As David saw Naomi in the gas chamber for the first time, I saw her face pasted onto historic images of enslaved people. Under the photos, she was labeled an "n-glet" and a "dindu." I'd never heard those words but knew they were horrific.

"What is happening?" I asked. Against my better judgment, I kept scrolling. I needed to know what was out there about us—about my family. One White nationalist website purported to explain why they were attacking David, and it had to do with adoption.

"The word cuckold comes from 'cuckoo,' the bird that lays its eggs in the nest of a different species," one White nationalist website explained. "The other mother bird can't tell the difference, and feeds the cuckoo chick along with her own. The chick rewards her by pitching the other babies out of the nest, so it gets all the food. A cuckold is a man whose wife had an affair, had the baby, and the poor sap thinks it's his. The cuckold is a figure of derision and contempt because he's been tricked into lavishing care on a child that's not his."[13]

The writer went on to explain why they were labeling David a cuck. "Instead of having another child of their own, they deliberately decided to adopt someone who is as alien to them—genetically, racially, culturally—as possible." He went on to question whether David's "Little Ethiopian" can truly love America.

Another alt right website explained that "the cuckservative is often fanatically in favor of transracial adoption. He sees it as some divine calling. In a sense, this is cuckoldry at its essence, since these Whites are usually forgoing their own inclusive fitness to adopt someone from another race . . . they're race-cucking their own families."[14]

Their crass, negative, inaccurate characterization of adoption filled me with anger. It reminded me of Isaiah 5:20. "Woe unto them that call evil good, and good evil; that put darkness for light, and light for darkness; that put bitter for sweet, and sweet for bitter!" (KJV).

My phone rang. "Hey, just checking in on you," my friend said.

"What do you mean?" More urgently, I added, "Tell me."

"I saw the online images today," she said. "Thought I'd check in."

"Okay, yeah." I put her on speaker. "I'm sitting here with David. We've seen them."

"I mean, they're obviously fake," she said. "No one's gonna believe that's you having sex."

My stomach lurched within me, and I swallowed bile in my throat. Me having sex? I stared at the phone, and lost focus of everything else in the room. What had she seen? What had all of Twitter seen?

"This is David." He picked up the phone. "What are you talking about?"

My friend texted us links to pornographic photos of me photoshopped to look like I was having sex with—according to the caption—several "Black bucks." They'd edited David's face in an open window as if he was helplessly watching the infidelity.

With one pornographic image, they branded David a "cuckservative." With one pornographic image, they branded me as someone who has sex with multiple partners outside of marriage. We sat in silence. David rubbed his hand over his face.

"What is happening?" I asked again.

"The alt right hates international adoption." David spoke calmly, but I could tell his manner did not match his emotional state. "So they're either saying we are intentionally 'raising the enemy' or they're saying we did not adopt Naomi. They're saying the adoption thing is a lie, and that . . ." He paused. "That we have a Black daughter because you were unfaithful to me while I was deployed."

I felt my heart beating in my face. The idea that people were talking, speculating, and laughing about me sexually made me want to crawl into bed, pull the covers over my head, and never get out. The comments were disgusting, speculative, and X-rated. They didn't stop. They kept coming at it—through email, my website, and Twitter. It was all both very public and very private. The alt right tried to inflict as much personal pain as they could on us, in the most intimate ways possible. These radicalized Trump supporters harassed us, mocked us, maligned us, and believed we should lose our jobs, and—at least according to our email inboxes—even our lives.

The alt right was not the Republican Party, but it affected the Republican Party. It influenced the Republican Party. Alt right cheerleader Bannon was Trump's most trusted advisor, and Trump himself retweeted the same sort of alt right accounts that had attacked us.[15]

I tried to explain this public humiliation to my friends, but they stared at me in shock. It was so far outside their experiences they couldn't offer much advice. They weren't sure how to process or fix this. When we mentioned these attacks to other friends, they doubled down on their Trump support.

"That's only a radical fringe," they assured us. "I hope this doesn't make you tie this to Trump."

The message was loud and clear. While we were being punished, ostracized, bullied, and sexually humiliated, many Christians' main concern was whether we would still support their candidate of choice. Since we were Republicans, almost all of our friends supported Trump. Since almost all of our friends supported Trump, they ignored these attacks on us.

But my client Ethan did not ignore them. One day, after seeing all the online hate, he called me.

"Hey, are you okay over there?" I was touched that he'd reached out via phone. Even though we'd had some Trump-related conflict, he seemed genuinely concerned.

"Yeah, we're okay," I said as Ethan listened to all that had happened. Finally, he said, "To be honest, I don't think the alt right is a thing."

"You don't think it exists?" This was not a "friendship" call to check on my welfare. This was another attempt to try to convince me that Donald Trump and his supporters were fine.

"Look, the media wants us to believe conservatives are racists," he explained, "so they're bringing all this attention to this group that's not even about racism."

"The media?" Ethan knew, and I knew, that David had written an article in *Time* about the alt right. That's what started it all. "Are you saying David's fake news?"

"I'm saying this is all smoke and mirrors to distract Americans from the real stuff that's going on."

I swallowed. This felt "real" to me. It felt like a real movement with real people posting photos and real people laughing at me. But Ethan and I disagreed more and more. His political views were established by consuming media I never read. Mine were established by consuming news he never read. When we tried to talk about a disagreement, we didn't even have a set of shared facts on which to build. I was in despair over the alt right's attack, and he believed the "alt right" was more like a monster under my bed than a political movement. Apparently, he believed we'd brought all of this on ourselves.

The next day, an editor at the *Washington Post* asked me to write about this harassment.[16] I wasn't sure if this was the right move. If I wrote about this in such a prominent newspaper, my attackers would realize they hit their emotional mark and might escalate their attacks. If I didn't, people would see these images and undoubtedly think the worst. I decided not to shrink away and to publish the article. Since most of the attacks against me were so vile, the editor could not allow most of the alt right's comments to me to be quoted in the article. However, I hoped this definitive piece would end the matter.

A few days later, I went to Washington, D.C., for a veteran's event for an organization which had hired me to write about charity, values, and service. I went alone to this gig, leaving David at home with the kids. The event started by singing the national anthem in front of the Lincoln Memorial as the "dawn's early light" peeked through the clouds. People within earshot—even those who weren't in our group—stopped in their tracks when they heard the first notes. The joggers running around the reflection pool paused their morning workouts and put their hand over their hearts in silence for the duration.

"Come do push-ups for America!" we said to passers-by. "Support our troops!"

Boy Scouts, bicyclists, moms with strollers, and marathoners all stopped and gave us twenty. As I watched them doing push-ups—standing with a veteran who had lost both legs defending American values, like the right to free speech—my heart swelled with patriotic appreciation. That's when my phone rang.

"Do not go to your blog," David said.

"What?" I walked away from the memorial. "Why?"

White nationalists had filled my blog with images and videos of Black men shooting other Black men, Black men dying via suicide, and videos of horrific executions.

"I've been to war, and I'll never unsee what's posted there," he said. "It's bad."

I shuddered to think about the readers who had gone to my blog that day and seen all of that evil. For weeks, the online MAGA supporters continued to target us with sexually charged, disturbing accusations. Every time I opened Twitter, I saw people bragging about having had sex with me.

My vacation Bible school–related abuse was not something I thought a great deal about, but it bubbled below my consciousness. Every time I saw people bragging about having sex with me—no doubt to provoke David into a response—I felt like I died a little, overcome with shame and grief.

And the promiscuous label followed me relentlessly. A conservative magazine called *American Greatness* published a blatantly racist poem called "Cuck Elegy"—which accompanied a photo of David and Naomi. Apparently, they knew this would not drive away readers, this would attract them. Also, by putting a photo of David and Naomi as the featured image, it further cemented the notion that she was the result of my supposed infidelity.[17]

This was not fringe. David's *National Review* colleague Victor Davis Hanson writes for this magazine.[18] And the Aspen Institute, one of the most prestigious gatherings of thought leaders, invited *American Greatness*'s editor Christopher Buskirk to participate in their panel discussion about the alt right.[19] (This was akin to asking an arsonist to give advice on putting out fires, but they did not ask me for my advice.) Even though Buskirk peddles in racism and mocks our daughter, he has written for the *New York Times*, the *Washington Post*, and contributes to *PBS Newshour*, NPR, and CNN.

This casual racism and brutality was not pushed by a fringe element, it had become the main political strategy of many conservatives. These people spouting conspiracy theories and shouting invectives were now embedded, wrapped up, and intertwined with mainstream Republicanism.

And, I sadly realized, so was I.

THE OPPORTUNITY

The heat from the 850-square-foot Manhattan apartment hit me as I opened the door. Sun poured through the skylight and baked the wooden floors. The East Thirtieth Street apartment smelled of cigarette smoke and Chinese takeout. Its elevator was so small it fit only two of us at a time, if we both held our breath. It was so slow I envisioned a guy in the basement lifting us with a pulley. There was no washer/dryer, but we were allowed to use the one in the Persian restaurant next door.

"It's perfect." Sweat trickled down my brow as Naomi crawled onto the fire escape. I snapped a photo and posted it to Instagram.

Camille and Austin unpacked their stuff and claimed their corners. It'd be tight, but that was part of the fun. Since Camille was about to go to college, we planned to spend the summer in New York so they could experience the city and have some quality time as a family.

The apartment was right next to the Empire State Building. No matter where the kids were, they could look up, spot the building, and know how to get home. Every day, eighteen-year-old Camille and sixteen-year-old Austin set off alone to explore—by going to Central Park, a Yankees game, and musicals like *Hamilton*. David and I looked for out-of-the-way Vietnamese restaurants and went to my old Greenwich Village stomping grounds.

"Bill Kristol invited me to dinner," David said one day. Bill was the editor of the *Weekly Standard*, the person who first floated the name Sarah Palin to the world as a possible running mate to McCain in 2008. At their dinner, David and Bill talked about the dismally unacceptable state of politics. It was now 2016, and Trump had secured the GOP nomination; Hillary Clinton had secured the Democratic nomination. As much as I disliked Trump, Hillary was not acceptable either.

The next morning, we turned on our phones and were surprised we'd missed many messages.

"Did you see what Kristol wrote?" a typical text read.

We quickly opened the *Weekly Standard* to read his morning essay, in which he lamented America's awful presidential options.

"Resist the decline of America by finding a serious and credible independent candidate," he wrote. He went through a list of capable, famous politicians who wouldn't run because of various political pressures. My phone buzzed, alerting me to more texts, and my heart beat faster.

"Take David French," he wrote. "I know David. To say he'd be a more responsible president than Clinton or Trump is to state a truth that would become self-evident as more Americans got to know him. There are others like him. There are thousands of Americans who—despite a relative lack of fame or fortune—would be manifestly superior to our current choices."[20]

I put down my phone and looked at David. "Well, that doesn't happen every day."

Still, after fielding all the texts and calls of friends who'd seen the piece, I put it out of my mind. It was a nice compliment, a kind word. But soon, David's phone rang. It was a political strategist named Malcolm who'd talked to Kristol.

Kristol had been serious, and Malcolm asked David to at least consider running for president as an alternative, Hail Mary candidate.

We laughed. Not only did we have no money, we had no national name recognition, no infrastructure, and no desire to enter into the political fray. But a few minutes later, Kristol contacted David privately and asked him to run.

Suddenly, this preposterous question needed to be considered.

David called several prominent people to get their advice, including Mike Murphy, the former political advisor to John McCain and Jeb Bush; Senator Ben Sasse; and evangelical leader Russell Moore. David was doing laundry in the Persian restaurant's basement when Mitt Romney returned his call. David answered while sitting on a potato bag in a restaurant's dark innards as Iranian busboys pulled off their shirts, aprons, and pants and tossed their items in the laundry. David strained to hear Romney's advice as nude men ran around yelling in Farsi.

By the afternoon, donors had pledged millions for a possible run. Not enough millions to run a successful presidential campaign, but more millions than we had—which was, after my calculations, precisely zero millions.

David wrote out all of the reasons he could run, all of the reasons he shouldn't run, and all of the things that could embarrass him if he did run.

He had a compelling story. He grew up in a small town in Kentucky—the son of a public-school elementary teacher and a math professor at the small Baptist college in town—went to a Christian college where he finished first in his class, and was the first student from the school to go to any Ivy League law school. He'd worked in law before joining the army. Unlike most JAG officers he was "boots on the ground" with a combat unit throughout his deployment. He ran detainee operations, conducted drone operations, made rules of engagement decisions, patrolled streets, met with tribal leaders, and spent serious time "outside the wire."

But did he have any skeletons in the closet?

I did. I'd kept my own sex abuse a secret. David knew, as well as school friends, but I'd pushed it into the recesses of my mind. For decades, I wrongly put my relationship with Conrad into the same mental category as "illicit affair," reflecting the way my church framed such encounters. Women—even twelve-year-old girls—were supposed to stave off the desires of men by wearing modest clothing and rebuffing their attempts. I'd failed to do that. I was responsible. As an adult, I would not have drawn that conclusion, but this was buried so deeply I never took it out to evaluate in the light of day. It was just an open wound, festering without my realizing it. I didn't have the courage to look at it.

This was the secret that jumped to mind during David's possible presidential run. But David wasn't going to run, was he?

David's "skeletons" were not skeletons at all.

"I'm a nerd. A nerd's nerd. I love computer games, *Star Wars*, and *Game of Thrones*. I can speak for hours on both the politics of Westeros and the competing philosophies of Jedi and Sith," he wrote in an email.

173

"And I mean hours. I would be the first 'Nerd-American' presidential candidate."

After he'd sent his message to a small team of advisors, he met with big-name political operatives. Top secret. Since Kristol had mentioned several other people who could challenge Trump, no one suspected people had approached David to seriously consider the idea. Mainly, because it was not serious. Was it? David had never held political office.

Yet the calls were serious, and David had to give it serious thought. This was not a simple decision, since much consideration had to go into ballot access at this late date. Since he had not made a decision yet, we prepared as if he was running.

"The advisors are going to assign some people to evaluate our social media accounts," David said. "So we'll need all of the kids' accounts—Twitter, Instagram, Facebook, TikTok."

I submitted our family's accounts for review, wondering what politically incorrect things lurked out there.

"Do you want to run for president?" I asked David.

"Want to?" He paused. "No, but I have to consider it."

On May 29, 2016, Kristol was about to jump on a plane to Israel, when he casually tweeted, "Just a heads-up over this holiday weekend: There will be an independent candidate—an impressive one, with a strong team and a real chance." Kristol turned off his phone and boarded the plane. He slept contentedly all the way to Israel, unaware of the political chaos he'd unleashed back in the states. His tweet set a thousand laptops ablaze in journalists' efforts to find out the identity of this "impressive" unknown candidate who had a "real chance."

We were at dinner when David checked his phone. His face fell as he showed me the tweet.

"Is he talking about . . ." I turned around in my seat to see if anyone was listening. "You?"

I was no political strategist, but this was precisely the wrong way to tease the presidential run of a relatively unknown, Hail Mary candidate. You don't overpromise. You might say something like, "Just a heads-up: There will be an independent candidate who has no chance but you can pull the lever for him without throwing up in your mouth."

Yet there it was, a tweet leading people to believe it was someone known, someone with loftier chances. David would be a great president, but he wouldn't have even been his own first choice. In our nation's time of crisis, however, something needed to be done.

As I was looking at David's phone, it rang. He didn't answer it but listened to the voicemail.

"It's Robert Costa from the *Washington Post* asking me if I am the unknown candidate."

"What?" I asked. "How?" I assumed Costa could've read Kristol's article, which mentioned David—but it had mentioned others as well. It seemed like Costa had insider information.

"I don't know."

Our world closed in on us with every bite of pasta. The tweet had dramatically pushed forward the already-accelerated time frame. Not only did they have to move fast to beat ballot-initiative deadlines, they had to beat the reporters desperate to break the story.

David agreed to meet the political operatives in Vermont to determine if a viable path to getting his name on the ballot even existed. I didn't go because I couldn't leave the kids in Manhattan by themselves. Also, because I couldn't wrap my head around the idea that David could possibly run for president. However, with every passing minute, it seemed more and more possible.

David spent several days with some of the best minds in politics. He learned that the ballot-access challenge could be met with modest effort, by activating a preexisting network of willing people; the polling for an independent was better than most people knew; and people with outstanding political talents were willing to quit their jobs to help provide the American people with an alternative.

While David was in Vermont, I navigated Manhattan with the kids. The kids knew little of what was going on because this process demanded absolute secrecy. Since GOP leaders had not endorsed Trump yet, the team had to scurry to get much-needed financial commitments. If news leaked, the whole thing would blow up in their faces. I found comfort in the secrecy. As long as this remained off the radar, I wouldn't have to face it.

Then Donald Trump poured gasoline on the whole thing.

"Bill Kristol is a loser," Trump said at a news conference when asked about Bill's tweet. He later told Sean Hannity any independent candidate would lose. "I don't think [Kristol] has anybody, because now he's saying 'it will come someday, it will come, you know, in the future.' Well, if you read his tweet, his tweet was almost like it was imminent, like it's going to be announced this morning. And then all of the sudden he announced 'well, maybe not so fast.' Who would do it?"

I swallowed hard. I knew who might. As I watched people on television speculating about this mystery candidate, I was filled with terror.

What was happening? Was my "summer in New York" plan being turned into a presidential launch? We hadn't packed for this. David had brought one button-up shirt, and it wasn't even ironed. The kids and I didn't have nice clothing, since we'd packed for hot summer days in Manhattan.

"This is getting real." David called me one night from Vermont.

"What are you thinking?"

"I don't know."

We sat in silence, both of us exhausted. My heart raced, but I couldn't find words to explain how much I feared the public scrutiny if he chose to run. Who would put their family through such a public ordeal? To prepare for the possible onslaught of media attention, I had to be "vetted," so I met Malcolm the next day.

"Can you tell me more about what this is?" I asked him in a conference room. I didn't meet his eyes.

"Vetting is an old racing term." Malcolm opened his laptop. "Before they'd put their horses in a race, a veterinarian would make sure they were healthy enough to run. A horse might look good, but the doctor made sure the race wasn't sabotaged by some unknown problem."

"In this analogy, you're the veterinarian and I'm the horse?"

He smiled.

"Tell me anything embarrassing—or potentially embarrassing—so our team can figure out how to deal with it in advance."

"You mean . . ."

"Financial, political, romantic." He eyed me narrowly. "Don't worry. Your skeletons can't be worse than the bones clanking around in closets of Trump or Clinton."

He said it as a statement, but it was a question. My stomach dropped.

"I have relatives on the mountain who belong to the KKK," I blurted. "And if television vans showed up on Monteagle, my family might shoot them."

He jotted some notes on his iPad. "Everyone's got the crazy uncle," he said.

"But my uncle killed his wife."

"You had nothing to do with that, I assume?" Nonplussed. He asked me about all aspects of my past: financial dealings, any conflicts with neighbors, and every boyfriend I'd ever had—how we broke up, whether it was public, whether anyone had compromising photographs of me, and so forth. It was like going to confession, except Malcolm offered spin instead of absolution. Malcolm evaluated whether the ex would have an impetus to come forward, based on his occupation, political disposition, and financial needs.

I told Malcolm about my college boyfriend, who would be the most apt to come forward and try to humiliate me on a national stage. He didn't say a word, just took notes.

"And where is Jacob now?"

"I don't know." His parents had told me never to call them again, and I hadn't.

"We're going to need to locate him," he said. He wrote down his full name and hometown.

"Okay, so there's one more." I felt my face immediately redden with shame. "My vacation Bible school teacher, Conrad." Malcolm wrote down his name.

"How did it start, what exactly happened, who knew about it, and so forth." He had as much emotion as an actuary. I wasn't used to talking about this, especially with a political operative whose main goal was to get David to run.

I stumbled over my words but finally spilled my deepest, darkest secret.

Malcolm listened. "That wasn't a 'relationship,' technically. He's not likely to admit to being a pedophile, right?"

Pedophile. The abusive nature of this relationship seemed clear to Malcolm. I nodded.

"People are abused all the time. In fact, it might even make you more relatable."

I swallowed. "I've never considered my sexual abuse as an asset."

Malcolm shut his laptop. "I've seen worse."

I left the meeting feeling shamed but comforted myself by believing David's presidential run wouldn't happen.

That evening, I sat in front of my laptop in that sweltering apartment with one mission: to finally find out what happened to Jacob. His last words echoed in my ears. He told me that one day I'd hear he killed himself. And rest assured, his death would be caused by me. "No matter how many years later."

For hours, I googled his name. Nothing. I checked all the social media sites and found scant evidence that he'd ever existed. Finally, I messaged a friend from back home.

"Oh, Nancy, you were close to him?" she asked. "You didn't know he killed himself?"

I was suddenly right back in my college dorm room listening to his recording on my answering machine. Had I caused this?

"When?"

"It's been a few years."

She had no other details, and neither did anyone else. I messaged Malcolm. "You don't have to worry about Jacob making a statement to the press."

For the next few days, the kids and I continued to explore New York, while David was in Vermont. However, my vision narrowed into a possible presidential run. As the kids explored museums, I called friends to seek advice. It all seemed improbable, but I felt I needed to emotionally prepare.

On June 1, David's phone rang in Vermont. Believing the 212 number was from his magazine's office, he answered it.

"This is Mark Halperin, from Bloomberg," the caller said. "Are you running for president?"

David had not decided whether to run, so he'd attempted to dodge the press. And he attempted to dodge the question in this call. It didn't work.

"'Um, well, um,'" Halperin repeated. "May I quote you on that?"

David laughed. "No, I'd rather you didn't."

"Okay, let me put it this way," Halperin said. "Do you *deny* you are considering running for president?"

David had a choice to make. He could lie to the reporter, which politicians do all the time, or tell the truth. Lying had its disadvantages: it was wrong, and he couldn't call out Clinton and Trump for dishonesty while misleading a reporter. But the truth had its disadvantages: confirming this would sink whatever chances he had. The GOP, once alerted of the possibility of a third-party candidate, would circle the wagons to ensure he wouldn't splinter the Republican vote. When those wagons circled, money would dry up. That would be that. The decision would be made.

But like George Washington at the foot of the fabled cherry tree, David could not tell a lie.

"I don't deny it," he said. And with that, his fate was sealed.

"The story will drop in fifteen minutes," Halperin said before hanging up.

I was on a bus with Naomi when David called me.

"Gather the kids," David said. I had a hard time hearing his voice over the roar of the engine. "The news is about to break, so call your parents and mine and tell them not to answer the phone under any circumstances. You have fifteen minutes."

I texted the kids: "Meet me at Times Square Church at 51st and Broadway." This was where David and I attended church when we were first married. It was as good a place as any to rally the troops while the world closed in around us.

I called my mom and dad on the bus ride to the church.

They had no idea we'd even been considering David running for president. I'd only told them we were in New York to see *Hamilton*.

"So it's a Broadway musical in rap?" My dad had spoken slowly. "And the Founding Fathers are Puerto Rican?"

"Not all of them," I said. "George Washington's Black."

That conversation had happened only a few weeks ago, but it felt like a million years had passed.

"Daddy, listen carefully," I said into the phone. "A news story is about to break about David, and I need to tell you about it."

I tried to explain the situation while the bus rolled through Manhattan, periodically coming to stops while we waited for others to get on. Would the media dig into my parents' family? Would they find out about their mountain roots and depict them as knuckle-dragging hillbillies? Hearing his voice—his mountain accent while I was sitting on a NYC bus—filled my heart with sorrow and trepidation.

"Okay, so David might be running for president?" He said the words slowly. "So don't pick up the phone?"

"He hasn't decided yet, but don't accept any new Facebook friends," I said. "Even if you think you know them. Turn on the television, and you'll see the news."

"What channel?" he asked.

"Any of them," I said. "All of them."

By the end of the call, my phone had blown up with texts, Google notifications, and phone calls.

Halperin hadn't even waited the full fifteen minutes. It dropped in five.

23

THE SPOTLIGHT

The next morning, the national press discussed David's possible candidacy. Since David didn't have any clean clothing, I dropped off his shirt at the cleaners for an express cleaning. I was with the kids for breakfast at the Gramercy Diner on Third Avenue when my phone rang, a 212 Manhattan area code. I figured it was my landlord telling me it was a health code violation to talk to Mitt Romney while leaning on the potatoes and doing laundry, so I answered.

"Nancy, this is Robert Costa with the *Washington Post*." My eggs fell off my fork. He must've gotten my personal cell phone number from someone who knew me. "Has your husband decided to run for president?"

I wasn't going to lie, but I also knew I had to keep the deliberations secret.

"If my husband was running for president, I'm sure I'd know it," I said. I fielded a few more questions, and the kids stopped eating as they saw my panicked face. Costa asked if he had the correct number for David's cell phone. I swallowed as I heard him rattle off the familiar Tennessee number.

As soon as I hung up, I called David.

Voicemail.

"Do not answer the phone." My face grew hot as I left the message. "Robert Costa has your number," I texted him.

My heart raced as I paid our bill and walked home, dry cleaning on my shoulder. Nine-year-old Naomi was on a scooter, joyfully wheeling her way down the street, when I saw a gaggle of reporters and a film crew standing outside our apartment. Their cameras were pointed directly at us.

"Dear God," I prayed. "Please stop this from happening."

But it *was* happening. I did a quick assessment of my appearance. I hadn't put on makeup or brushed my hair. I cursed myself for not splurging on a doorman building. They'd already spotted me, and I didn't want them to film me running in the opposite direction.

I walked slowly as I reached into my purse and fumbled for my keys. My hand landed on a package of gum, a tampon, and then—

"Mrs. French, is your husband running for president?"

I had no keys. I had no way out.

"He'd make a wonderful president." I smiled. How had they found us? Had they seen the photo of Naomi sitting on our fire escape and been able to ascertain our location through the buildings in the background? If so, they deserved the scoop.

The reporter asked me why America needed an alternative to Trump and Clinton, a question I could answer even as I searched for my keys. As I answered, a person approached us. Had God answered my prayers and sent an angel to interrupt the interview?

If so, the angel hadn't opted for a flowy robe and a sword. He was wearing the smallest bikini I've ever seen. I didn't have time to inquire properly about this person's pronouns, but this angel appeared to be a man, possibly in his early seventies and had perkier breasts than I did. He must've been hovering on the outskirts of the interview, waiting for his moment to shine. I'd never been happier to see another person in my life.

"I want you to know," he said to me as the cameras rolled, "I support your husband for president."

He gave me a fist bump. It was like we had a long-standing relationship, and he, fully briefed on all of David's political positions, found them satisfactory.

"Well, there's one vote," I said.

The reporter wrapped it up quickly, and I could tell he believed his report was sullied by the appearance of my bikini-clad angel. I grabbed Naomi's hand and disappeared into our apartment.

When I got inside, I sank into the sofa.

My phone rang. Malcolm. I described the scene outside my apartment. "Why don't you have a doorman?"

"We're not made of money." This, of course, was the number one reason David shouldn't run for president. I planned for many vacation complications—extra money in case I lost my credit card. A fanny pack so the kids didn't get pickpocketed. I neglected to get a doorman in case my husband up and ran for president.

"You can't stay there," he said. "I'll have someone call you later today with a list of new apartments. Find one by tomorrow. Donors will pay for it."

"Is he running?" I thought about my line to Costa. If my husband was running for president, I'm sure I'd know it. Now I wasn't so sure. Malcolm said that David was close to making the decision, and he thought he'd do it.

David and I connected later on the phone.

"Are you running?" I asked.

"I don't know." He explained that he was genuinely uncertain.

Which meant we still we had to plan for that eventuality. That evening, I stood in a multimillion-dollar apartment in Manhattan. Malcolm had given me a list of available apartments for rent, so I attempted to look like I belonged there. I did not. Our home in rural Tennessee had a playset, a trampoline, and a chicken coop full of birds: Mrs. Frizzle, Malefactus, Mrs. Featherbottom, and Johann Sebastian, because it made the sound *Bach*.

In a less stressful time, I would've relished looking at this gated midtown residence built on the former grounds of the J. P. Morgan Carriage House. Normally, I had to satisfy my "how rich people live" curiosity by watching HBO dramas and looking at a real estate app when I drove through rich parts of town. The agent showed me around, and I looked at the place skeptically, trying to camouflage my wide-eyed wonder at its sheer opulence.

"Push this button and you magically get another room." A wall emerged from the floor, turning the area into a private living space. The condo also had east and west views, huge closets, two master bedrooms, and marble bathrooms.

"When can you move in?" she asked.

I tried to be noncommittal because I was under strict orders not to tell the agent of my "situation." That's how I thought of this possible presidential run. Something to be managed. No building, out of courtesy for the other residents, wanted press outside hounding a possible presidential candidate's family.

I imagined us living in Manhattan—far from our Tennessee home—and my throat got thick. I wanted to sink into myself, to disappear. Even though this place was amazing, I felt exposed. Would the entire nation soon be discussing my relationship with Conrad? Would there be opinion pieces and news segments inferring the wife of the "moral candidate" David French had an illicit affair with her pastor?

"How did apartment hunting go?" David had called me when he got a chance to break off from his constant meetings. "And the vetting process?"

I began to cry.

He was surprised by my reaction. "Malcolm said everything went well."

"He wasn't the one baring his soul."

"What specifically bothers you?" he asked. "You need to tell me now. What's going on? No matter what it is, I can take it. I need to hear it now."

No telling what he was preparing to hear—an affair, nude photographs? It felt like one of those serious marital moments in which I could confess a million things and we'd have to deal with them with political consultants instead of marital counselors.

"Conrad." I could only say that one word, but his name conveyed everything. David didn't speak for a moment, and every moment was critical. His advisors had pulled in professionals from other campaigns, and they were trying to get him back to meetings. He covered the phone with his hand and told them he needed more time. "What if people find out?" I added.

"They'll have compassion for what you went through." His voice was soft.

"But what if they construe it as a he-said-she-said thing?" I readjusted on the apartment's cheap couch. "No one ever believes victims, especially if it serves them politically to shrug it off."

I'd lived long enough to know how this would play out. Our critics would get a false narrative out there fast and let it ride. Damage could be mitigated by telling my side of the story, but would anyone believe me? And even if they did, at what cost?

David knew about the abuse, but he didn't know it had been weighing me down for years, a burden I couldn't put down. He was quiet for a moment.

"No normal person would hold your sexual abuse against you," he said gently. "You were the victim of a pedophile. If people find out about it, I get it. It'll be awful. But we can handle it."

Something about his tone, his assurance, disarmed me. Saying it aloud robbed it of its terrifying power. People would understand.

"Are you sure?" I asked.

"I'm not sure how people will react to it, but—to me—this isn't a thing. I'm proud of you and the person you've become. It makes you even more impressive."

A sob emerged in my throat. Though I wasn't sure if America would, I loved David French. My abuse had been bubbling underneath the surface of my consciousness for so long, forcing me into a room of isolation and loneliness, even when I was surrounded by people who loved me.

I knew people wouldn't blame me for my own sexual abuse. Instead, I worried they'd hear of my abuse and see me like my abuser had seen me: as unworthy of dignity, trash to be thrown away.

My conversation with David, after not talking about my abuse for decades, helped. He didn't do anything remarkable or say magic words. Instead, his acceptances and assurance were enough to pronounce the sacred truth. I was loved. I had dignity and worth.

I spoke with an uneven voice. "If you decide to run, I'll support you." I hung up the phone and looked at the media coverage. All of the channels covered the new development of David's potential candidacy:

- *Washington Post*: "Conservative Tennessee Attorney David French Is Urged to Enter Presidential Race as Independent"[21]
- NBC: "Who Is David French and Is He Running for President?"[22]
- POLITICO: "What Does David French Believe?"[23]
- CNN: "Kristol's White Knight: David French"[24]

Reporters scurried to our hometown of Columbia, Tennessee, only to discover we weren't there. Undeterred, they parked news vans at our house and interviewed our neighbors. Though they could easily talk about how we didn't keep the flower beds up or how we didn't remove our garbage cans from the streets promptly, they weren't snitches.

"David is a man of integrity," said our neighbor. "I know he would run a principled campaign if he got involved." My son's football coach went on record: "We know David well. Our families are good friends and go to church together. He's intelligent and loves this country."

Reporters went to local diners and asked people if they knew us. Most didn't but had the good manners to support the local guy anyway.

The *Washington Post* described our hometown like this: "The chicken processing plant looms large in Columbia. The smells it produces waft through a town square centered around a big, pillared courthouse when the wind is right." I'd never smelled a chicken processing plant in Columbia, but that might explain why Mrs. Featherbottom was always so jumpy.

Reporters went to Lipscomb University to interview his former professors. Though they did not find his *World of Warcraft* magazine feature, a writer for *GQ* did mention David's enthusiasm for television: "David French's Conservatism, as Revealed by His *Game of Thrones* Recap."

That night, the thing I most feared happened. A reporter's attention turned toward me. A POLITICO reporter mocked me after mischaracterizing a summary of the "rules" David and I jointly agreed upon during his Iraq deployment. "So when David French was in Iraq," he tweeted, "he wouldn't let his wife email men or use Facebook."

Out of all the possible attacks, I didn't expect that.

"Are you okay?" my friends texted me. "We saw the POLITICO guy's thing."

But I was elated, full of relief. After gearing up for news of my abuse to surface, or ex-boyfriends popping up to say who knows what, the false accusation of subservience was invigorating. Sure, the reporter made us sound like fundamentalist puritans, but he was pulling words out of context. David and I did agree on some basic principles during this deployment, because we'd seen many marriages break up over such long separations. I agreed not to drink while he was away (he couldn't drink by military policy), we both agreed to be extremely careful about forming new friendships with people of the opposite sex, and we set boundaries on nonprofessional interactions with people. These were not hard-and-fast rules but simply wise considerations we had gleaned from military families facing long deployments.

Still other publications ran with this false narrative. In "Nancy French, David's Wife: Five Fast Facts You Need to Know," number two was "When her husband was in Iraq, she wasn't allowed to use Facebook or email men."[25]

Sure, it was irritating, but the accusation was so dumb it didn't matter. However, the next time I posted on social media the trolls came out in full force:

- @DavidAFrench u bullied your wife @NancyAFrench and treated her like a whore. i would have trusted Nancy if i was lucky to be married 2 her—Matt Heath, June 2, 2016
- @NancyAFrench @DavidAFrench It is tough. Is it worth it 2 b locked in a closet while hubby runs around making an ass of himself?—cool gloo, June 2, 2016
- @NancyAFrench @DavidAFrench hi David I'm talking to your wife online—reptoid, June 2, 2016

Now that the nation was paying attention to us—and the media knew where we lived—we had to leave our sweltering apartment. It would take a week to secure one of the nicer apartments, so we relocated to a Park Avenue hotel with a doorman, three bedrooms, its own washer and dryer, a pool, a working air conditioner, and no nude Iranians. (A hotel can't have everything.)

David wasn't the best candidate. We knew that. But no framework existed—not even emotionally—for evangelicals to consider supporting a candidate outside the GOP. While we thought they might jump at the chance to support a candidate without serious moral flaws or accusations of sexual misconduct, that was not the case. For the past three decades, the "religious right" was firmly ensconced in one political party, and not even a rape allegation was going to change that.

Just as journalists, party leaders, and politicians weren't thrilled with David being floated as an alternative to Clinton and Trump, neither were evangelicals. We'd thought many Christians were simply holding their nose to vote for Trump. Turns out, they quite liked him.

Americans frequently wring their hands at their political options. "Surely, these aren't the best America has to offer," they say. "How do we end up with these people?" I was beginning to solve that mystery. Anyone who would voluntarily endure this process had to be insane.

We received some kind, public encouragement. "I know David French to be an honorable, intelligent and patriotic person," Mitt Romney tweeted. "I look forward to following what he has to say."

This fueled the fire even more, and the media scrutiny increased.

What did David have to say? Was he going to run?

I had no idea.

———

Our lives were being uprooted, undermined, and mocked, and David was growing more and more wary of accepting the third-party presidential slot. He called me from Vermont and told me he didn't feel like Clinton or Trump should be president, but he also didn't want to be the Ross Perot of 2016. He knew he couldn't win the presidency but could glean enough votes from vital states to be a spoiler.

"I'm not going to run," he said into the phone.

As news of David's potential candidacy spread like wildfire, the GOP—as predicted—circled the wagons. Even though House Speaker Paul D. Ryan had refused to endorse Trump, he formally endorsed him.[26] Senate Leader Mitch McConnell endorsed the GOP candidate in an interview. "He's not going to change the platform of the Republican Party, or the views of the Republican Party," McConnell said. "We're much more likely to change him."[27] Reince Priebus said those involved in the independent effort were "embarrassing themselves."[28]

When David confidentially told Malcolm and the other political strategists he wasn't running, they were crestfallen. However, they encouraged him to have one more meeting with a gaggle of people from many other former campaigns who were coming to meet us in New York the next morning. Maybe we could help create another party for the future? Maybe we could use this moment to reflect on the inadequacies of a two-party system?

Reluctantly, we agreed to this meeting, and I scurried to find something to wear. The next morning, we walked into a conference room at our hotel, and energy was in the air. People treated me like I was a celebrity, not a rural Tennessee ghostwriter.

"There she is," someone said. "Our future First Lady."

I stopped right next to the coffee service cart. What was happening? People introduced themselves after taking the red-eye from California. A documentary filmmaker showed up. Why go to such lengths to meet with a guy who was *not* running for president? The nation's eyes were on our family, since David had not officially responded to the possible bid in public.

I nodded silently at their innocent accolades and supportive words, unable to speak. All of these high-ranking operatives had canceled everything to come to New York. They seemed to have come under the false pretenses of getting new jobs on the David French campaign. They'd been tricked to get them to this meeting, and so had we.

I'm not sure of the motive. Maybe Malcolm hoped David would see all of these potential teammates and change his mind. Maybe he wanted to launch a different third-party effort. Maybe he wanted to continue the drama. Regardless, these people had been deceived, and I was furious.

For a long time, I'd believed evangelical Trump supporters had lost their collective minds. But #NeverTrump fervor could be as irrational. These strategists were so committed to undermining Trump, they'd do it at all costs. My family's reputation was acceptable collateral damage to stop Trump.

When the meeting began, Malcolm spoke in lofty terms—about America and the untenable condition we found ourselves in, about how we needed to forge a new path.

But David did not participate in the ruse.

"I am not running for president," David interrupted. Malcolm's face reddened at the direct proclamation, but people immediately got out their phones and furiously texted. The news was about to break, and David needed to get in front of it.

We left and David quickly sent an essay to *National Review* formally declining to run. He didn't have time to wordsmith since reporters everywhere were ready to pounce on any new developments. After he published the article, all the chaos was over.

The next morning, the streets were remarkably desolate when we tried to hail a cab to LaGuardia. Having been rejected by liberals, conservatives, the GOP, and the #NeverTrump strategists, we were utterly alone.

I scanned to the right and to the left, hoping to say goodbye to our lone, bikini-clad supporter, but even he was nowhere to be seen. I guess I shouldn't have been surprised. Angels, as well as all of our perceived political allies, had a way of disappearing.

24

THE RALLY

S o, anything going on in the news lately?"

My Trump-supporting client and I kept abreast of every political development relating to the presidential race, and the only news was that my husband believed Trump was so unacceptable that he almost ran for president.

"Not much to speak of," I said.

Silence.

Under normal circumstances, my client would have asked me to write an essay or an article for her speaking out against this unknown Tennessee lawyer attempting to challenge the GOP front-runner. But she knew me. She knew David.

Words cannot adequately describe the discomfort of my husband almost running for president while I worked for Trump's main supporters. Etiquette books did not cover this, and I was left to navigate it alone.

Though my clients knew we weren't "enemies of America," they didn't like us criticizing their candidate one bit—especially since many of their futures were interwoven with Trump's success.

If he was elected, they might receive political appointments. If he was elected, they'd have a seat at the table of power. My clients viewed me more as a fly—an annoyance that they couldn't swat away—ruining the potential feast set out before them.

One client called me immediately after all the drama. "I want you to know I support you." She was a huge Trump promoter and a Fox News personality, so this was a surprise.

"Really?"

"This is not about politics, this is about friendship," she said, "and you and me? We're friends no matter what."

But not all of my clients reached out. Some moved on without any confrontation or discussion. They stopped calling because they knew I could not write what they needed me to write. Though I disagreed with their political endorsement of Trump, I cared for them and watched from afar as they traveled with him on the campaign trail, made speeches for him, and sang his praises on television.

Others took a different route and confronted me over my stance.

"You and David are actively hurting Trump's chance at winning. You have a binary choice," one told me. "You gonna vote for Hillary? No, so quit bellyaching about it."

"I'm not voting for Hillary *or* Donald," I clarified.

"Well, not voting is a vote for Hillary."

"Do you believe that?" I asked.

"I do."

"Should I go ahead and vote for Clinton then?" I didn't wait for him to respond. He and I both knew he didn't want me casting a vote for the Democrat. It's not that I didn't value the privilege of voting. Rather, I valued it so much I wasn't going to use it to honor either of these unacceptable candidates. Supporting bad candidates was a guarantee we'd keep getting bad candidates, so I decided not to comply with either of the two options the parties handed down to me. Not voting, for me, was an act of speech—a way to send a message.

"So not voting is not the same as voting for the other candidate?" I asked. "Apparently, one is better than the other?"

This awkward dance between my clients and me was clumsy, and I stepped on a few toes. However, I eventually achieved some level of peace with my various clients.

Except one.

A larger-than-life media personality and pundit had hired me to write his book well before Trump was a viable option. Now—in the middle of writing the book I was contractually obligated to finish—he was a conductor on the "Trump Train" while David and I were "Never Trump" vagabonds. Because this client was forceful and opinionated, I was worried this contention might threaten the book. I braced myself for the moment when we'd have to acknowledge the "GOP elephant" in the room, but—as brash as he was—he never brought it up. He talked to me like nothing had happened, like David hadn't almost run for president, like we weren't suddenly on opposite sides. Since our political differences seemed irreconcilable, avoidance—though a bad relationship strategy—was an acceptable occupational one. If I did my job, it would soon be over.

"Hey, change of plans," he told me one autumn afternoon over the phone. "You know how you were going to come hear my speech at that Reagan Dinner in Kansas? Well, Trump asked me to introduce him at a rally in Colorado. He offered to fly me from his rally to my speech so I could do both." He paused, and added—more slowly, "On his plane."

He said the last part with such a forced casualness that I knew he was trying to hide his excitement about Trump's tricked-out homage to *Air Force One*. "Since you're stuck with me," he laughed, "I guess that means you get to ride on it too."

A few months ago, David was on every television channel explaining why Trump was an unsuitable option for Republicans. And now I was planning on attending a MAGA rally and flying on Trump's jet. Life was a lot of things, but it was not dull.

Within a week, I found myself waiting in line for a Make America Great Again rally. The people in line were dressed like it was the Fourth of July—red, white, and blue clothing. Funny, patriotic hats. Vendors sold American flags, signs, and shirts with Hillary Clinton's scowling face.

As I waited in the line, I chatted with people. Mothers with children on their hips. Fathers with eagle-themed T-shirts. In some ways, these were "my people"—they could've been in my family, in my neighborhood, in my church. But I felt an ever-widening gap between us. I felt counterfeit. Hatless. My insides churned as people stomped photographs of Clinton into the pavement with their snakeskin boots.

A group gathered on the lawn carrying a sign with a gigantic face of

Hillary with a portion of Revelation 17 written beneath it: "Babylon the great, the mother of prostitutes and of the abominations of the earth."

I'd gone to church my whole life, but what was all this?

One young man carried a sign which read "Bill Clinton is a rapist." And an older man carried a sign that had a photo of a young, smiling Hillary Clinton standing next to Vince Foster, the White House deputy counsel during the Clinton administration. He was yelling, "What really happened to Vince Foster?"

Foster died via suicide, causing many to speculate the Clintons had murdered him. (Both Attorney General Janet Reno and Kenneth Starr investigated Foster's death and concluded Foster committed suicide.)

"The Clintons happened to Vince Foster, that's what," the man carrying the photograph yelled as people high-fived him.

I'd cut my political teeth on the Mitt Romney presidential campaign bus, which was like riding the trolley in Mister Rogers' Neighborhood. Everyone was good-naturedly engaged in thoughtful conversation and maybe drinking chocolate milk.

But this atmosphere was not like your typical church potluck. It had the energy of a rave, but the drug animating the fervor was not ketamine or LSD. It was hatred. My "journalist" press pass was in my pocket, and I kept it there.

"Why *can't* I take a gun into this rally?" Someone pointed to a posted sign. "Ever heard of the Second Amendment?"

The police officer looked straight ahead, eyes on the hundreds of people shouting and chanting. They had overbooked the venue, and thousands of people who'd signed up would be left outside. Violence felt like it might erupt at any second.

"Trump believes in the Second Amendment, so this sign seems a little odd to me," the man continued. "You know, for a Republican rally."

"Get in line," the cop said.

People in front of me and behind me chanted "USA" repeatedly as the excitement outside the arena reached a fevered pitch. When the doors finally opened, people ran inside, jostling to get the best seats. Three thousand people made it into the arena, but a couple of thousand were left outside.

I went to the press section, which was partitioned off with metal bars like we were zoo animals. Huge American flags hung on the walls.

Once people settled in the balcony, people chanted.

I listened to the words, and finally made out that—over and over—a hundred or so people were screaming, "The whore of Babylon." Chill bumps raised on my arms. It was unnerving to feel so much unmasked hatred.

Another group yelled, "Lock her up! Lock her up!"

I watched all of this from the elevated platform labeled "Reserved for Press," which felt like wearing a "Kick Me" sign during elementary school recess. People took one look at us and yelled, "Fake news!" Others hurled profanities.

Then a friendly face peered over the railings. It was one of my client's friends, who'd been assigned as my "handler" for the week.

"Hey, do you want a selfie with the next president?" He smiled. "Before everything starts? You could show it to your grandchildren one day."

I considered what these future grandchildren might say if they saw a photo of Donald Trump and me. How would history judge this man? How would they judge me?

"Thank you so much, but I shouldn't leave," I said. "The rally is about to start."

"Oh, okay." He looked disappointed. "Cool about Trump's plane. Take photos. I heard the fixtures are twenty-four-carat gold." He shook his head and left to get his own photograph.

Finally, it was time for the rally.

"Dear Heavenly Father, we come confidently before you," a speaker prayed, "because we know that Donald Trump's righteous goals for America line up with your Word." After the prayer, the crowd said the Pledge of Allegiance and sang the national anthem.

The crowd cheered as my client strode on stage. He was larger than life and strode back and forth. Every eye was on him.

"Are you guys ready to kick the door down to vote for Donald J. Trump?" he asked. What a curious question. Why would an American need to kick a door down to cast a vote in a peaceful election? The imagery felt at odds with the democratic process, but the crowd hollered. Energized by their enthusiasm, my client compared Trump to George Washington, Abraham Lincoln, and—even—Martin Luther King Jr.

The crowd raised their fists in the air. "USA! USA! USA!"

I put my head down. Trying to prevent my eyes from rolling felt like I might be harming myself. I didn't need to broadcast my dismay at this sort of rhetoric, but I did need to figure out how to live as a conservative political writer and fulfill my contracts now that my tribe considered me a traitor. I pasted a blank look on my face and watched the stage.

Rudy Giuliani—introduced as the "Mayor of the World"—came to the podium, and the crowd erupted into cheers and chants. This led to Lee Greenwood's voice drifting out of the loudspeakers. Everyone seemed to be proud to be an American as they belted out this famous song, phones aloft in the air in their attempt to catch Trump making his way onstage.

"There's nothing better than a Trump rally," Donald Trump said when he finally made it out to the microphone. "Or safer." This strange addendum was because fistfights had broken out at a few of his rallies. Nonetheless, people loved him. They cheered, they laughed, they clapped. His rambling red-meat speech lasted for forty-five minutes.

When he was finished, a song by the Rolling Stones blasted across the arena: "You Can't Always Get What You Want." A strange song selection, but it worked for me. I was not getting what I wanted in this year's presidential contest, and I figured many other Americans felt the same way.

After the rally, I made my way to the front of the crowd. My client, invigorated, smiled when he saw me. "Ready for the *Trump Force One*?"

I had forgotten the Trump campaign had nicknamed their plane a moniker echoing *Air Force One*, but of course they did. And I had to admit, I was curious.

My client rubbed his hands together. "I guess ole Donald must've really wanted me to introduce him," he said as we were driven to the airport, "to go to all this trouble."

By the time we drove out to the runway, the sun had gone down. A small, twin-engine aircraft—not even a turboprop—waited for us.

"Is this," my client lowered his voice, "is this the 'Trump plane'?"

Apparently, we were flying in the equivalent of an old VW van. It was ancient—maybe thirty years old—and I half expected the interior to be covered in shag carpet.

I took one look at it and surmised this was a more accurate representation of the man's character and promise-keeping abilities than the twenty-four-carat gold showpiece we expected. I crouched and climbed into the plane. Was this jalopy safe? If this plane went down, people would see it on their television screens and say, "Yeah, that plane didn't look air worthy." However, my client climbed in behind me, and I was stuck.

"Have fun listening to the next president of the United States back there?" If he was disappointed in our plane, he did not indicate it.

"It was an experience." The pilots turned on the engine and took us into the air. Though I attempted to interview my client by getting two inches from his face and yelling questions, my recording device could not pick up our conversation over the deafening engine.

The sun had gone down and the plane was dark and cozy, but mostly I felt trapped. I closed my eyes, listened to the engine, and made a vow. Once I fulfilled my contract, I'd never put myself into this position again. I would never attend a Trump rally. I would never be on a Trump plane—fancy or otherwise. I would never be here—whatever this was—again.

When we arrived, a car was waiting to take us to the next rally.

"Ready to settle up?" the pilots asked.

My client looked surprised. "Donald told me he'd take care of it."

They looked at each other. "Well, he didn't." Though Trump often portrayed himself as a working-class messiah, he was notorious for not paying contractors. I pretended not to notice my client surreptitiously handing them his credit card, but I was embarrassed for him and for our party.

At the Reagan Dinner, I sat at a table with my client as he was glowingly introduced and strutted to the podium. His speech detailed Hillary Clinton's many failures before he switched gears.

"That's what I don't get about Never Trumpers," he said into the microphone. The audience laughed at the way he spat the term. "They refuse to get over their egos and put their country first."

Was it my imagination or did he look in my direction?

The crowd applauded, and I looked at my dinner plate. Ever since

David's name was floated as a possible third-party candidate, the conversation surrounding the Never Trump movement was getting a lot of attention.

After an hour, he walked off the platform to thunderous applause. People approached him for autographs. Finally, our rickety plane was ready to take us back to my client's hometown. But before we left, a man who worked for a famous radio personality pulled us aside in the lobby.

Apparently that radio guy was wavering on whether he could continue to support Trump.

"This Never Trumper movement is dangerous. That David French guy—the one who almost ran for president?—he won't shut up, will he?" He rolled his eyes.

The staffer had no idea I was married to David. He assumed, since I was there with my client, we shared the same views, that I was his assistant, that I was "safe." Or maybe, since I was a ghost, he didn't see me at all.

My client loved this and waxed eloquent about Never Trumpers' lack of patriotism, occasionally stealing glances at me to see if his comments struck as intended.

On the plane ride home, my client looked at me sideways. "You survive?"

"Oh, I've been to a lot of those Republican dinners," I said nonchalantly. "The chicken was delicious."

The old, loud, rickety plane left the ground. After witnessing the adoration people had for Trump and the contempt they had for half of America, I knew I'd made the right choice in rejecting him. I knew—even as my bones rattled in this plane—that I was not stuck.

When I got off this plane, I would stay off it—and the Trump train. And I would never ever put myself in this position again.

WAFFLE HOUSE CONFESSIONS

G rowing up in rural Tennessee, I was more likely to hear someone dealing with their anxieties by shooting squirrels off the porch than seeking counseling. Preachers derided "psychology" as a dangerous brew of self-indulgence and extrabiblical, heretical teaching. When David and I got engaged, we refused all premarital counseling and navigated our lives like everyone before us in the history of the world: without professional assistance.

But by the time we were raising Naomi, I had begun to see its value and went to counseling to learn how to parent an adopted child in a trauma-informed way. I filled out an intake form: name, birthdate, medications, the reason for my visit. But my pen hovered over one question: have you ever been sexually abused?

I hadn't come to talk about me. I'd come to talk about Naomi. Still, I checked the box "yes," with no intention of bringing it up. For several months, I received parenting tips but my counselor eventually broached the topic.

"On your intake form," he said, "you mentioned you'd been sexually abused." My cheeks flushed red. "Do you want to talk about that?"

"Is it relevant?"

"It might affect you in ways you don't realize."

By this time, I'd gotten used to counseling and was willing to talk. However, when I opened my mouth, the words wouldn't come out.

He waited.

"It's not a big deal, really," I said.

"What's not a big deal?" he asked.

We sat in silence until he threw me a lifeline. "Here's an idea. Go home, write it on a piece of paper, and bring it in next week. I'll read it, and you don't have to tell me." This suggestion wasn't preposterous, since I was a writer. But still. It felt intrusive.

"Write out what happened and how it made you feel," he said. "We'll deal with it next week."

After my session, I drove to Waffle House, ordered an omelet, and opened my laptop. Writing has always been a safe place for me to say anything, and I figured writing it in such a public space would make it more palatable. Words flew onto the screen as easily as insults from the lips of my waitress to her cook. As she berated him for undercooked hash browns, I jotted down the basics.

But as I wrote, accusatory words bounced in my head. *He didn't do anything wrong. You caused this. You enjoyed it. You deserved it.* I wasn't able to catch them to properly evaluate their veracity, but they filled me with dread.

"Another coffee cup, please?" A customer held a mug to the waitress. He was wearing a MAGA hat and a T-shirt emblazoned with a gigantic eagle superimposed over the words, "One Nation, Under God." "Hold the lipstick stains?"

He caught my eye and gave me a what's-wrong-with-these-people look. I withheld the approval he sought. I used to work at the Huddle House, where—at least weekly—I'd take a lipstick-stained mug away from a customer who thought it had never happened before.

I had something else to worry about. My assignment was to write about what happened and how it made me feel. I'd documented the first part. Now, how did I feel?

I tried to remember. I thought of the confusion I'd had when he'd shown interest, about the grief I felt when he lost interest and moved on like nothing had ever happened.

Sexual abuse robbed me of my ability to think correctly about such things, to feel the right things at the right times. It awakened me to things I shouldn't have known. My home—which should've been a place of comfort—became a place of abuse. Everything about me changed: my outgoing personality turned bitter; my innocent faith turned skeptical. I hid what I was feeling—first as a way of hiding the relationship, then as a matter of habit. Everything settled around this abuse-masquerading-as-romance, until I was unrecognizable from the girl who'd made pinkie rings out of butter cookies at vacation Bible school.

The waitress thudded another cup in front of the MAGA-hat-wearing customer. He took a sip of coffee. In the past, I might've felt a connection to this stranger. I was a Christian Republican, too, after all.

But why was the party of "family values" rallying behind the guy who made a Playboy cameo? Hadn't Trump bragged on video about doing to women what the preacher did to me so many years ago?

"This is how men talk," prominent evangelicals said. "Let him who is without sin cast the first stone," said another. But I didn't recall that sort of rationale during the Clinton years. Had they objected to him only because he had a (D) by his name?

The "religious right," which I'd defended my whole life, had abandoned the posture of "family values" when they had the chance to gain a seat at the table. It confused me to hear the values preached from the podium but ignored in real life. It was all a lie, and so was the "lesser of two evils" myth. Coffee Cup Man was proud of his candidate or he wouldn't be wearing that hat. Lipstick stains are unpleasant, but moral stains are more dangerous.

By the time I'd left Waffle House, five cups of coffee later, I'd created an essay that revealed my sex abuse and lamented the state of our political affairs. Something about the process of writing it down made it slightly more manageable. Plus, I suddenly felt desperate to talk to my fellow Republicans about what we were doing to the party of Lincoln. I was tired of sitting in the MAGA crowds and going along with it. David had spoken out, and now I was ready to speak out, too.

A woman dressed in a Waffle House uniform pulled into the parking lot. I watched as she moved a car seat into a waiting Jeep, the toddler crying when she handed him over.

"Sorry I'm late." She burst through the door, an unlit cigarette in her hand. "But Kevin didn't pick up the kid like he promised. Probably out all night."

Anytime anyone had a problem at Waffle House, you couldn't help but be drawn into the drama. Her manager, a man with a tattoo sleeve, flicked his spatula. "You deserve better than that shit."

I deserved better than this shit, too. And American women deserved better than the two options of Trump and Clinton.

My story broke out of its emotionally sealed box. My counselor was right. All of this was related. I buttered my toast and kept writing. I'd spent my whole life pretending I had not been hurt. I'd never let anyone see me cry, never admitted I'd been humiliated, never asked for sympathy or pity, never let anyone know I was a victim. Even the word *victim* carried its own stigma in my mind, a contempt predicated on shame. All of that was my own feeble attempt at creating a shell of protection. But at Waffle House, for the first time in my life, I documented the truth.

"My party—which should've been a place of a certain set of values— now shelters an abuser," I wrote. I ended my story by asking Republicans to please—please—consider what their support of Donald Trump would do to conservatives like me who had been victimized.

When I finished, I did not obey my counselor's request. Instead of printing it out and bringing it to my next session, I decided to publish it. I was conveying an important perspective, one I hadn't seen in major newspapers. Though many liberal women had expressed distaste for Trump, most conservative women stayed quiet. I decided to publish my article anonymously, which would get the message out there without any personal embarrassment or risk.

That evening, I submitted it to the *Washington Post* and heard back immediately.

"This is powerful," the editor replied, "but we don't do anonymous articles. Are you okay using your name?"

I shut my laptop to make the question disappear. Though it had felt invigorating to write the piece, did I want the label of "sex abuse victim" to follow me for the rest of my life? Would people believe me? Would people in my hometown know who my abuser was, even though I didn't name him? What would my parents say?

For hours, I turned the editor's question over in my head, but my story—both with words and in print—was connected to me like a rubber band. As I tried to get it out, it bounced back to snap me into silence.

It was the rubber band of shame, but what did I do that was shameful? I'd always eschewed the label "victim." No one wants to be a victim, and I didn't either. That's at least part of the reason I didn't tell adults about my abuse. It's why I didn't tell that junior high counselor. It's why I didn't raise my hand in my class at NYU when the professor asked who'd been victimized.

The word is culturally loaded with shame and blame. No one wants to have a "victim mentality," a catchall phrase the culture uses to encapsulate some Eeyore-ish "poor-is-me" mindset. An article in *Psychology Today* characterized people with a "victim mentality" as social "vampires" who are "allergic to taking responsibility for their actions." Additionally, "I refuse to be a victim" entered our lexicon and subconsciouses, and we applaud anyone who proclaims it. The NRA even used "Refuse to Be a Victim" as a title for one of their self-defense programs.

But by tossing the word *victim* in these phrases, people unwittingly lump victims into a category of people who should've done something different, who could have simply "refused" their victimhood, and—at the very least—should get on with their lives without being such a drag.

These phrases stigmatize into silence, because they demonstrate a lack of empathy for the suffering and a toe-tapping impatience for people who've been hurt. Though it might feel empowering to proclaim, "I'll never be victimized again," that's a promise we can't make. We can't even promise our kids they won't be hurt, as even the most fastidious parents can't protect our children from the world's evil, barbed intentions.

Our impatience with sorrow and trauma has seeped into our language and into our culture, so that a victim might hesitate to identify as one. Sometimes I see victims of horrific abuse describe themselves as "survivors." Fine. However, that word has an embedded positive spin designed to, yes, empower the afflicted. But more often than not, it's used as a benefit to the listener, to gloss over the evil that was done to make everyone within earshot feel better about the world.

In high school Latin class, I learned that the word *victim* comes from the Latin word *victima*, which means a living being killed and offered as a sacrifice to a god. That seemed about right to me. The Republican Party worshiped the god of political expediency. Once political power became their idol, they lost control. Mitch McConnell seemed to think that the Republican Party would change Trump, not the other way around. But the party had unknowingly ceded too much ground. Idols have a way of gaining power over their acolytes, and they always demand sacrifice—often women and children.[29]

I am a victim, but being a victim is not the only thing about me and not the primary thing about me. It's a part of my story, and I no longer was ashamed of what happened.

When I asked David for advice, he told me he supported my decision either way. With his support, I put aside my reservations and published this alarm bell to help save the Republican Party I'd loved my whole life.

I decided to use my name, and the article was published the day after I hurriedly wrote the piece in Waffle House. The headline read, "What It's Like to Experience the 2016 Election as Both a Conservative and a Sex Abuse Survivor."[30]

I had presented an offering to the world, everything I'd hidden that no one knew even existed. Why was I able to write such a personal story for public consumption? Was it because I could imagine people all over the nation reading it? Was that the greatest privacy? Like an actor on stage looking into a packed house, unable to make out the individual faces?

My phone buzzed as a reader tagged me on Twitter. It buzzed again and again. Hundreds of people—many of them Democrats—left encouraging comments under the article. In fact, it went viral, an eventuality for which I wasn't emotionally prepared. Days earlier I wasn't even ready for my counselor to know the truth, and now I'd announced my abuse to all of America.

The publication broke the walls within me. The facade of "compliant female Republican" fell and shattered into a million pieces. I swept the remnants into a corner, knowing I'd burned this bridge and would never need them again. I took a moment to enjoy being my true self, even if that true self was a defiant political troublemaker. A rock thrower.

Okay, here I am, I thought. *This is me. Take a good look, conservatives. Look at the wreckage of my life and see if you can ignore it.*

I'd lose all of my political clients, but I wanted to cross that Rubicon. Some of my clients were shocked, but so were even my closest friends.

"I've known you for twenty years," one friend wrote. "Why didn't you tell me?"

A bouquet of roses appeared at my door, with a kind note from another sexual abuse victim. Also, I received many notes of kind encouragement, especially from other survivors of both political persuasions.

But I had to deal with another unanticipated consequence. With every passing minute, my inbox was flooded by messages from complete strangers who told me their own stories of abuse. They were painful and horrifying. Readers reasonably assumed I was more emotionally healed than I was. Who'd publish such an account if they hadn't already moved past it? No one knew this was supposed to be a jotted sketch to show my counselor for the first time ever.

The hundreds of abuse stories, even though they were supportive, put me in a place of despair. People were sharing sacred pain, and I wanted to respond. But what to say? I had no wisdom, nothing to say other than "I'm so sorry."

With all of this out in the open, I felt worse than ever. I walked around in an almost catatonic state. I didn't talk. I didn't move. I wanted to sleep all the time.

"Are you okay?" David asked gently.

I was not okay. I felt exposed, vulnerable, and ashamed. Every action, every small movement, took concentration: *I'm going to put one foot on the floor. And another. Now I'm going to stand up. Just a few steps to the sink. Okay, I'm going to turn on the water. I'm going to brush my teeth.* Some days, I didn't even accomplish all that. The day moved in slow motion, yet I could not keep up with it.

A few days after I published my article, I walked into counseling—carrying a copy of the article, weighing me down like a cannonball.

"Did you get around to writing what we discussed?" he asked.

"Yes," I said, placing the article in his hands.

He looked up in surprise.

"Okay," he said. "This isn't the way people usually go about it, but we can work with this."

As much as it hurt, I didn't regret publishing that article. After so many years of silence and shame, I needed to do something dramatic to yank me back into the land of the living. And I was back, sort of.

I still had to put one foot down. And another.

But before I knew it, I'd taken a big step toward healing.

THE CANARY IN
THE COAL MINE

O ne candidate I really dislike is going to win tonight," David joked as we settled down for the long election night. We were in downtown Nashville with some evangelical leaders and friends who'd opposed Trump. No matter which way the election went, we felt like America was losing something.

Around six o'clock, David looked at me. Hillary was winning the popular vote—we later learned she would win it by almost 2.9 million votes, receiving more votes than any other defeated presidential candidate in our nation's history. But around eleven o'clock, Trump took Utah. Ten minutes later, he won Iowa.

Other than people in that room, almost every single person I knew had voted for Trump.

As America's Christians let their voice be heard, had I made the right decision to reveal my sex abuse? I'd hoped the article would dampen evangelical Christians' enthusiasm for him. Sure, it was only one *Washington Post* piece, but we were dealing with such slight differences in the polls. If the article could've changed a few people's minds in key states, it might have helped. But it didn't.

The slight margins sparked another question. Had David made the right decision about running for president? He would not have won. But he could have possibly taken enough margin in states like Pennsylvania to have changed the results of the Electoral College and the course of history. Hillary would have become the next president, and what was happening on our screens before us would be quite different.

Had he made the right decision? We'd have to wait to find out—I didn't want Hillary to be president, but I wasn't sure under Trump's leadership that the nation would be okay. Before Trump was announced the victor, we left and drove home. We hoped—for the sake of our nation—that Trump could be a good president.

When Trump took office, MAGA Republicans said David's protests about Trump were ineffectual and worthless and that my *Washington Post* piece was indulgent. Since we'd taken a stand against the man who now sat in the Oval Office, we were going to be pushed to the edges of political conversation and the "true conservatives" would finally have their moment. Many friends angled for a position in the government, and an excitement energized the Republican stalwarts.

We'd been a part of the conservative movement for so long, and suddenly we were the uncool people standing outside the car, telling people not to climb into a vehicle with a drunk driver. I still felt like a "true conservative." When asked why I didn't support Trump, I always responded, "I'm too conservative to support him." But now Trump Republicans viewed us as either traitorous or liberal or both.

Now that Trump was president, David continued to call "balls and strikes." This meant sometimes official White House communications quoted David at length. Other times, Democrats promoted David's criticism of the president. David's critics from the right never saw his criticisms from the left. His critics from the left never considered his criticisms from the right. Both sides seemed to equally hate him.

I rarely got involved in local politics. But when my little sister ran for president of the Williamson County, Tennessee Republican Party, she asked me to cast a vote for her. When I got to the door of the community center, the person at the front desk looked at me sideways. "Nancy French," she said my name slowly. "Are you even a Republican?"

I paused and bit my lip. In the state of Tennessee, we didn't have to commit to one party to vote. When I decided to split with the GOP over

Trump, there was no membership card to burn. I simply drifted away, or the party drifted away from me. I woke up one morning and I was far, far away from the place I'd always been. This woman was trying to make sure that everyone who voted for the county leadership was a member of the GOP. That sounded reasonable. Wise, even.

But I didn't know how to respond. I'd written several books for Republican politicians, written barn-burner speeches, traveled to Fox News to allow my clients to "own the libs," and briefly lived with Sarah Palin. I was married to a pro-life attorney who served his country in uniform. I supported the troops, was for limited government, and loved God.

"No," I told her, "I don't suppose I am."

The Tennessee Speaker of the House—a friend of my sister—walked by and saw the interaction.

"Oh, hello, Nancy." He smiled at me. Then to the lady, "This is Nancy, Mary Kate's sister. She and her husband are great conservatives. Come on in."

This man, because of his position in the GOP, had the power to simply usher me into the hall. I knew a little about him. He'd already attempted to file a lawsuit to force Barack Obama to produce a copy of his birth certificate. He'd already rallied for Trump. Little did I know that—within a few weeks—he'd lose his powerful position in the state of Tennessee. Racist and sexist memes in a text thread would be revealed. His fabricated evidence against Black activists in Tennessee would emerge. The FBI would raid his offices.

However, getting inside the inner halls of the GOP required his stamp of approval. That seemed about right.

I'd spent years attending, sponsoring, and working at Republican gatherings and conventions. I'd organized straw polls. For years, I was on the speaking circuit, delivering speeches to Republican women across America, sharing the stage with Rudy Giuliani. Now I didn't even meet the basic requirements for entry. "I shouldn't be here," I told him. "I'm no longer a Republican. That lady was right."

"Oh, sure you are," he said, waving at my sister across the room. When he got her attention, he said, "Look who I rescued."

He was offering me a lifeboat. *Sure the election was rough, but we're all conservatives here. We're all southern. We're all Christian. This is your tribe. There's no one else. What are you gonna do, be a Democrat? We'll still accept you if you simply stop making such a big deal out of all your objections.*

I lived in one of the most Republican areas of America. My neighborhood is what the *New York Times* calls a "bubble area," since 85 percent of my neighbors are Republican. It was not easy to casually befriend Democrats, because I rarely ran into them. It was like I'd taken a stand against what was happening in the GOP, Jerry Maguire–style, except no one was coming with me, and I wasn't able to leave the office building. I was left there, holding a goldfish, saying, "There is such a thing as manners, a way of treating people." I knew I looked insane.

But in 2017, I realized Trump was not the actual problem. He was merely a canary in a coal mine, an early indicator of the danger that was already all around us.

"Hey, quick favor." Ethan had the manner of someone who was about to run out the door. "Can you write me an endorsement for Judge Roy Moore? He's running in a special Alabama Senate race."

"No, no, no," I said. "Do not endorse Roy Moore."

"Why?" Ethan and I had disagreed on several issues, but every time one of these issues came up, it was surprising. Ethan usually embraced conflict because he believed it was important for people to work out personal issues in order to have true friendships. Though we'd had many heart-to-heart conversations, these did not move the dial for us. We still disagreed and were in conflict over an ever-growing list of issues. "He's the guy who put up the Ten Commandments in the courtroom, right? He's one of us."

Judge Moore had erected a two-and-a-half-ton monument of the Ten Commandments in the rotunda of the State Judicial Building, and used taxpayer money to maintain it. Eventually, a federal district judge had the display removed, but not before many evangelicals rallied around Moore for his "religious persecution." But his two-and-a-half-ton monument was neither wise nor constitutional. Judge Moore was a blight to true religious freedom.

"He's the kind of guy who poses as a warrior for Christian virtue, but he damages the culture," I said. "Wolf-in-sheep's-clothing type thing."

Over the hour, my client kept peppering me with questions. People, politicians, and pundits in his circle were rallying around this Alabama judge, and he wanted to endorse Moore as well. However, my client knew that David was a First Amendment expert who had worked for religious freedom for years. It was hard for him to believe we were soft on this issue.

"I'm saying this in the strongest way possible," I said. "He's bad news. You will regret an endorsement. I'm watching out for your brand."

Eventually, he relented, and our relationship stretched even thinner. I had exceeded the limits of the acceptable amount of pushback for a ghost. Two clients took my advice not to endorse Moore, but others endorsed him wholeheartedly.

Within a few months, however, multiple women accused Moore of unwanted advances and sexual assault when he was in his early thirties and they were in their teens. I knew his Ten Commandments posturing was enough to disqualify him, but even I was shocked at these allegations of abuse.

Leigh Corfman, fourteen at the time she said Moore abused her, said, "I felt responsible. I felt like I had done something bad. And it kind of set the course for me doing other things that were bad."[31] After her life spiraled "with drinking, drugs, boyfriends," she attempted suicide two years later. In fact, she didn't come forward earlier because she worried that her three divorces and poor financial history would make people doubt her story.

Her quote lodged in my soul. That's how sexual predators work. They attack the weak, make them weaker, then discredit them because of their weakness. They go on to bigger and better things, leaving a collection of wounded people in their wake.

Now that these victims were speaking out, I felt like I should support them. I wrote an article in the *Washington Post*[32] and appeared on NPR's[33] *All Things Considered*. Most of my clients were Roy Moore endorsers or fans, and they were beginning to see me as a liability. Ghosts were supposed to be invisible, nonthreatening blank slates. Yet there I was in newspapers and on the radio saying things that made people uncomfortable. I was uncomfortable too.

I spent many hours talking to my clients about the allegations, which they seemed keen to dismiss. I never convinced their staffers, who were always trying to prove their conservative *bona fides* and be more strident than the next guy to impress "the boss."

Moore attempted to address this situation by saying he'd "dated a lot of young ladies." Though he denied abusing the fourteen-year-old, he didn't deny dating teens when he was in his thirties. Eventually, Donald Trump and the Republican Party reaffirmed their support.

"I don't see what the big deal was." A friend grabbed me after church to discuss Moore. "Back then it was common for people to date younger women."

"Were you not alive in the 1980s?" I was incredulous. "It *was* weird for a thirty-year-old to date a fourteen-year-old. I remember. I was there."

Another church member told me Moore was a "man of God," that Alabama would be lucky to have him as a senator, and that I was harming the gospel.

Though I'd been dismayed at the rise of Donald Trump, he was not the GOP's main problem. He was simply an indicator that something was dangerously off. And the tone-deaf, calloused response to abuse kept coming up.

The next indication that something was wrong was when President Trump nominated Brett Kavanaugh to fill a Supreme Court vacancy, and Dr. Christine Ford accused Kavanaugh of sexually assaulting her in high school.

Conservatives, once again, had a choice. They could have listened to the evidence presented in the hearings and moved on from there based on the results. However, Republicans had a knee-jerk, defensive reaction. Many argued Kavanaugh's guilt or innocence was not important. They argued he'd done so many good things since high school, this should be a nonissue.

But victims who've been abused by clergy, the wealthy, or the philanthropic are frequently assured their predators are overall "good people." How much money does a person need to donate to a women's shelter to make up for striking a woman in the face? How much for a rape? Who determines the value of innocence? Who determines the price to be paid?

I believed Supreme Court justices—and presidents—needed to be held to a high standard. As much as I wanted good conservative justices, I still did not believe we should simply overlook possible sex abuse to get what we wanted.

I sank into despair. Professional pundits mocked and dismissed Dr. Ford, a posture which made sex abuse victims feel invisible and irrelevant, and so did my friends from church. The message from the GOP was clear: if "one of our own tribe" abused women, we don't want to know.

But couldn't we spend a little time trying to figure it out? With every mocking post or tweet, my own emotional wounds opened wider. As this drama unfolded, I wrote another article for the *Washington Post*, saying I had no idea whether Dr. Ford's accusation was accurate—the hearings had not yet been conducted. However, if they were, none of Kavanaugh's subsequent good deeds could wipe the slate clean.

I held my breath with the rest of America during the hearings. In the middle of the hearings, a *Time* magazine reporter reached out to me for comment. I didn't want to comment on Kavanaugh's guilt or innocence because we were only partially through the evidence, but the circus filled me with a dull ache. I anticipated her asking me about the merits of the evidence. She didn't. Instead, she apparently heard me sniffle.

"Are you crying?" The kindness in her tone took me off my talking points. "What's going on emotionally for you right now?"

It was hard to watch this hearing, where so much emotion was laid bare. And apparently, others felt this despair too. The National Sexual Assault Hotline experienced a 147 percent increase in calls on the day of the hearing. But this is the quote I struggled to give her: "As a sex abuse survivor, you're marginalized your whole life—like no one is listening to you."

That's it. That's all I said, but it was enough. A writer for *American Greatness* named Julie Kelly read this quote and decided to try to destroy me.

"OK—Nancy French screwed around with her preacher when she was a teen," Kelly tweeted. "Again, ladies: Your personal experiences have nothing to do with this. And shame on you for exploiting it to help destroy a decent man."

That tweet was a punch in the stomach. I wasn't trying to destroy Kavanaugh. In fact, I repeatedly declined to speculate on the veracity of the claims, deciding to let the process work out. To discredit me, Kelly used the common tactic of the alt right: cruelty. She sexually weaponized her insults instead of dealing with my actual arguments. Though, by now, I was familiar with these tactics, Kelly's attempt at silencing me was well beyond normal political discourse, even by today's polarized standards.

Her followers called me "the seducer of preachers." Once again, people online were discussing me sexually, mocking me sexually, and humiliating me sexually. This was the price conservatives wanted me to pay because I wrote a *Washington Post* article? Yes, according to Kelly, I deserved all of this.

"If you exploit your personal experiences—including adopting a baby—to score political points, you have no moral high road," she tweeted. "And if you use it to smear a SCOTUS nominee for attention, you deserve blowback."[34]

What did my comments on the Supreme Court hearings of Brett Kavanaugh have to do with the fact that we had adopted a baby? Again, the attacks never made sense because logic was never the point. They were after complete and total emotional evisceration and would strike at the tenderest parts of my story.

I tried to shut this out of my mind, but my attempts were like trying not to hear the dripping faucet. I knew, every second, someone would read that I had seduced my preacher. Someone would believe that. The haunting, accusatory words came back to me. *He didn't do anything wrong. You caused this. You enjoyed it. You deserved it.* But now they weren't amorphous self-condemning thoughts bouncing around in my head. They were now a part of the national discourse. They were now a part of Julie Kelly's Twitter feed.[35]

Alienated and humiliated, I folded into myself in my attempt to keep the world out of my head. I'd been mocked online before. People have told me I sound like Barney Fife, that my teeth look equine, and that I'm fat, stupid, and morally preening. I've been harassed by White nationalists and threatened by extremists. But nothing prepared me for the laserlike hatred of some conservative pundits.

By writing about my own abuse in the *Washington Post*, I'd revealed my soft underbelly. I'd made myself vulnerable. I'd expected some sort of pushback, some sort of criticism. But I had not anticipated that people would blame the twelve-year-old me for seduction. I'd shared my story, hoping people would understand why a conservative like me could not support

Trump. I presented myself to the world, hoping they'd at least hear my political perspective, even if they disagreed with it. But I overestimated my audience. They didn't read my article and attempt to know me. They read it and saw an opportunity to sexually humiliate me too.

David made sure people knew about this writer's attacks, but some conservatives yawned that their friends had taken the side of the pedophile. These were not "fringe" conservatives. Many of our friends whom I'd met at Alliance Defending Freedom gatherings of Christian journalists and activists—and even one of David's *National Review* colleagues—sided with Julie Kelly. They even helped her promote her book.

My political home both shrank and expanded. My formula for determining the good guys and bad guys became more complicated. I could no longer claim Republican churchgoers were good, and everyone else was suspicious. Especially since most of the people who showed me support were Democrats.

My heart could no longer perform my job. I'd worked out a truce with my clients that I could write "general conservative" articles without writing about Trump. But suddenly, it all felt shallow and weird. Sure, maybe conservatives have the better take on taxes, but their lax opinion on pedophilia sort of mitigated any sort of intellectual advantage. I would no longer prop them up.

In a job where "an edge" is required, I'd lost mine. I could no longer blast the Democrats, many of whom had shown kindness to me during this debacle. This caused problems with my clients who wanted zingers.

"I don't know, Ethan," I said during one conversation in which he had asked me to write something that conflicted with how I perceived political reality. "This isn't right."

"Well, maybe you shouldn't work for me if you disagree with every single word I try to say." Ethan was impatient. He'd tried to make this work with me, believing if we could iron out our differences we would both come out stronger. But this chasm between us could not be traversed.

I still don't know if I was fired or if I quit, because I responded, simply. "You're right." We sat in silence on the phone for a few seconds, said words I don't remember, and it was over. And my long-standing relationship with this client—and friend—came to an end.

I had gradually lost so many of my friends and colleagues, but Ethan was the worst one because we'd tried so hard to make it work. He was my last "holdout"; however, our disagreement couldn't be resolved, couldn't be worked out, and also couldn't be ignored.

Also, I wasn't great at my job anymore. Political pundits usually want hired assassins, someone to make their political point with as much memorable punch as possible. Instead, I'd tapped out. I'd hung up my gloves.

And now that Kelly had sexually humiliated me over differing views on the next Supreme Court justice, the last little bit of fight drained out of me. I'd naturally been a person who was ready for some verbal sparring, ready to engage in rhetorical battles. A previous iteration of me would've weighed in on Twitter, would've clapped back, would've fought. I would've presented myself as bulletproof and swooped in with a righteous fury.

But I had none of that. This new version of me had no defenses. I'd told my story, and now I felt I'd never be strong enough to fight back anymore. I'd revealed my true self, and my fellow conservatives had found me contemptible.

I sank into this new landscape without a tribe, without backup, without a political home.

"Do you think you'll have friends after all of this?" a friend asked.

"Maybe," I said. "But they're going to be totally different friends."

27

NORDSTROM

Don't peek."

Naomi looked at me and laughed. She knew I'd grabbed her yoga pants at the Nordstrom Rack and hid them under my jacket in the cart. Even though I never told my kids that Santa Claus was real, I hid the gifts and wrapped them so they would be surprised on Christmas morning.

"Go over there." I pointed out the accessories department to Naomi, full of Santa earrings, snowman necklaces, and pricey sunglasses. She walked away, and I slid the yoga pants to the cashier. Out of the corner of my eye, I saw a uniformed police officer walk up to her. I hurriedly made my purchase but when the cashier handed me the bag, the officer was already standing next to me. He was holding her arm.

"She claims you're buying her yoga pants?" the officer asked.

"Yes, sir," I said. "She requested them for Christmas."

Naomi looked at her shoes.

"What's the problem?" I turned to him in an attempt not to look intimidated.

"Yoga pants?" His voice was laced with incredulity, as if he doubted Black people did yoga. He leaned over and opened my bag. I'd never had my bags searched at a department store, but I had nothing to hide. I felt the eyes of other shoppers on us as the officer inspected my purchases. "Rudolph the Red-Nosed Reindeer" was playing over the loudspeaker.

I knew what was happening. He'd suspected a Black child of stealing jewelry, apprehended her, and came to check out her story. I wanted to model appropriate behavior toward a police officer to my daughter, in case this ever happened without me. In case she was in one of those situations that go bad, the types of situations that have been caught on viral videos. I wanted her to see me react respectfully. Quietly. Calmly.

But I wasn't calm. Would an outright confrontation relay to her that this mistreatment was unacceptable? Or would it set a bad example? I kept my mouth shut. He pulled out the yoga pants and held them up to the light. Finally, the officer stuffed them back into the bag. "You can go."

Even though we hadn't done anything wrong, it felt embarrassing that an officer had suspected us of stealing.

"Hey, so let's talk about what happens if a police officer approaches you again," I said when we got into the car. I squeezed the steering wheel and exhaled. "You did great today. Just remember to maintain eye contact, don't have any sudden moves, and be polite. *Yes sir, no sir.*"

She nodded and eyed the bag with her "surprise" Christmas gift. "Is it okay if we admit I know you bought me yoga pants?" She smiled.

"Guess there's no reason to pretend anymore." I handed her the bag and she feigned surprise. We drove home and told our family at dinner what had happened. Otherwise, we kept it quiet.

Later, I heard a storyteller[36] encouraging people to tell their stories of racism to build public awareness and help keep Black people safe. Or at least, it would show them they weren't alone.

Inspired by his story, I went to Twitter and created a tweet thread[37] of what happened at Nordstrom. I didn't have many followers, but Nordstrom contacted me via message and soon I was emailing with the store's manager.

"Thank you for providing feedback about your experience in our Nordstrom location. The experience you described is embarrassing and against everything we hold dear to our Nordstrom culture."

By looking at my receipt, I determined the day and time of the incident, which allowed the manager to determine which officer had been working at the time.

"Thank you for this information. I will be sharing your story with my entire leadership team and address this in the strongest terms. I can also assure you this employee does not work for our company any longer."

For years, I'd worked for clients who did not support Black Lives Matter. I'd investigated this organization on their behalf. I'd read about the founders' goals of disrupting the nuclear family. I'd read about their demands to let domestic terrorists go free. I'd agreed with my clients that this organization was questionable even if their slogan seemed innocuous enough.

But now—suddenly, in spite of my reticence—I'd joined the cause. Not the organization, but the cause. Surely all Americans could agree on this cause.

In May of 2020, I was sitting at our kitchen table when David came from his upstairs office.

"Something terrible happened in Minneapolis," he said. "I watched a video of a man named George Floyd who got arrested for using a fake twenty-dollar bill. The police officers . . ." He stopped, getting choked up. "One had his knee on the man's neck for nine minutes. Floyd kept saying he couldn't breathe, but the police officer wouldn't move his knee from his neck. He died. This is really bad."

Soon, the video went viral, and the world was outraged by Floyd's killing. Protests broke out all over the globe.

A few days later, my son Austin—who was now nineteen years old—told me a protest would be held in honor of Floyd in Nashville. "I'm going."

I wasn't sure if this was a good idea. Some protests had become violent, and cities were under siege.

"It'd be a shame if the only people who cared about George Floyd's death were Black."

He had a point. By this point, conservatives were decrying the Black Lives Matter organization and not dealing with the tragedy of Floyd's death. Some even maligned him in their refusal to acknowledge what was happening to our Black friends and neighbors. After all, their White neighborhoods were safe, so what's the big deal? Their reverence for police prohibited conservatives from looking honestly at what was happening. Though I still believed the claims and demands on the original BLM website to be misguided, the movement had morphed from its radical nature into a collective sigh of despair felt by many Americans. But most people who adopted the "Black lives matter" language were simply terrified by what was happening to Black Americans. And I was more concerned to show my love and concern to Black Americans than I was concerned about failing some sort of ideological litmus test with conservatives.

"Can I go?" Naomi asked.

David and I sought counsel from friends and family. David would be out of town, so would it be wise to take our twelve-year-old daughter to Nashville's rally? Most of our friends advised us not to take her because these rallies might attract racists. But we decided I would take her anyway.

We wanted her to experience what it's like to take racism on—to go on the offensive, with her family by her side, surrounded by people who stood with her. No doubt she'd eventually encounter racism alone, but we wanted her to be able to confront it with her family supporting her. We wanted her to learn how to fight, or at least brace against, evil.

On Friday night, we stayed up late making T-shirts and signs. One sign had the Tennessee seal as the "O" in the word "LOVE." Another we painted red, like the MAGA hats, and wrote "Make Racism Evil Again."

"If any violence breaks out," David texted me from out of town, "I want you to leave immediately."

The next day, we attended the rally and listened to the speakers: the mayor of Nashville and several state senators—all Democrats. When a scuffle broke out, the crowd chanted—"We want peace!" More than four thousand people attended the event, which was simultaneously filled with goodwill, disappointment, and grief.

When people marched, someone yelled out the names of African Americans who've been killed by police brutality. The crowd yelled back, "We will not forget." Others chanted "f—k Donald Trump," "hands up, don't shoot," and "no justice, no peace, no racist police."

I pulled Naomi aside. "The 'hands up, don't shoot' chant is based on false witness accounts. Also, we do not say 'f—k' anybody."

Suddenly, I heard a loud sound behind me—not loud enough for a gunshot, but the protesters, already on alert, scurried. A person had thrown a brick at one of the Nashville buildings, but the glass held.

The protesters came to a stop in front of the Metro Nashville Police Department's Central Precinct, where my late uncle had worked. Bricks flew through the air and hit the windows.

It was time to go. The police came through in riot gear.

"We need White allies!" someone screamed. My son—who was a high school football player—volunteered to help make a human barrier between the cops and the African American crowd. But I saw other White people pushing an officer, throwing bricks, and smearing horse excrement on a police car.

"Don't do that," a Black man yelled at the adult, White troublemakers, explaining that people would blame the Black protesters. "Y'all ain't f—ing grown."

People screamed at officers, kicked their horses, sprayed them with water, and hit them with full water bottles. A brick bounced off a window and hit an officer in the head. Some blew marijuana smoke in the police officers' mask-covered faces, taunted female officers about their children, and called Black officers "traitors." The visibly upset officers stayed in formation and did not retaliate.

We left, and the riot escalated. The mayor issued an emergency order, police issued a curfew, and our governor mobilized the National Guard. Order was quickly restored, and the Ryman Auditorium—a sacred place for country music fans—suffered only a single broken window. Only one person was eventually arrested for setting fire to our historic courthouse—a twenty-five-year-old White male.

It was poignant to walk past officers as the crowd yelled "f— the police" repeatedly. In a time of national angst, it was good to remember how much freedom we have and how many police still show admirable restraint and discipline.

But that notion wasn't a comfort to George Floyd or the millions of people mourning his loss. Because it was obvious from that horrific video that went viral across America. He—with his hands in cuffs and an officer's boot on his neck—couldn't brace himself against evil.

28

COUNTING TO TEN

A few months after my 2016 *Washington Post* article, people began sharing intensely personal stories of abuse and tagging them with the hashtag #MeToo. I read a few, then scrolled, then read some more. But the hair on my arms raised. My heart sped up. All of these people sharing such intimate stories felt dangerous. When I'd shared my story, I'd been eviscerated. Who was going to help all of these people when the haters showed up? It didn't take long.[38]

Rude, insensitive, trauma-ignorant comments appeared beneath these stories. Critics derided the hashtag and movement saying that victims were lying, attention-seeking, or just whores. I'd never used the hashtag, but the pushback made me feel as thin and insubstantial as wax paper. The world was not a safe place for abuse victims, and I feared this ridicule might send all these women right back into a spiral of shame. When people I knew started posting insulting comments under friends' #MeToo posts, it sent me into despair.

Yet one by one, these women—individually, collectively—demanded to be heard. Though this was inspiring, I'd made up my mind. I would not re-engage on the topic of sexual abuse ever again. I would scroll past this cultural conversation.

But even as I tried to ignore this phenomenon, the world didn't. Miraculously, people paid attention. Victims revealed a lifetime of wounds, and—one story at a time—the movement changed the conversation surrounding abuse.

With #MeToo becoming a cultural movement, a publisher contacted me and asked me to write a book about abuse in the context of the church. Newspapers asked me to write articles. Two prominent Christian denominations asked me to help on their newly created abuse task forces. I said no to every opportunity.

I was still being mocked online as the "seducer of pastors," people were posting fake pornographic images of me, and people on Twitter were bragging about having sex with me. Plus, I felt like walking into a church to talk about abuse—where my abuse had originated—might undo me. I cheered for (and feared for) the women brave enough to speak out, but I had no more fight.

These decisions were not great for me financially. Writers are supposed to write, but—for the sake of my emotional health—I couldn't write a word. My occupational options seemed to be shrinking by the day.

I *had* written some books that were blessedly free of politics. I worked with "America's favorite Bachelor" on a book that allowed me to go to a live ABC televised wedding. I'd written a book for a mother who forgave her daughter's killer and pursued restorative justice. I'd worked with an Olympic gold medalist from the bleachers of a training center. I'd worked with a Chinese political dissident who fled as Communist agents attempted to kill his baby *in utero*.

However, I was mostly known for political books, and—once you're in a lane—it's hard to switch. Most of the people who contacted me for books were related to the Republican political world, which led back to Trump. I could still theoretically write for conservatives—I was one, after all—but most conservatives didn't want a writer with so much political baggage. Having me associated with their books might make conservative book buyers hesitant. I understood the game and took a step backward. Ever since I was contractually obligated to finish a book that eventually landed me at a MAGA rally, I was completely forthright at the outset of any potential project. I never wanted to be in that position again. Of course, these awkward conversations ended in the same way—without a book deal.

People frequently criticized David and me for being "grifters," for opposing Trump because of the money. But our stance cost us dearly. Without a college degree, I had limited occupational options. Though I was able to pick up a few nonpolitical books, quitting the GOP screeched my normal income stream to a halt.

With three kids' educational needs, I needed to make money in a different way. I went online and filled out applications for jobs that had nothing to do with politics. I applied for any jobs that might require good writing skills. I applied to work in communications, marketing, and corporate correspondence. After applying to several different organizations, only one called me back. And that, I soon learned, was a curiosity call. I could tell my interviewer wanted to find out why on earth a person who had five *New York Times* bestsellers was applying to help an electricity company with brand management. I didn't get the job. I didn't get any job.

I must've been grifting wrong.

One morning in October 2020, I received an email from Gretchen Carlson. She was Fox News's former morning show host who sued Roger Ailes, the founder of Fox, for sexual harassment. She became a crusader against nondisclosure agreements as she spoke out about what she experienced. When I wrote my *Washington Post* article about my abuse, she emailed me and explained that she'd read my article on the train and it had made her cry. When I saw her stand up to Roger Ailes, I emailed her explaining that I supported her and was inspired by her stance.

"Your name came up yesterday." She'd heard about a Christian camp in Branson, Missouri, called Kanakuk where horrific sexual abuse had been happening—all hidden from unsuspecting parents by NDAs. "Let me know if you can look into this," Gretchen wrote, "and I appreciate you and your bravery."

I didn't want to look into this, and I wasn't brave. However, I didn't want to admit my hesistance to Gretchen, who was standing up to an entire multibillion-dollar media organization alone. Though I'd declined offers from publishers, newspapers, and denominations asking me to write about abuse, the least I could do was look into this for her.

Gretchen emailed, asking if she could connect me to a woman named

Elizabeth. "Sadly, her brother was abused at Kanakuk as a child," she explained. "And he committed suicide last year."

My fingers hovered above my keyboard as I processed this request. The last thing I wanted to do was talk to a grieving sister about pedophilia and suicide, but I agreed to take that call. If this woman had lived through her brother's abuse and death, I should be able to live through a conversation about his abuse and death.

When I finally talked to Elizabeth, I expected an emotionally charged conversation. Instead, her manner was professional and businesslike. In a calm voice, she told me that the Christian leaders who ran Kanakuk had turned a blind eye to red flags for years. The camp caught a predator nude with children during basketball, swimming, and riding four-wheelers. Parents called to complain about this abuser's behavior—describing how he encouraged boys to disrobe in front of him. Even worse, a young camper witnessed him abusing another camper.

As she described the details, I couldn't concentrate. The story was complicated, foggy, and hard to follow. Plus, I didn't want to absorb the details and planned to expunge them from my mind as soon as I'd made enough of an effort to appease Gretchen. I tuned back in to the conversation.

"Kanakuk didn't fire this guy. Instead, they promoted him. And that was just *one predator*." Elizabeth paused for me to consider the scale and scope of abuse at this camp. The way she told it, the abuse was massive, ongoing, and being covered up by camp leadership. "Anyway, an investigative journalist should look into all this."

"If what you're saying is true, this would be one of the largest evangelical sex scandals against children in American history," I said. "And no one's ever even heard of it."

"Exactly."

"Are the same people leading the camp today?"

"Yep." She waited for me to catch up.

"So . . . campers are still at risk."

"Twenty-five thousand children are coming to camp in," she paused, "seven months."

I felt a throbbing in my throat.

She also told me the camp used NDAs to silence victims and to keep all of these abuse stories out of the press. "This meant my brother wasn't comfortable describing his abuse to his therapists," she said. "Victims are taking this secret to their graves. My brother's not the only one."

"If the victims talk to me as sources, they'd get sued." I was processing the difficulty of this task aloud.

"And you will too, but you could help victims get their voices back."

I wasn't keen on a multimillion-dollar camp in Branson suing me over people I didn't know. Plus, I was a college dropout, not a journalist. If I took this job, I'd be doing it on my own—without pay—since I didn't work for a publication. And since the money had gotten tighter since I stopped ghosting for politicians and pundits, this would be a move in the wrong financial direction. Something needed to be done, but I was not the person to do it.

"If the camp hadn't ignored all of these red flags," she said, "my brother would still be alive."

I considered this and decided to help, albeit in the most minimal way possible.

"Alright," I said. "I'll try to find someone to help you."

Over the next few days, I contacted everyone I knew in journalism. However, they questioned the camp's significance in the broader, emerging story of Christian abuse. They didn't understand why a camp in Missouri merited scrutiny. No one had the resources for such a large investigation, especially if the camp was litigious.

Soon, two things became glaringly obvious. First, if half of what this grieving sister shared was true, this story would be a bomb in the evangelical world. Second, if I wanted someone to investigate Kanakuk, I'd have to do it myself.

"Are you sure you want to get involved in this?" David asked. He'd seen me after my *Washington Post* article and didn't want me back into that emotional morass.

"No," I said. "But if the camp knew of this superpredator's behavior and hid it, kids are in danger."

I sought advice from my counselor, who listened to the details and furrowed his brow. "It echoes your abuse. The Kanakuk abuser taught about sexual purity while he was abusing children. Your VBS teacher taught about sexual purity while targeting you. Not to mention the suicide element."

He was right. This topic had haunted me ever since Jacob constantly threatened to kill himself to keep me around. It put me on edge, made me nervous, and especially made me want to avoid the topic. If I investigated this, I would not be avoiding it. And I might even be making the situation worse. Dredging this into the public spotlight might retraumatize victims and possibly even cause more death. "It'll be hard," my counselor said.

"I don't want to do this," I told him. "It's hard, complicated, and outside my professional wheelhouse. I'm no journalist."

But when he tilted his head, without saying a word, conviction descended on me. I processed aloud.

"When Conrad abused me, none of the adults in my congregation intervened. Maybe because it would've been too difficult. Too complicated," I said slowly. "And here I am, a grown adult, thinking the same thing."

He nodded. I kept thinking of all the kids who were heading to Branson that summer. Just as I wished someone had intervened and kept abusers out of my vacation Bible school, someone needed to intervene and keep abusers out of Kanakuk. But it seemed there were no other someones. There was only me.

I vowed to give it a month and hand my work off to real journalists. "But I won't use my name, because I don't want to forever be tied to this abuse," I told Elizabeth. "Not even in footnotes."

———

"What does 'off the record' mean?" I did a Google search.

Though my ghostwriting work taught me to pay attention to details and corroborate facts under public scrutiny, I had no idea how to pull off an investigation. I read about the distinctions among "on the record," "off the record," "on background," and "on deep background"—and combed through comments on blogs mentioning Kanakuk, searching for people on whom to use my new interviewing skills.

The comments were rich with sources. People mentioned more abusers and identified as victims. Some people were forthright and adamant—one posted her full name and phone number. Others were cryptic, offered scant details, and used fake names.

One heartbreaking pseudonymous post was by someone claiming to have been abused at Kanakuk. I read his post over and over, trying to figure out who he was, where he lived, how to get in touch with him. He was frustratingly difficult to find. When I googled his username, however, I found someone on a Japanese anime site who went by the same handle. On a hunch, I joined the anime site, tracked down that user, and sent him a message within their system. I feared that jumping through all of these hoops to contact him might scare him away, but I felt like I could understand more if we had a conversation.

"Are you the same person who had information about Kanakuk back in 2009?" I sent via the anime site. "I'm investigating this and would appreciate if you could tell me what happened to you." He didn't respond, and I had no way of knowing whether the anime site user was the same person who'd posted about Kanakuk years ago. After a few days, however I received an email with the subject "Kanakuk abuse." It was short and to the point, but the first words will forever dwell in my soul—they lodged there permanently and I'll never unsee them or be able to erase their impact.

"I've been waiting eleven years to hear from you."

A chill went down my spine, and tears filled my eyes so much I had to wait to respond. The victims were like Hansel and Gretel, leaving breadcrumb clues, hoping someone would pick up their trail. They didn't care that I wasn't a professional journalist. They just wanted someone to hear them, to believe them, to find them. I would keep searching.

I created several Excel spreadsheets to keep track of what I learned. One was for victims (and included the dates, locations, methods of abuse as well as the name of the abuser) and one was for people who were suspected victims who later died via suicide. When friends casually asked me what I was working on, hoping to hear about the latest celebrity-book gossip, my answer was less glamorous and more dire. I figured most wouldn't know about this camp, but people had intense reactions when I told them about my investigation.

"What?" a friend said, her eyes wide. "I sent my kids there. But that's a Christian camp." People seemed to think the "Christian" designation would protect it from evil—or at least from my scrutiny. It was easy enough to believe people in Hollywood abused kids, but no one would even consider this would happen at a Christian camp.

"But the camp's CEO spoke at Promise Keepers rallies," another said. "He's a friend of James Dobson." Another asked, speaking of one of the most successful Christian music artists, "Isn't that the camp that Michael W. Smith sent his kids to? Doesn't he write songs for this camp every year?"

All of these people were correct. The camp's CEO was "evangelical famous"—a man who spoke at Promise Keepers rallies, Liberty University convocations, and wrote a ton of books published by Focus on the Family. Many celebrities were associated with the camp or its leaders by endorsing the CEO's books, writing forewords to his many study guides, sending their kids to the camp, and singing the camp's praises in public—including Amy Grant, Michael W. Smith, Steven Curtis Chapman, Tim Tebow, and Lecrae.

These people had given Kanakuk cultural prominence and credibility, so my fellow Christians were shocked that I was investigating the camp.

"You're being led astray," said a Christian friend, a former vice president of a huge Christian relief organization. "The CEO of Kanakuk is Joe White, and he's one of the best Christians on the planet. Throughout his life, he's not only been spiritually strong, he's physically strong." He went on to describe this man's ability to lift weights.

It was such a strange conversation. The level of praise would've felt more appropriate for a North Korean citizen describing Kim Jong Un. The man told me he flew his children on private jets to meet with the camp's CEO for one hour. "I wanted my kids to see his spirituality, his faith in person," he said. "If just some of his goodness would rub off on them, the trip would've been worth it."

During our long conversation, he told me about the attributes of this wonderful Christian man. But never—not once—did he ask me, "Hey, so why do you think Joe is involved in a massive sex abuse cover-up?" Not once. He simply said I was wrong and should not look into it.

"And by the way, have you talked to him as Matthew 18 encourages?" he asked. He was referring to a passage that encourages Christians to work out their disagreements in person and in private to preserve the peace of the church.

I had to admit, I hadn't. "But I'll fly to Branson and sit down with him to speak to him in person if he'll agree to it." Not only would this be spiritually good, it would be journalistically good. We could sit down, I could ask him questions, and he could clear up any misunderstandings.

After I sent an email, the camp declined my invitation citing the CEO's health issues. He was too sick to even receive visitors, the camp explained. However, a few days later, I saw on Instagram that he was about ten miles from my house performing a wedding.

When I mentioned this to my friend who admired Joe White so much, he shrugged it off. "Well, he's been very sick," he said, "So it makes sense he can't travel to see you."

"But he's ten miles from my house," I said. "He's traveling. Plus, I offered to travel to see him."

Nothing added up, but people's confidence in the camp's inherent goodness was unshakable.

The next week in church, I was about to walk to my seat when a person caught my arm and whispered, "I heard you were investigating Kanakuk. Just a quick word: our church is full of people who love the camp. They're *very* powerful in the Christian world."

Was that a warning?

Over and over, I got the same message: you're on the wrong track. Stop now before you go too far. The way people spoke about the camp was how I imagined some people used to talk about the mafia.

They're good people. Cross them at your peril.

———

I planned to pass the information I learned to other journalists. However, no matter how much evidence I collected, I couldn't get any professional journalist to take interest in the case. Without other options, I kept investigating alone.

On my report card as a kid, teachers always checked the "talks too much" box. Now I decided to use this character flaw as an asset. Around the clock, I talked to victims, witnesses, and even convicted pedophiles.

Some were eager to unburden themselves, while others wanted to prove their innocence. Some were reluctant but their reticence softened as we developed a rapport. I patiently waited for my sources to meander around their own guilt, trauma, and shame on their way to telling me what they needed to tell. Others wanted to pursue justice, even though they risked social alienation if their assistance was ever made public. Most people were vaults, and it took me months to find the right key to unlock their information. Eventually, I had more than three hundred sources in my phone labeled "Kanakuk," and that did not include the people I reached out to via Twitter, email, Facebook, texts, Instagram, and in person.

I became friends with victims, offered a listening ear to guilt-stricken parents, and laid conversational traps for clever sources trying to protect the camp. Just as my grandfather mined for coal, I mined for information. However, he attempted to avoid the explosions of the dynamite. I was hoping to find something to blow this case wide open.

After months of work, I knew the narrative, but there were missing links in the evidence. I had to show readers proof, to remove any doubt.

"I'd help you, but you don't have the guts," the father of one victim told me over the phone. I learned he had a thumb drive that had all of his son's court information on it. If he handed over that thumb drive, I'd be able to prove what I only suspected. But first I had to earn his trust.

"The camp is litigious," he said. "They legally threatened us."

"Wait, what?"

"They tried to force us to sign an NDA and sanction us for speaking to the media. They didn't even want my son to give his testimony at church," he said. "We had to spend tens of thousands of dollars to protect ourselves. They'll sue you, I guarantee. And you'll back down."

"I won't back down," I said.

"Plus, you don't understand the scope of all this," he said. "My son's abuse affected the whole family. Because we were so concerned about putting him on the right track after Kanakuk, we ignored his brother. Abuse affects entire families, not just the victim. I'm afraid if we cooperate with you, it'll be like opening Pandora's box. I'm afraid my other son might have to relive the trauma, and—honestly—I'm afraid it might kill him."

This shook me to my core. The idea that my work could destablize traumatized families haunted me when I laid down at night. And this man's statement activated the part of me that had worried about inadvertently causing Jacob's death. However, by this time, we'd been talking for three hours, and it was time to get off the call.

"Look, my husband, David, sued the Obama administration, the Trump administration threatened us, and then he joined the army after 9/11 and sat knee to knee with al-Qaeda terrorists," I said. "We are not afraid of a Christian camp director in Branson, Missouri." I wanted to put it as clearly and directly as possible. "And if it came down to it, I'd be honored to be sued by Kanakuk on your behalf."

He paused, and I thought I'd convinced him. I hadn't.

"I need to look you and David in the eye." This man might be the most stubborn person I'd ever met, but I understood. He feared for the lives of his sons—both the Kanakuk victim and his brother who'd been innocently caught in the blast radius.

By this time, my investigation had gone on a year, and I wasn't even close to cracking it. Though I'd said I wouldn't even put my name in footnotes, I was now conducting the whole investigation alone without anywhere to publish it. What was I doing spending all this time, money, and emotion without a viable plan on getting this information to the public?

David and I climbed on a plane to fly to Texas to meet with this father and his family and try to convince him that he could trust us to stay the course. The meeting was intense and emotional, and the victim's father had his Texas swagger on full display. David and I attempted to show him our intentions and—yes—we looked him in the eye. But even after all of that, this man had been so burned by the camp that he had a tough time trusting us. Again, he mentioned to me that he worried about the life of his other son, who had turned to drugs after all the Kanakuk drama infiltrated his home.

We left without the thumb drive, but by the time we arrived home, he'd had a change of heart. He agreed to let us look at the materials.

When we finally got our hands on this treasure trove of information, I knew that I'd finally done what I'd set out to do. The evidence was buried in sixteen hours of video depositions, damning emails, and so much corroborating evidence that I would never be able to include all of it in an article. I had my smoking gun.

Now I just had to write, but I happened to have a surgery planned. This was inconvenient timing, since I now had a single-minded determination to write this article and expose the truth. However, my investigation had become so all-encompassing that I sometimes missed meals and showers over the past year. Though I was driven by a fierce desire to protect children, I had to take a week's break.

On the day of the surgery, David held my hand as the nurse administered medicine into my IV. As the medicine took effect, it dawned on me. I had not shared my evidence with anyone. Though David helped me get the thumb drive, he didn't know the ins and outs of my investigation. If I died on the operating table, no one would be able to piece this story together.

David smiled at me and squeezed my hand. "I'll be here when you wake up."

"If I don't wake up, my investigation is labeled . . ." I tried to remember the names of my Google documents, but the medicine had already fogged up my mind. The last words I heard before I succumbed to the anesthesia were from the nurse.

"Does she work for the FBI?"

And in my mind, I laughed, because the truth was more preposterous. I didn't work for anyone.

———

"Hello, my name is Nancy French, and I'm investigating the sex abuse at Kanakuk Kamps in Branson, Missouri. I believe you have firsthand knowledge of this."

I paused and looked at the text on my phone. I was texting someone I believed was a pedophile, but I wanted to give him a chance to explain himself. I also didn't want to catch him off guard in some sort of cheap journalistic move. Even though I'd invested months of my life pursuing the truth about Kanakuk, I still wanted to treat all of the people I encountered with dignity. That meant giving them the option of speaking, but not attempting to trick them into a confession. I continued to write my text.

"I am going to call you in 120 seconds. If you would like to talk to me, please pick up. If you don't want to speak to me, I'll leave you a message and you can respond later."

I pressed send and set the timer on my phone. My heart raced. Over the course of my investigation, I had interviewed several pedophiles who had been at Kanakuk and were now in prison. But I'd never caught one myself. I watched the timer count down to zero and dialed the number. I didn't expect him to pick up. The phone rang twice. Then he answered.

"Oh, hello," I said. "I honestly didn't expect you to answer. This is Nancy French."

"Now, how do I know you, Nancy, dear?" He had a charming, folksy voice, and I could not imagine uttering the syllables I had to utter. But I had no choice. I explained what I was doing and then—to emphasize—I added, "To be clear, I'm investigating you. And I should let you know, I've already talked to two of your victims, their parents, and to a Kanakuk leader who heard you confess to your crimes."

This guy was caught and even confessed to abusing a camper, but the camp—instead of alerting the police— moved him to a different Kanakuk-related children's ministry. I was calling him three decades after he should've been arrested. And during those ensuing years, he'd worked at four schools and was now a girls' volleyball coach. To my surprise and his credit, he did not hang up on me.

"Did you abuse these two girls?" I asked.

"I'm busy doing the work of my Lord and Savior, Jesus Christ," he said.

"Do you *deny* abusing these girls?"

"I'm busy doing the work of my Lord and Savior, Jesus Christ."

"I'm writing down that you refuse to deny the abuse."

"Don't put words in my mouth," he demanded, his casual tone disrupted by a flash of anger. Within seconds, he ended the call.

I sat on the bed when the line went dead. My hands were shaking so violently that I stuck them between my knees to control them. I sucked in a massive amount of air and held my breath. I was trying to reset my nerves, but nothing helped. For the next hour, I would shake—from lament, from anger, from grief, for fear. This investigation required all of me and it would take a toll.

My phone buzzed, and I picked it up.

"Hey, this is Carol. Making sure you're still bringing cookies for the concession stand?"

I spent so much of my life chasing down bad guys, tracking predators, writing letters to prisoners, and listening to victims that it was getting hard to switch back to "real life" without serious cognitive dissonance. Every crevice of my life became filled with trauma. And the more I dug in, the darker the situation became. Once, I tracked down a source I'd wanted to talk to for more than a year. But when I spoke to her, the details she provided were so horrific, I dissociated from the interviews and could not hear the information I so desperately needed.

Was I losing my grasp of reality, or is this what journalism feels like? Over and over, I felt trepidation about the whole thing. Having been abused myself as a kid, I still heard the words of my abuser: *Don't tell anyone about abuse. Don't mention this or else.* Every day of this investigation, I had to fight this tinnitus of self-recrimination ringing in my ears. Though I knew it was right to fight for these kids, it filled me with dread.

Plus, over the course of the year, the number of suspected suicides of Kanakuk victims had grown as concerned, grieving parents and siblings suspected their loved ones had been abused and later died. Some victims were addicted to drugs and struggling with suicidal ideation. After we talked, some disappeared for months without responding to texts or calls. I was paralyzed by fear—of the camp suing me, and of not being able to get the story right, but mostly of these sources dying. Not because of me, but I had reopened these terrible chapters of their lives.

One family member of a Kanakuk victim who later died by suicide sent me a piece of art which depicted John 1:5 in beautiful calligraphy: "The light shines in the darkness, and the darkness has not overcome it." I snapped a photo and used it as the cover photo on my phone.

"I won't change this until I'm done with this investigation," I said, thanking her for the reminder. This investigation forced me to face death head-on. But I wasn't defying death, like some warrior strapping on a sword and grabbing a shield. I felt death was wrapping itself around me for the first time since I'd gone through the grief of Virginia's death. It was everywhere, which I should've seen coming. My childhood preacher spoke of it at the end of every sermon.

On Easter, I got a text. It was about the family of the Texas man who reluctantly handed over the thumb drive. The one who didn't trust me that I'd stick to my journalism once the camp threatened me. The one who worried that talking to me might further traumatize his children to the point of suicide. The one who'd made my corroboration possible. The one who wanted to look into my eyes.

His son had overdosed. He was dead.

Overwhelmed with grief, I also felt shame that my investigation might've pushed him back emotionally. I felt responsible, guilty, and powerless. Since I have limited skills, the only thing I could do was help the family write the obituary. Then I hopped on another plane to Texas to once again look this father and mother in the eyes. I owed them that.

I packed my bags slowly. I couldn't figure out what shoes to bring, what clothing. What had I gotten myself into by agreeing to look into this camp? This investigation was well beyond my professional and emotional capabilities.

Plus, I'd done all of this work but had nowhere to publish my investigation. I didn't work for a newspaper, and nationally prominent newspapers were not eager to publish such an enormous and potentially litigious freelance investigation. Since my husband wrote for *The Dispatch*, the magazine's founders Steve Hayes and Jonah Goldberg allowed me to publish my investigation as a coauthored piece with David.

Finally, I could breathe more easily because I knew this information—at least some of it—would be made known. This article turned out to be the most challenging writing I'd ever done. I needed to present a great amount of confusing evidence in a compelling way, do justice to the victims' experiences, and write with perfect accuracy.

In late November, more than a year after I got the email from Gretchen, David and I spent two full days in his office checking and double-checking all of my claims. On the evening before publication, we were still doing last-minute edits when it dawned on me. I was about to drop a journalistic bomb on a multimillion-dollar organization.

"You're going to have to take over," I told David. I held up my hands, trembling so much I couldn't type.

"You okay?" He steadied my hands between his and brought them up to his face.

"I'm second-guessing every single piece of evidence. But I've documented every detail and corroborated it with several sources, right?"

"This is one of the most impressive feats of journalism I've ever seen." David smiled encouragingly.

The next day, we published "'They Aren't Who You Think They Are': The Inside Story of How Kanakuk—One of America's Largest Christian Camps—Enabled Horrific Abuse."[39] Apple News disseminated it across the nation. Hundreds of thousands of readers flocked to the site.

The response from many was thunderous and unequivocable. Democrats, liberals, and progressives almost uniformly expressed the same sentiment: this camp needed to be shut down and investigated by the FBI.

But some Christians were not so supportive. When friends read it, they told me this was "old news," since the main superpredator had gone to prison in 2010. "The camp has done so much good," they said. "This is so unfair, ungracious, and unforgiving to attack people who've brought so many people to Jesus."

My response was always the same. There is no statute of limitations on truth or for individual and institutional accountability. Nobody resigned as a result of the failure to stop a decade of abuse, no disciplinary action was taken against any of the superpredator's supervisors, and Joe White is still the head of the camp today. They still used NDAs against victims and refused to acknowledge their role in allowing this abuse to occur.

I was correcting the false narrative which has circulated about Kanakuk for more than a decade, because I wanted parents to have access to material facts before they sent their kids to worship in the same place where other children were raped. I was not attacking the church, I was protecting children.

I liked to believe Jesus would be okay with that, even if individual Christians—shockingly—were not. Plus, the Christian media, other than repeating my claims, largely ignored the story. I approached *Christianity Today* to see if they were interested in publishing my additional follow-up investigative pieces. I had a good relationship with them, since I'd published a popular article about faith as it was represented on reality television years ago. However, they declined.

"I'd love to work together in the future," wrote the then-executive editor. "I still think about that *Bachelorette* piece as an example of the kind of culture analysis I wish we were doing more of."

This response both infuriated and devastated me. I was wrong when I thought that if I could prove a fraction of what these sources were claiming, it would be a bombshell on the church. "The church"—or at least the mainstream manifestations of the church—didn't seem to care at all. They wanted to talk about reality television, not the reality of abuse.

Conservative Christians who were convinced of conspiracy theories like a White House–led pedophile ring dismissed my well-documented article. A camp enthusiast messaged one victim's family member: #IKnowAndIStillGo.

I'd taken on this investigation because my hometown church hadn't intervened when I was abused so many decades ago. And here I was, asking the Christians to care again about abuse on a massive scale, and they shrugged it off.

I grew up near Kentucky Lake and had heard a saying. "If you see a fish go belly-up in a lake, you try to find out what was wrong with the fish. You see a thousand fish go belly-up in a lake and you better take a look at the lake." I looked at the lake of Christian churches and wondered what was wrong with the baptismal water.

Three days later, a FedEx delivery man showed up on my porch with a package which required a signature. I ran upstairs to David's office, opened the package, and saw a cease and desist letter from Kanakuk's attorneys. Tears immediately filled my eyes, and I couldn't read the document. The camp demanded we "correct" several mistakes in the article within ten days or else they would pursue legal action.

David took the package from me. I regretted dragging him into this. If we got sued by the camp, it would be a huge hassle and financial burden on his publication. I felt woozy, like I might hyperventilate. My hands shook as I handed the package to David.

He took one look at it and laughed. At first, it was a chuckle, but with each "correction" the lawyers demanded, he laughed harder. He read some of the attorneys' objections aloud, barely able to contain himself. David's confidence allowed me to relax a bit too.

"What do we do?" I asked.

"Nothing. These demands are absurd." David tossed the envelope on his desk.

Immediately, I called the Texas man who'd given me the hard drive.

"Remember when I told you I'd be honored to be sued on your behalf? I'm about to prove it to you," I said.

I'd felt bad for victims going through this process with me. After I proved everything I set out to prove, Christian parents still sent their kids to the camp, churches still partnered with the camp, and none of the famous Christians associated with the camp spoke out. My investigation had taken me years, made no societal impact, and now might get me sued.

"I've got ten days to comply with the camp's demands," I explained.

The man, for all his bluster, turned into a gigantic teddy bear. He'd lost so much. "I can't tell you how much this means to me." He was crying. So was I.

Ten days came and went. That's when I realized Kanakuk, like the ineffectual mother counting to ten, was going to do nothing.

Sadly, neither was the church.

29

THE CALL

My phone buzzed as I sat in the waiting room of a doctor's office, continually alerting me of tips about Kanakuk victims, predators, and possible suicides. After the publication of my first Kanakuk article, victims across America learned for the first time of the camp's complicity. Many reached out, eager to share stories they'd held alone for years. I had no idea what to do with this information. Not emotionally, not journalistically. I'd already written my main article about Kanakuk. Was I just supposed to continue investigating this as more abuse surfaced? How many of these stories were there?

"John abused my friend, and I told Kanakuk's CEO about it," one source said. "Joe White didn't call the cops and he's still around kids all the time."

"Steve, a leader for a Kanakuk ministry, took compromising photos of my son when he was a kid," another wrote. "He was never arrested."

"Conrad is working as a high school girls' basketball coach in Kentucky," read a message. "And he's up to his old tricks."

My phone slipped out of my hand and fell into my lap. Conrad? As I was inundated with tips on Kanakuk predators, had I gotten one about my own?

The nurse hadn't called my name, but now I might really need a doctor. I picked up my phone and clicked on the message. My vision narrowed so I couldn't see the tile of the waiting room floor under my feet or the mother

240

holding her newborn. I could see only the message on my phone and the threat it held.

How could this be? My mother had told me Conrad had been arrested for raping the mother of my high school friend Jason. That was a long time ago, but I remember that conversation clearly. How could he now work for a public high school with a criminal record? I wanted to ignore the tip and put this chapter of my life behind me, but I mentioned this to a Kanakuk victim.

"You've given us our voices back," he said. "Maybe it's time to find yours."

That's why—while I was investigating Kanakuk—I opened a parallel investigation of Conrad. I started online. Immediately, I went through his school's Facebook page where multiple videos showed him hanging out with students. On one video, he talked about students' rear ends and laughed, and a chill ran through me. Seeing this man again—hearing his voice and witnessing his larger than life mannerisms—was like opening a time capsule. He hadn't changed one bit, but I had.

Next, I tracked down my hometown friend Jason—whom I'd not talked to in thirty years—and messaged him to call me. Within thirty seconds, my phone rang. Urgency permeated the conversation, and I got right to the point. "A long time ago, my mother told me Conrad raped your mother and was put in prison," I said. "Was that true?"

"Yes and no." Jason explained Conrad had broken into their house and assaulted his mother. "I was going to call the cops, but someone from the church showed up at our house to 'handle it.' Said it was best to deal with such things without law enforcement, said they'd fix it within the church."

I took a moment to process the eerie similarities to the way Kanakuk handled—or didn't handle—abuse. I'd gone to Sulphur Well Church of Christ my whole life, and I couldn't imagine anyone I knew who would cover up an attempted rape. "Who was the guy who came to your house?"

"He was tall, lanky." He paused to try to remember. "Sorry, it's been so long ago. Wait, his name was Jimmy."

It took me a second for this name to register. Jimmy Credell. Our main preacher. The wonderful man who'd taught me about God as a kid. "You're sure?" He was sure.

I swallowed bile rising in my throat. By this time, I was all too aware

241

that Christians shoved abuse allegations under the rug. But was this true of my hometown church's preacher? Was this true everywhere?

I knew I was imposing on Jason by calling him out of the blue and asking him about such a painful incident decades later. But I had one more question. "May I use your name with the police and high school principal?"

"You give them my name *and* my phone number," he said. "I want to stop him."

I did more digging and then emailed the Kentucky high school principal, the athletic director, the superintendent, and a local police officer requesting a meeting. Though my statute of limitations had passed a long time ago, the presence of law enforcement would provide a record in case other victims came forward. Undoubtedly they granted the meeting because I was a journalist and they wanted to avoid negative press.

One week later, I drove down the interstate, gripping the steering wheel so tightly my knuckles were white. I drove through rural Kentucky, past Confederate flags, and onto school property. I was suddenly so very tired, and my eyes grew heavy.

I walked into the high school and sat in a room with the principal, the police officer, and David's cousin Bob, who lived in the same town. I explained I grew up right there in the adjacent county, but this hometown connection did nothing to soften them toward me. Judging from their emotionless eyes, I was the ultimate outsider. Giving up my feeble attempts to earn their favor, I simply described what happened after vacation Bible school and then said what I'd already told them in the email. "The man who abused me is your girls' basketball coach."

Their faces remained blank.

Beads of perspiration formed on my forehead as I described the emotional effect this abuse had on me. I was embarrassed to connect myself sexually to this man even conversationally, but it was necessary to protect the girls in this school. I'd been immersed in abuse stories for months now, but I hadn't spoken of mine. I stumbled over my words. I fought back tears.

The principal's eyes narrowed and she spoke in a monotone voice. "Conrad's popular with the students. Plus, when I got your meeting request, I talked to him about you. Your story and his are different."

David's cousin nodded at me in encouragement across the room. They didn't believe me. They were disregarding my story. I was humiliated. After an hour, I gave up. It was fruitless. They had not smiled at me or been kind to me. As the meeting wrapped, the principal asked me one more question.

"If Conrad had abused you, why didn't you mention his name in the *Washington Post?*" she asked.

"My article was a political opinion piece, not a sex abuse investigation. I couldn't expect my editors in D.C.—in order to publish an opinion piece—to first prove I was abused decades ago in rural Tennessee."

"But you expect to prove it to me?"

The police officer looked at his hands, and the futility of my effort settled on my chest. Now, on top of everything else, I had to explain how journalism worked.

"Conrad has not been formally charged with a crime," I said. "It wasn't possible to name him as a potential suspect in the article. Since I figured you guys were unaware of his past, I came here to alert you. To warn you."

"Why wasn't he charged with a crime?" she asked.

Deep within me, I knew I hadn't done what I should've done to alert the public about my abuse, but I'd only been a kid. My ears burned and my face flushed red with shame.

"Your *Washington Post* article is hardly evidence." She emphasized the word *evidence*. "His name's not even in it. But you expect me to take your word for it?"

But now, after the Kanakuk case, I knew something about evidence. I dug deep into my soul and mustered every ounce of dignity I had left. Then I reached into my folder of documents. "You don't have to trust me. Here's a copy of my *Washington Post* article." I placed the papers in front of the principal and the police officer. They did not pick them up. "I didn't name Conrad in this piece. You're absolutely correct."

Next I pulled out a letter.

"However, this is a signed letter from the current pastor of Sulphur Well Church of Christ identifying Conrad as the abuser in the *article*." Jimmy had retired, but his replacement verified Conrad's abuse with church elders. I placed the letter, written on church stationery, on the table. The principal's eyes remained solely on me.

"Last, here is a statement of a man named Jason. Conrad attacked his mother," I said. "With his permission, I've included his contact information, and he's ready to tell his story."

They knew and I knew: I'd handed them a pile of potential litigation. If Conrad abused someone at the school after this well-documented warning, the victim could sue them for all they were worth. I stopped at the door, turned around, and smiled. "Thank you for your time."

I was able to hold in my tears until I made it to the parking lot and broke into sobs. When I was a kid, I'd done nothing and Conrad continued abusing others. Now, as an adult, I'd done all I could and still wasn't able to stop him. On the long drive home, I felt ignored, humiliated, and embarrassed.

But mostly, I felt betrayed. I kept thinking of Jimmy, my beloved hometown preacher who had now retired. I thought I'd had an idyllic church life—maybe too fundamentalist in their theology, but the people were salt of the earth. Had I been wrong? Had I been living with people who covered up abuse like the leaders at Kanakuk had? The miles ticked by, and I couldn't stop thinking about Jimmy. Though I'd not spoken to him in decades, I decided to track down his phone number from mutual friends and call him. He answered.

"Well, how are you, girl?" There are some sights, aromas, and sounds that bring you back to a certain place and time. His voice—surprised but laced with warm affection—was the sound of my church by the lake, spiritual formation, childhood, and, I'd thought, love. Hearing it broke me wide open. "Great to hear from you."

"I'm calling about Conrad." My voice sounded childlike and feeble, and I didn't know how to soften the awkwardness of this conversation. I had to find out the truth of what had happened so long ago. "I talked with Jason this week. Do you remember him? He went to school with me—a year ahead of me. Anyway, he told me Conrad tried to rape his mom, but the church stopped him from calling the cops. He said someone tried to cover it up." I veered from one interstate onto another, and took a deep breath before uttering the next sentence, which was really more of an accusation. "He said it was you."

I waited but Jimmy didn't respond. He was out in the hay field. I heard a tractor in the distance. I'm sure it took him a moment to transition from farm work to answering a rape cover-up accusation.

"Is that true?" I asked gently. "He described the man as tall and lanky. He said his name was Jimmy."

Just asking the question felt arrogant and disrespectful. I'd been brought up to be respectful of my spiritual leaders, an inclination still firmly rooted in me. Also, I'd been conditioned not to talk about abuse, not to reveal it, not to hold it up to the light to examine it. Feelings of self-recrimination filled my soul, but they stopped as soon as Jimmy said the next words.

"Yes, Nancy," he said. "That was me."

This knocked the breath out of me. I couldn't speak and he didn't either. We let it sit between us for a moment.

"Conrad was always getting in trouble and his dad bailed him out of everything. One day, he asked me to go with him to visit Jason's family. I didn't know what it was about, but I felt this wasn't a normal church visit. Only when I got there did I understand what happened. Conrad's dad was trying to fix the situation, and having me there made it seem like all of that was church-approved. I didn't want to go, and I didn't like it while I was there. I didn't feel good about it at all."

I was surprised that he and Conrad's dad—an elder at my church—covered up an attempted rape. I was even more surprised that he admitted this. He explained that after this happened, he vowed to tell people the truth if they ever asked.

And there I was asking.

I felt a rush of gratitude for someone, finally, talking to me straight. But just as I let the gratitude seep in, I reprimanded myself. I shouldn't be thankful that a preacher told the truth. That's Christianity 101. I should be angry—outraged—that he covered up this attempted rape in the first place, letting Conrad go to continue harming more people. But the anger had drained from me years ago. Now I had only a deep and abiding grief. Tears filled my eyes, and I cleared my throat to steady my voice.

"But you have to understand," he continued. "The first meal I ever ate in this county was with Conrad. He was about table height." I imagined Jimmy using his hand to show how tall Conrad was. He always used his hands during sermon illustrations. For one moment, I let myself imagine being a kid on a pew, Bible opened in my lap, hanging on every word the preacher said. I was still hanging on his every word, but now for different reasons. "I've watched him grow up."

"You watched me grow up," I said. "Did you know Conrad abused me?"

"I did," he said. "And the others." He said Conrad abused approximately twelve to fifteen other victims in his congregation. *Fifteen?* I had no idea.

"Were they all . . ." I hesitated to ask this, since I knew everyone in our congregation. "Children?"

"No, you were the youngest. They ranged in age from middle school to, well, old enough to be his grandmother. He drank a lot."

I put on my blinker and changed lanes. I shouldn't have had this conversation while driving.

"I dealt with Conrad the only way I knew how," he said.

"Why"—and now tears were rolling down my face—"didn't you call the police?"

"Oh, some of the victims did," he said. "But you know this county. His family knows everyone. I honestly didn't know what to do. What do you do when the police won't act and you've got a guy running rampant through the congregation?"

I didn't know. As a kid, I wasn't supposed to have the answers. But it would've been great if someone somewhere knew what to do. We sat on a silent line for a few seconds.

"I considered shooting him. I didn't, but I thought about it pretty hard," he said. "It might seem obvious to you I should've done this or that, but I did the best I knew how."

I thought about that for a moment. I'd taken a concealed carry class at Sulphur Well Church of Christ, and many of the little old ladies carried pistols in their purses on Sunday morning. Since guns were just a part of rural culture, people would've understood if Jimmy had shot Conrad. Some behaviors are just not acceptable. But what about holding someone responsible, alerting authorities, notifying the congregation, and helping victims overcome the trauma of abuse? That was an untrodden path.

"Wasn't there a middle ground between killing him and letting him run rampant?" I asked.

Jimmy acknowledged there probably was, but he wanted to focus on redemption, forgiveness, and positive change. This was the same theological justification that allowed my predator to operate undetected all these years: only "redemptive" stories can be told, and everything else must be squelched.

"Shouldn't you speak up so he's not coaching girls' basketball now?"

"He's told me he's sorry and I think he's changed," he said. "And he's teaching those kids the gospel in a Bible study."

"You think he's changed? You are gambling with *people's lives*," I cried. "He taught me the gospel, and I almost killed myself."

I hoped that people like Conrad could change, but his actions made me dubious. If he was truly in recovery, he would have chosen a different occupation. Conrad's getting a job at a high school was like an alcoholic seeking employment as a bartender.

He waited for me to catch my breath. His voice was soft, but he didn't apologize.

"I don't know where the balance is between letting somebody move on with their life and giving them a second, third, fourth, eighteenth, or twentieth chance," Jimmy said quietly. "I don't claim to have the answers. But Conrad can do a lot of good, and he's doing that."

I swallowed back bile in my throat and ended the conversation. When I got off the phone, I wept so hard I had to pull over. For decades, I'd held my abuse so tightly, in a vice of secrecy, that I couldn't even articulate it to my therapist. It never occurred to me that it was all public knowledge, that my community knew and did nothing to help me or warn others about his tactics.

Just as people in my small town weren't warned, students in this Kentucky community didn't know the truth about their coach and teacher now. Consequently, older victims didn't come forward because no one would believe such a prolific abuser had gotten away with it for so long. Newer possible victims didn't come forward, because he's one of the most popular teachers at his school. The police couldn't investigate old claims because of statutes of limitations.

I knew how to hold abusers accountable more than most people, and I'd utterly failed. But I hadn't done everything. In a last-ditch effort, David's cousin Bob filed a Freedom of Information Act (FOIA) request about

Conrad's employment history at the school. To my surprise, the information had all of his disciplinary infractions over his entire career.

My eyes scanned the documents. He hadn't reformed as Jimmy had hoped. Not even remotely. He'd been suspended already at the school on several occasions without pay for egregiously disqualifying behavior. He'd told the kids he'd done cocaine; allowed female students to skip class to hang out in his classroom; made fun of Asians; used racial slurs about Black people; called a student "whore"; and made students feel uncomfortable with continuous talk about religion. In the most bizarre incident, a female student was late for class because she'd been cutting Conrad's ingrown toenails.

It was a veritable human resources manual on how not to be a teacher. Really, how not to be a human.

But the most troubling details came from the classroom. He had students fill out a sexual inventory paper describing their romantic experiences; asked students to raise their hand if they've ever had a sexual thought; described possible sexual pairings in the classroom; brought up masturbation, referring to it as "happy time"; and asked students to raise their hands if they had used porn. He also taught homosexuality was the same as pedophilia but warned the students not to tell their parents. "I don't need any mommas calling me," he was quoted as saying.

When he talked about child pornography in class, a student expressed disgust.

"Don't judge," he corrected. All of us are perverted in some way."

Even worse, the information indicated Conrad got "close to" a group of girls every few years. One student, who had visited him several times since spring break, didn't show up for one of her classes, and another teacher found her alone with Conrad in his classroom. After he was instructed not to have female students privately in his room, he immediately went back into the room with her and shut the door. In another incident, a teacher discovered him with several female students. "It felt weird," the teacher said. "A locked door with a room full of girls."

Two months before I went to his high school, Conrad sent sexual text messages to students. The principal—the same one who had treated me as if I was insane—had the screenshots, suspended him without pay, and made him take classes on sexual harassment.

In the corrective memoranda portions of the FOIA request, he was told not to make comments about women, LGBTQ students, or immigrants; not to use historical racial slurs in class; not to retaliate against students; and not to initiate conversation with them about sex. In addition to sexual harassment training, he had to undergo training to prevent discrimination.

How did Conrad have a job at a public high school after all of that? The principal had some gall to accuse me of not having evidence of Conrad's sexual impropriety when her own personnel file was bursting at the seams with years of evidence.

It reminded me of the movie *Spotlight*, a movie about a team of *Boston Globe* reporters who revealed the Catholic church's sex-abuse cover up. In one scene, the attorney said, "If it takes a village to raise a child, it takes a village to abuse a child."

That's what got me. During this process, I was forced to confront an entire village of people—my preacher, this high school principal, the school superintendent—who saw glaring red flags and did nothing to stop Conrad. Worse than nothing, they gave him a job, a platform from which he could operate. They handed him the keys to an ice cream truck, flung open the gates to the neighborhood, and watched the unsuspecting victims flock to him.

I was upset at abusers but was even more upset at these seemingly normal people who allowed predators to stay free because they refused to see what was in front of them. Instead of acknowledging the truth, they looked at the victims and shook their heads ruefully, casting doubt on their experiences. When I published my *WaPo* piece, many people from my hometown church knew immediately who I was speaking about. I didn't have to name him because the puzzle pieces were there on the table, laid out. In disarray? Yes. But an image emerged, and normal people turned their heads away from the truth and hid evidence through spiritual manipulation and outright deceit.

Now I had a folder of evidence too. I filed a report with Kentucky's Education Professional Standards Board, which triggered an automatic investigation, taking my complaints outside of his immediate circle of friends. The next day, Conrad announced his retirement. One year later, the Kentucky Board of Education revoked his teaching license.

This development was good but hardly satisfying. Before I heard of Kanakuk, I had no idea how to investigate sexual abuse, corroborate facts, or get people to pay attention. But after I'd acquired those skills, I put them to work. It took every skill I possessed as an investigative journalist to get Conrad's license revoked. What about all those people out there being abused who don't have those resources, who won't be believed, and who will be silenced?

I didn't have to imagine them, because I was one of them. As a kid I wasn't as important as the charismatic preacher. I was collateral damage. They just assumed I'd go away quietly, without causing problems. They never assumed that the little girl with lopsided bangs would be able to fight back. They were essentially right, since Conrad has been out there for decades without accountability, with full access to vulnerable women and children—and, though he no longer teaches, still is.

I did what I could, but it wasn't enough. It's never enough.

During this time, I was so despondent a friend of mine—a theologian—called to remind me that my job was never to exact justice in either the Kanakuk case or the Conrad case. I didn't have the power to do that; only God does. He reminded me that one day everything would be made right, justice would reign, and every tear would be dried. But today wasn't that today. Today my only job was to remind people—and myself—that justice is coming and that everything that has been lost will—ultimately—be restored.

That was all I could hope to accomplish, and—if I did that—it would be enough. This message resonated with me. Though I never stopped trying to get the culture or the church to pay attention to abuse, I no longer felt powerless.

I knew what to do. When I received a message from someone who had been victimized and wanted to share this burden with someone else, I wrote back to them and scheduled a call.

For the next few months, though I no longer had investigative work to accomplish, I waited for my phone to ring. When people honored me with their stories, I believed them. I listened. I added their names to my Excel database on my laptop. I kept score on their behalf.

At the end of my investigation, I wasn't able to publicly document all of the incidents I'd been told happened at that camp. But I did what I could, and to my surprise I was able to hold their stories and mine too. The investigation didn't completely break me.

Throughout it all, I remained in the land of the living. But there is also a land of the dead, a great cloud of witnesses, populated by people I've never met but whose names are also on my Excel spreadsheet under "suicide." People like Elizabeth's brother, who died when he was only twenty-nine years old. People like the young Texas man who overdosed at Easter.

These people were mourned only by those who knew them, and the public will never know their names. But all of us involved in this saga—the good guys and the bad guys—will one day meet the same fate and finally succumb to death. I can't control the eternal destinies of anyone and have to work out my own salvation with fear and trembling. But I do know that the most important thing that I could do while in the land of living is love.

I started my investigation driven by a righteous fury and ended it in a grievous lament. But after all I did which failed to bring abuse to light, I now know that love will have been enough. Even justice is not necessary for love. I couldn't solve anything for these victims, but I could tell them that I loved them. In these cases, "I love you" sounded like "It wasn't your fault," "You didn't deserve it," "You did nothing wrong," and "I believe you." I thought of that old proverb which says, "Shared joy is a double joy; shared sorrow is half a sorrow."

And so I scheduled calls, sat by the phone, and waited for the caller's name to pop up on my iPhone's cover photo: "The light shines in the darkness, and the darkness has not overcome it."

I read that message quickly and took a moment to hope it is true.

Then I answered the call.

30

LISTEN

I walked onto the stage of Lincoln Center and squinted in the bright lights. The audience would arrive soon. Signs outside on the New York City streets announced the performance. If anyone had told me when David and I were newlyweds and living in the city that one day I'd be there, I wouldn't have believed it.

I was there to tell a story.

For months, I worked on a story for The Moth, a New York City–based storytelling organization. The Moth doesn't allow notes or memorization, so I practiced it over the phone with producers. I skipped vital parts, stammered over words. And yet I was about to tell my story in public. Lin-Manuel Miranda, the creator of *Hamilton*, had told a story for The Moth the previous month. They must've made a serious mistake asking me to tell my story.

In an hour, I had to deliver a story, without notes, in front of two thousand people after our rehearsal the day before. The other storytellers included a woman who integrated the Arkansas public school system in the 1960s, an octogenarian British comedian, a trans/queer/obesity activist, and a college professor/poet. When the producers asked for volunteers to tell their stories during the preshow rehearsal, I went first. I didn't want to sit there comparing myself to these professional storytellers. So I popped out of my chair, stood in front of the room, and told the story of when—as a newlywed—I thought David was cheating on me.

"One day the phone rang. It was a woman with a sultry voice asking for David. I explained he wasn't there, and she hung up without leaving a message. The next day, the phone rang again. It was a different woman asking for David. That time, he was home, so I handed him the phone. I hovered nearby so I could eavesdrop. Wrong number, he said. But the phone rang at 3:00 a.m. And at 4:00."

I told my story, more or less, as I'd intended—forgetting one detail or the other. I explained how we'd gotten married quickly in spite of protests, moved to New York, where I fielded calls from breathless women asking to speak to David French (I thought) when they were really asking for David Lee Roth (the lead singer of Van Halen). The room was supportive and offered helpful critiques.

"You might want to explain who Van Halen is," a younger person suggested. "In case the audience isn't familiar with the 1980s. And you might mention caller ID didn't exist."

I incorporated these suggestions and was nearly immobilized at the prospect of telling my story to people who'd paid for tickets, gotten dressed, and worn pantyhose to this event. Before anyone arrived, I walked onstage with the other storytellers and looked into the theater.

"I'm terrified," I told the British comedian.

"You bloody well should be." He looked out into the seats. "This is Lincoln Center."

I tried to keep my mind off of what I was about to do. I ate snacks in the green room and chatted with the producers and musicians. I prayed. My prayer life had been stunted. After all these years, I was so disappointed in the church and I realized I didn't understand God. But in the green room, I prayed more earnestly than I'd prayed in years. Evidently, my faith in God had not been totally shaken, just my faith in my fellow Christians, my faith in my fellow Americans, and myself.

The comedian walked up to me. "What the hell are you doing?"

I didn't want him to know I was praying, so I said I was trying to calm my nerves. "I've never done this before."

"When the f—k are you going to drop the I-don't-know-anything shtick, delivered in that southern drawl of yours?" He contorted his Oxford voice into a southern accent. "'Aw, shucks. I don't know anything.' You're exhausting."

I was taken aback by his inexplicable animosity. I barely knew the guy.

"Wait, don't pull the accent card on me. You've been bedding women for decades by simply opening your mouth and being British," I said.

The producer indicated it was time for the show. The storytellers and I sat in the front rows of the audience and the host introduced me. I was the opener.

"When our first speaker was in elementary school, she met a story-teller and told him she wanted to tell stories when she grew up. The man looked at her and said, 'Do yourself a favor and get a real job.'" The audience laughed. "Put your hands together for Nancy French."

I walked out on stage, the bright lights in my eyes. I was overcome with gratitude. I was thankful that, after the years of investigating abuse, I was able to do something fun. I was thankful that I, after coming from a hillbilly family in Tennessee, had the chance to perform at Lincoln Center. And I was thankful that the man I married so spontaneously was sitting with my three kids and son-in-law in the audience.

I took one moment before I launched into my story.

The audience sat in rapt attention. When I told them about all the women calling the house, they seemed full of trepidation. I enjoyed spinning the yarn, making them believe I'd made the worst decision of my life by marrying this stranger. Then it was time for the big reveal. I had to get this right. I made sure to speak clearly.

"Are you calling for David French, the attorney?"

"He said, 'No. I'm calling for the singer, David Lee Roth.'"

"David Lee Roth? The lead singer of Van Halen? Big hair/spandex/rock star David Lee Roth?"

That was the part I added to make sure the younger members of the audience knew who the singer was. I explained the confusion: we had David Lee Roth's old phone number and he was still using it. When I revealed the mix-up, everyone roared in laughter, in relief. I took a second to enjoy their delight and applause.

"But during the short time it took for David Lee Roth to transition to a new telephone number, I'd doubted the man I married. How precarious love is. Surprisingly, it turned out to be quite resilient. Our marriage survived disappointments and health scares. It lasted when jobs, friends, and vehicles didn't. It survived when the months kept going after the paychecks ran out. It's thrived through horrible heartbreak, and unspeakable joy.

"I wasn't wrong to believe in love. If anything, I didn't believe in it enough. My idea of love was less robust, less romantic, and less amazing than it turned out to be. I was a small-town girl who learned how to shoot guns at church and dropped out of college, who wanted roses and romance, but I got a man who speaks Elvish but who's been by my side for twenty-six years."

I paused here, because the audience clapped, but I still had one more line.

"That's why I'm thankful I decided—in the immortal words of David Lee Roth—to 'go ahead and jump.'"

I'd added this closing line after the producer and I strategized over how to end the story. Since Van Halen with David Lee Roth as lead singer had a 1984 hit called "Jump," it seemed like a good enough conclusion. It must've worked, because the audience loved it. I didn't miss a syllable.

I made my way back to the empty seat next to the comedian. "Do you hear the applause?" He paused to let me listen. "It's all for you, and it's the most addictive sensation you'll ever experience," he shouted over their applause. "It's better than sex, it's better than everything. I spent my whole life seeking that sound. Don't make the same mistake I did. Don't get addicted to it."

It was a surprisingly authentic moment. There was more to him than met the eye.

After the event, I went to the cast party. So many people milled around. The comedian and I were stuck at a table together—neither able to get up. But as the drinks came and the hours passed, we chatted about our lives. He told me anecdotes about coming from London in a boat and starting his comedy career in New York City in the 1960s. I told him about my mountain family and living in Tennessee.

We marveled at how different two people's lives could be, and several hours later, we said our goodbyes.

"I'm eighty-two years old, and I don't know how many more years I have left in this world," he told me and David as we parted ways. "But I would be honored if your family was a part of my life between now and then."

This man was not a Christian. He was not a conservative. And honestly, he was not very nice. But I knew I had a lifelong friend in Los Angeles. We exchanged numbers and emails and promised to keep in touch. We have.

In the past, I felt uneasy around unbelieving liberals, and I immediately felt I should share the gospel with them—the one in the Bible or the one about Reagan's trickle-down economics.

Throughout my life, I desperately wanted to identify the "good" people and the "bad" people, so I could walk more confidently among them—befriending the good ones, avoiding the bad ones. I'd categorized people into tribes according to their political views, their church attendance, and their voting patterns. But this line was fuzzier than I'd originally believed. "If only there were evil people somewhere insidiously committing evil deeds, and it were necessary only to separate them from the rest of us and destroy them," Aleksandr Solzhenitsyn wrote. "But the line dividing good and evil cuts through the heart of every human being."[40]

That line cut through me.

Though I fiercely wanted people to be one thing and not two for simplicity's sake, people—as Walt Whitman wrote—contain multitudes. Me included.

I also subscribed to the view that life was too short to deal with complicated people, but aren't we all? Instead of categorizing people according to their collective beliefs like I used to, I tried to look at them as individuals. I tried to love them. If needed, I tried to forgive them. If needed, I asked them to forgive me.

To truly love our fellow Americans, we have to stop averting our eyes at the first sign of disagreement. We must look at them and truly see them. "With our imagination as well as our eyes," writes Frederick Buechner, "like artists, we must see not just their faces but the life behind and within their faces."[41]

By overlooking people's sometimes rough exteriors and truly seeing them, I'd found friends in places I never expected. But they have to overlook my edges too. Most of us aren't willing to put in the effort, especially since people's stories are so complicated.

And speaking of complicated stories, I decided to dive into my family's stories with my parents. They never really spoke about the mountain. When they moved off that big rock, they'd sealed everything off into an airtight compartment labeled "the past" and had moved on to their present and future. When they turned eighty, I realized, with a tightening of my throat, that they had more years behind them than in front of them.

And so I decided to treat them like my celebrity clients. I was going to ghostwrite a book for my parents before they died, to leave a written record of where our family had come from.

"Now what are you doing?" my dad asked. He looked at the recording device suspiciously.

"I'm going to record your lives," I said. "Like I do for my clients."

"You're going to write a book about us?" he asked.

"No, we're going to write your story together." I could tell he still didn't understand, but he was willing to go along with it.

I went to their house, and I asked them everything I could think of. *What is your first memory? What did you fight with your siblings about? Did you have a nickname? Who gave it to you and how did you get it? Who was your first love? How much did milk cost?*

"Now, tell me again," Dad said, unused to having me sitting in front of them and listening to every syllable. Plus, I'm not sure he ever truly understood what I did for a living. "You're writing a book? For me?"

"Yes, I want your great-grandchildren to know about you."

Sitting in front of a screen and getting paid to type was difficult for my dad to understand. Because he hadn't learned his ABCs until his twenties, he wasn't much on reading. I doubt he's ever read one of my books. And though he faithfully reads David's columns, he frequently stands up afterward and says, "Well, I know that is smart, but I ain't got the mind to ponder all that."

For months, we sat together in their house, which is always too hot or too cold because they refuse to spend money to control the temperature. Eventually, the questions got more to the point.

What was it like knowing your family was in the KKK? Who was the first Black person you ever saw? What was it like to join the marines before you had your driver's license? What was it like to come back from the military and go back to high school? What was it like to grow up in a world of violence? When your cousin shot the other's arm off, were you afraid of him? What was it like for your own father to break your mother's leg? What was it like to refrain from hitting your father back when he attacked you? Were you at the bar the night that guy was almost decapitated?

My dad hesitated at first, but over the course of our days of interviews, his voice—thick with emotion—occasionally cracked. My mother has not been able to tell me what she had for breakfast for years, but she recounted incidents from seventy years ago with perfect clarity. Those moments in their hot house was like having her back again, completely. I'd almost waited too long to ask the questions.

I labored over our recorded conversations because my automatic transcription service could not properly understand my parents' thick mountain accents. My dad says "orta" instead of "ought to," for example, and added "I tell you what" and "I reckon" every few seconds for flavor. The transcription was indecipherable chaos. *Like life*, I thought.

I had to listen, to actually listen, to every syllable over and over as I documented our conversations. I had to see my parents in a new way, with the imagination of someone who wanted to understand them. I had to see their faces—wrinkled and tan from years of outside labor and that strong Cherokee bloodline—as well as the life behind and within those beautiful faces.

My people on the mountain always told me I had a nascent gift of "seeing." I was beginning to think they were right. Because looking at people with a pure heart and without grievance is as magical as anything I've ever seen in a crystal ball.

By the end of their story, I did see my parents—maybe for the first time. They described trauma that's hard for someone like me to imagine—their starvation, poverty, and violence. They never used the word *trauma* and insisted their lives have been blessed. They were simply describing the way life was on the mountain. Not hardship. Just life.

But the reason "someone like me" had a hard time even fathoming their circumstances was because they had—in a moment of bravery—broken the cycle for our family. They'd packed their bags and left their situation, though those hills were everything they knew. They raised three girls, below the poverty line, the best they knew how—through hard work and living morally and going to church.

It wasn't a bad plan. They'd done their best, and we were still standing. I owed them everything.

I'm grown and married to a Harvard Law graduate who is a *New York Times* columnist. We have three kids and two dogs and comfortable lives. Yes, this is because of my parents' decision to leave the mountain and force me into the college I loathed. I met David at that college after they'd saved their whole lives to send me there. I had the privilege of finding love because of them. I've had the privilege of affording counseling—something they've never had the money or inclination to avail themselves of—because of them. My parents raised me up on their arms, giving me a higher place from which to step into the world.

And I jumped.

But I couldn't turn around and judge my parents with the psychological and emotional tools I had (because of their bravery) which they did not have (because of their upbringing). They'd sacrificed so I could have a better life and a different perspective. It would no longer do to accept the abundance of their sacrifice, only to turn it against them. I wanted to love them as well as I could during the years we had left.

"So one more thing," I said. The next question had been a haunting question my entire life. "What was it like to know Uncle Jasper killed his wife?" This is what I worried the journalists across America would find out if David had run for president. This is what made me hesitate before writing this book. This is what made me cringe a bit every time I saw him until he died.

"Jasper?" Dad asked. He looked at me blankly. "Nah, Jasper never killed nobody."

"Yes," I said. "He did. Buck told me that years ago. I've heard it my whole life."

Daddy shook his head. "Nah, not Jasper. Jasper was a lot of things, but he weren't no murderer."

"He threatened to kill David, though," I told my parents. "When we got engaged, he called David and said he'd kill him if he ever laid a finger on me."

Dad told me that many tall tales sprouted up around his brother because mountain folk esteemed manliness over virtue.

"Remember that story I've told you all my life about how Jasper went to California, got in a fight, and got hit in the head with a baseball bat?" Dad asked. "He never was the same after that?"

I nodded.

"That ain't true either." Dad looked at his feet. "I believed that my whole life, but—turns out—Jasper was just . . ." He looked at my mom. "What's the word?"

"I don't know, Bob." She could remember things only from the deep past, and this was a relatively new revelation.

"Bi-something," Dad said. "Bipolar?" I'd never heard my dad use a psychological term in his life, and the word barely fell out of his mouth. "He had some sort of mental disorder that made him . . . different."

"And your parents were ashamed of him?"

"They never mentioned it. They made up this whole story about Jasper's violent streak including that California baseball-bat-to-the-head thing. Guess they'd rather people fear him than pity him."

I let that sink in. My grandparents would rather have people believe their son was a murderer than had a mental disorder. I'd believed a lie for decades. But in spite of my lifelong certainty, the truth turned out to be more complicated. Sometimes it's hard to tell what's true and what's not. Sometimes stories have to marinate a bit before you can figure out their meaning.

That was the case with my newlywed story when I thought David was having an affair, a story which had been sitting on the shelf of my memories, collecting dust until enough years had passed to make it funny.

The day after I told that story at Lincoln Center, I went to Central Park. I planned on walking the length of the park and hailing a cab. The day was bright and hopeful as I walked down the "Promenade," under the canopy of American elm trees. I looked at paintings artists were trying to peddle, fluffy dogs on leashes, people in wheelchairs being pushed by caretakers, mothers pushing strollers.

Twenty-six years ago, I'd come to this city as a terrified southerner trying to make it as a newlywed. And hours ago, I'd performed at one of Manhattan's epicenters of art and sophistication. I went over the story I'd told onstage, going over the lines that made the audience terrified and those that made them cackle.

My story was admittedly insane, marrying a stranger so quickly only to be horrified at the suspicion of infidelity. That terror was a gift now that I'd seen how everything played out. David hadn't cheated, my life was going to be good, and I got a pretty funny story out of it. Life is like that—interesting, if you can survive it.

I'd experienced many heartaches. Conrad's abuse, Jacob's hands tightening around my throat, Virginia's death, David's Iraq deployment, Camille's prebirth complications, Naomi's adoption struggles, David's almost running for president, harassment by White nationalists, friends leaving us over Trump, the Kanakuk investigation, and yes, the marital confusion over David Lee Roth's telephone number back in 1996.

I kept thinking aging would provide some resolution to all of my problems, and I could make sense of everything that had happened. But as I walked through Central Park, I was as confused as ever. I'd experienced those moments of heartbreak without seeing the fuller picture because it simply wasn't possible to see the full picture from my vantage point. My life had felt like a string of weird occurrences, one propelling me to the next. I never had a chance to sit down and look at all of them together, to wonder why my life had meandered aimlessly much like I was doing in the park that day.

"Time is the very lens through which ye see—small and clear, as men see through the wrong end of a telescope—something that would otherwise be too big for ye to see at all," C. S. Lewis wrote.[42] Had God arranged for me to experience all of these moments, but secretly embedded a future hope into them—hope I couldn't detect at the time?

Back in 1996 when I was fielding calls from the women hoping to connect with David Lee Roth and fearing for my future, had God foreseen last night's moment at Lincoln Center, rubbed his hands together, thrown his head back, and laughed? The thought that God was outside time and had been orchestrating my steps was both delightful and curious. Had God planned every single detail of my life?

"What are you like, God?" I asked as I walked through Central Park. People walked by me eating ice cream and kids tossed a football. I felt my heart softening toward this divine and frustratingly silent mystery. I was reaching out in a real way, in a conversational way. I wasn't asking him to do anything. I was hesitantly reaching out an olive branch, trying to understand him—if not to see his face, to see the face within the face. "Are you really that mischievous?"

I exited the park and came to a statue on the corner of Fifty-Fifth Street and Sixth Avenue. It was a gigantic statue—a man twice the size of a regular person. I stopped and looked at the statue, which was labeled "Listen." The statue had his finger to his lips as if he was imploring busy New Yorkers to pause and notice the noise around them.

It was strange to ask pedestrians to be quiet in such a loud city, but I stopped. Had God heard my question about whether he's directing my path and cheekily directed me to stop on that particular street in that specific moment? Was this piece of art an invitation from God himself? Was he finally answering my questions after all these years of silence?

Okay, God. I'll play your game.

After planting my feet next to the statue, I listened to the ambient noise at Fifty-Fifth Street: cars honking, people arguing, a police officer chatting with a hot dog vendor.

As I stood there, I was irritated at God, who was once again ignoring my questions. *God, do you control every detail of my life? Is everything a part of your plan? Please. Answer me.*

That's when I heard it. A bodega was located about ten feet from me. On its counter was a boom box from the 1980s, and from its speakers I heard a song from the radio quietly playing. Per the statue's instructions, I listened. The song had a driving beat and the voice singing was familiar.

I gasped.

A few hours ago, I'd ended my speech by quoting the hit song "Jump" on the stage of Lincoln Center. And in that moment, when I was questioning God about directing my steps, I heard that thirty-eight-year-old tune.

Now God was just showing off.

Over the years, I've been ghosted by political friends, spiritual allies, and even some neighbors. I've felt the sting of betrayal when those I loved turned their backs on me. But as much as I wrestled with God and tried to ignore him, he showed up and occasionally took my breath away. The old-time Christians called this the Holy Ghost, and I like that phrase. Throughout my life, God "ghosted" me, and being "Holy-Ghosted" is a much different experience altogether. Instead of shoving me away, God brought me in. Instead of sending a message of apathy, he showed loving care. Instead of disappearing in silence, he revealed his hopeful presence.

In that moment, I relented to that hope. God was God, not me. He knew, cared about, and understood every aspect of my life, and every step I took. He's in control of the strange details, the heartbreaks, and the joys. Since I am the created and he is the creator, I will never fully see his face this side of heaven.

But I heard his voice.

Right there at the foot of Central Park, God spoke, and—at least in that moment—he sounded an awful lot like Van Halen.

I laughed and uttered a silent prayer of wonder. Then I kept on walking, one step at a time, toward home.

NOTES

1. I first told this story in my book *Red State of Mind* and also in Nancy French, "I Ignored Warnings from Friends and Family Not to Marry My Husband. Was I Making a Big Mistake?" *Washington Post*, December 30, 2019, www.washingtonpost.com/lifestyle/2019/12/30/i-ignored-friends-familys -warnings-not-marry-my-husband-was-i-making-big-mistake/.

2. This story was first told in David French and Nancy French, *Home and Away: A Story of Family in a Time of War.*

3. Nancy French, "Perspective: Romney Was Never Christian Enough for Some Republicans. Somehow, Trump Is," *Washington Post*, April 26, 2019, www.washingtonpost.com/outlook/2019/04/25/romney-was-never-christian -enough-some-republicans-somehow-trump-still-is/.

4. French, "Perspective."

5. William Keller, "A Vote for Romney Will Lead 1 Million Plus Souls to Hell," Christian Newswire, April 25, 2012, www.christiannewswire.com /news/9714219522.html.

6. Jessica Valenti, "Is Bristol Palen's New Memoir the Story of a Rape Survivor Speaking Out?" *Washington Post*, June 24, 2011, www.washingtonpost.com /opinions/is-bristol-palins-new-memoir-the-story-of-a-rape-survivor-speaking -out/2011/06/23/AGLMzcjH_story.html.

7. Jesse Ellison, "Bristol Palin Memoir on How She Lost Her Virginity: Was It Date Rape?" *Daily Beast*, June 23, 2011, www.thedailybeast.com/bristol -palin-memoir-on-how-she-lost-her-virginity-was-it-date-rape.

8. Dan Savage, "Bristol Palin: Levi Raped Me," The Stranger, June 20, 2011, www.thestranger.com/blogs/2011/06/20/8720477/bristol-palin-levi-raped-me.

9. ABC News, "Bristol Palin 'GMA' Interview: My Virginity Was 'Stolen': Exclusive (06.27.11)," YouTube, June 27, 2011, www.youtube.com/watch?v=soieUrFMG1s.

10. Adelle M. Banks, "John Kerry Calls for Release of Saeed Abedini, Iranian-American Pastor Held in Tehran," *HuffPost*, March 27, 2013, www.huffpost.com/entry/john-kerry-calls-for-release-of-saeed-abedini-iranian-american-pastor-held-in-tehran_n_2959218.

11. Sarah Posner, "How Steve Bannon Created an Online Haven for White Nationalists," *Mother Jones*, August 22, 2016, www.motherjones.com/politics/2016/08/stephen-bannon-donald-trump-alt-right-breitbart-news/.

12. Joseph Bernstein, "Behind the Racist Hashtag That Is Blowing Up Twitter," *BuzzFeed News*, July 27, 2015, www.buzzfeednews.com/article/josephbernstein/behind-the-racist-hashtag-some-donald-trump-fans-love.

13. Bradford Hanson, "David French: A Cuck Begs for Mercy," National Vanguard, September 24, 2015, https://nationalvanguard.org/2015/09/david-french-a-cuck-begs-for-mercy/.

14. James Edwards, "The American Cuckservative," *James Ewards*, July 28, 2015. www.thepoliticalcesspool.org/jamesedwards/the-american-cuckservative/.

15. Chris Cillizza, "Donald Trump Retweeted an Alt-Right Conspiracy Theorist. Here's Why," CNN, August 18, 2017, www.cnn.com/2017/08/15/politics/donald-trump-jack-posobiec/index.html.

16. Nancy French, "Opinion: What It's Like to Be a White Conservative on Twitter When You Have a Black Child," *Washington Post*, September 18, 2015, www.washingtonpost.com/news/acts-of-faith/wp/2015/09/18/what-its-like-to-be-a-white-conservative-on-twitter-when-you-have-a-black-child.

17. Jane Coaston, "But Today the Journal of American Greatness (a Publication That Is Attempting to Put Meat on the Bones of Trumpism, so to Speak) Published This 'Poem,' by Someone Using a Pseudonym. It Is Entitled 'Cuck Elegy,'" Twitter, July 16, 2019, https://twitter.com/janecoaston/status/1151167468066525190.

18. Victor Davis Hanson, "Author: Victor Davis Hanson," American Greatness, author listing, accessed August 10, 2023, https://amgreatness.com/author/victor-davis-hanson/.

19. "Can the Republican Party Survive the Alt Right?" Aspen Ideas, accessed

August 10, 2023, www.aspenideas.org/sessions/can-the-republican-party -survive-the-alt-right.

20. Tina Nguyen, "Bill Kristol's Secret Third-Party Pick to Challenge Trump Is . . . Some Random National Review Writer," *Vanity Fair*, May 31, 2016, www.vanityfair.com/news/2016/05/david-french-presidential-bid-donald -trump.

21. Robert Costa, "Conservative Tennessee Attorney David French Is Urged to Enter Presidential Race as Independent," *Washington Post*, May 31, 2016, www.washingtonpost.com/news/post-politics/wp/2016/05/31/conservative -tennessee-attorney-david-french-is-urged-to-enter-presidential-race-as -independent/.

22. Jane C. Timm, "Who Is David French and Is He Running for President?" NBCNews.com, June 1, 2016, www.nbcnews.com/politics/2016-election /who-david-french-n583886.

23. Nick Gass, "What Does David French Believe?" POLITICO, June 1, 2016, www.politico.com/story/2016/06/what-does-david-french-believe-223777.

24. Dana Bash and Eric Bradner, "Kristol's White Knight: David French," CNN, June 1, 2016, www.cnn.com/2016/05/31/politics/bill-kristol-david -french-independent-presidential-bid/index.html.

25. Brendan Morrow, "Nancy French, David's Wife: Five Fast Facts You Need to Know," Heavy.com, May 31, 2016, last updated June 1, 2016, https:// heavy.com/news/2016/05/david-french-wife-nancy-who-is-family-children -kids-adoption-naomi-2016-election-independent-candidate/.

26. Paul Kane, "Paul Ryan Endorses Donald Trump," *Washington Post*, June 2, 2016, www.washingtonpost.com/news/powerpost/wp/2016/06/02/paul-ryan -endorses-donald-trump/.

27. Tom DiChristopher, "Trump Won't Change the GOP. We'll Change Him: Sen Mitch McConnell," CNBC, June 1, 2016, www.cnbc.com/2016/06/01 /trump-wont-change-the-gop-well-change-him-sen-mitch-mcconnell.html.

28. Nick Gass, "RNC Chairman Priebus: David French on 'Suicide Mission,'" POLITICO, June 6, 2016, www.politico.com/story/2016/06/reince-priebus -david-french-223822.

29. I learned a great deal about this from my friend Curtis Chang, as articulated in this article: "The Southern Baptist Convention Sacrifices Congregants on the Altar of Power," Redeeming Babel, May 24, 2022, https://redeeming

babel.org/the-southern-baptist-convention-sacrifices-congregants-on-the
-altar-of-power.

30. Nancy French, "Opinion: What It's Like to Experience the 2016 Election
    as Both a Conservative and a Sex Abuse Survivor," *Washington Post*,
    October 21, 2016, www.washingtonpost.com/news/acts-of-faith/wp/2016
    /10/21/what-its-like-to-experience-the-2016-election-as-both-a-conservative
    -and-a-sex-abuse-survivor/.

31. Stephanie McCrummen, Beth Reinhard, and Alice Crites, "Woman
    Says Roy Moore Initiated Sexual Encounter When She Was 14, He
    Was 32," *Washington Post*, November 9, 2017, www.washingtonpost.com
    /investigations/woman-says-roy-moore-initiated-sexual-encounter-when
    -she-was-14-he-was-32/2017/11/09/1f495878-c293-11e7-afe9-4f60b5a6c4a0
    _story.html.

32. Nancy Jane French, "Perspective: What It's like to Watch Men like Roy
    Moore as a Conservative and as a Sex Abuse Survivor," *Washington Post*,
    November 10, 2017, www.washingtonpost.com/news/acts-of-faith/wp
    /2017/11/10/what-its-like-to-watch-men-like-roy-moore-as-a-conservative
    -and-as-a-sex-abuse-survivor/.

33. Nancy French, "Nancy French on Implications of Alabama Election for
    Christian Conservatives," interview by Robert Siegel, *All Things Considered*,
    December 13, 2017, www.npr.org/2017/12/13/570603492/nancy-french-on
    -implications-of-alabama-election-for-christian-conservatives.

34. Julie Kelly, "If You Exploit Your Personal Experiences—Including Adopting
    a Baby—to Score Political Points, You Have No Moral High Road. And If
    You Use It to Smear a SCOTUS Nominee for Attention, Then You Deserve
    Blowback," Twitter, December 18, 2018, https://twitter.com/julie_kelly2
    /status/1074866497749729280.

35. Julie Kelly, "OK—Nancy French Screwed Around with Her Preacher When
    She Was a Teen, So If Kavanaugh Groped a Girl 36 Years Ago, He Can't
    Be on SCOTUS? Again, Ladies: Your Personal Experiences Have Nothing
    to Do with This. And Shame on You for Exploiting It to Help Destroy a
    Decent Man. https://T.Co/Aijk1lvnii," Twitter, September 21, 2018, https://
    twitter.com/julie_kelly2/status/1043116944935792643.

36. "Podcast: Black History Month 2020: Devan Sandiford and Al Sharpton,"
    The Moth, 2020, https://themoth.org/podcast/black-history-month-2020.

37. Nancy French, "After Listening to @DevanSandiford on @TheMoth, I'm Inspired to Tell the Story of What Happened When My 12 Year Old Black Daughter and I Were Shopping at Nordstroms in December. I Was Buying Her a Christmas Gift and Wanted It to Be a Surprise," Twitter, @NancyAFrench, March 3, 2020, https://mobile.twitter.com/NancyAFrench/status/1234851172349104129.

38. The Kanakuk part of my life spanned several years. Because I needed to simplify and shorten this story, as well as, in some cases, hide the identity of victims, I have moved events around from the original timeline.

39. David French and Nancy French, "'They Aren't Who You Think They Are,'" The Dispatch, March 28, 2021, https://thedispatch.com/newsletter/frenchpress/they-arent-who-you-think-they-are/.

40. Aleksandr Solzhenitsyn and H. T. Willetts, *The Gulag Archipelago* (New York: Harper and Row, 1978).

41. Frederick Buechner, *Whistling in the Dark: A Doubter's Dictionary* (San Francisco: HarperSanFrancisco, 1993).

42. C. S. Lewis, *The Great Divorce: A Dream* (London: Collins, 2015).